MCSE:
Windows 2000 Server

Exam Notes

MCSE:
Windows® 2000 Server
Exam Notes™

Scott Johnson
with Lisa Donald
and James Chellis

San Francisco • Paris • Düsseldorf • Soest • London

Associate Publisher: Neil Edde
Contracts and Licensing Manager: Kristine O'Callaghan
Acquisitions and Developmental Editors: Brenda Frink, Bonnie Bills
Editor: Carol Henry
Production Editor: Judith Hibbard
Technical Editor: Mark Kovach
Book Designer: Bill Gibson
Graphic Illustrator: Tony Jonick
Electronic Publishing Specialist: Susie Hendrickson
Proofreaders: Nancy Riddiough, Amey Garber
Indexer: Ann Rogers
Cover Designer: Archer Design
Cover Illustrator/Photographer: Natural Selection

To Robyn. With all my love.

Acknowledgments

I would like to thank Judith Hibbard, Carol Henry, Brenda Frink, and Bonnie Bills for all the great suggestions and edits. To Kevin, for getting my foot in the door. To Q, for helping me maintain sanity; now maybe you can work on your putting. Thanks!

—*Scott Johnson*

Contents

Introduction

Microsoft's new Microsoft Certified Systems Engineer (MCSE) track for Windows 2000 is the premier certification for computer industry professionals. Covering the core technologies around which Microsoft's future will be built, the new MCSE certification is a powerful credential for career advancement.

This book has been developed, in cooperation with Microsoft Corporation, to give you the critical skills and knowledge you need to prepare for one of the core requirements of the new MCSE certification program for Windows 2000 Server. You will find the information you need to acquire a solid understanding of Windows 2000 Server, to prepare for Exam 70-215: Installing, Configuring, and Administering Microsoft Windows 2000 Server, and to progress toward MCSE certification.

Is This Book for You?

The MCSE Exam Notes books were designed to be succinct, portable exam review guides that can be used either in conjunction with a more complete study program (book, CBT courseware, classroom/lab environment) or as an exam review for those who don't feel the need for more extensive test preparation. It isn't our goal to give the answers away, but rather to identify those topics on which you can expect to be tested and to provide sufficient coverage of these topics.

Perhaps you're already familiar with the features and functionality of Windows 2000. The thought of paying lots of money for a specialized MCSE exam preparation course probably doesn't sound too appealing. What can they teach you that you don't already know, right? Be careful, though. Many experienced network administrators have walked confidently into test centers only to walk sheepishly out of them after failing an MCSE exam. As they discovered, there's the Microsoft of the real world and the Microsoft of the MCSE exams. It's our goal with these Exam Notes books to show you where the two converge and where they diverge. After you've finished reading through this book, you should have a clear idea of how your understanding of the technologies involved matches up with the expectations of the MCSE test makers in Redmond.

Or perhaps you're relatively new to the world of Microsoft networking, drawn to it by the promise of challenging work and higher salaries. You've just waded through an 800-page MCSE Windows 2000 study guide or taken a class at a local training center. Lots of information to keep track of, isn't it? Well, by organizing the Exam Notes books according to the Microsoft exam objectives, and by breaking up the information into concise manageable pieces, we've created what we think is the handiest exam review guide available. Throw it in your briefcase and carry it to work with you. As you read through the book, you'll be able to identify quickly those areas you know best and those that require more in-depth review.

NOTE The goal of the Exam Notes series is to help MCSE candidates familiarize themselves with the subjects on which they can expect to be tested in the MCSE exams. For complete, in-depth coverage of the technologies and topics involved, we recommend the MCSE Windows 2000 Study Guide series from Sybex.

How Is This Book Organized?

As mentioned above, this book is organized according to the official exam objectives list prepared by Microsoft for Exam 70-215. The chapters coincide to the broad objectives groupings, such as Planning, Installation and Configuration, Monitoring and Optimization, and Troubleshooting. These groupings are also reflected in the organization of the MCSE exams themselves.

Within each chapter, the individual exam objectives are addressed in turn. Each objective's coverage is further divided into the following sections of information:

Critical Information

This section presents the greatest level of detail on information for the objective. This is the place to start if you're unfamiliar with or uncertain about the objective's technical issues.

Necessary Procedures

Here you'll find instructions for procedures that require completion on a lab computer. From installing operating systems to modifying configuration defaults, the information in these sections addresses the hands-on requirements for the MCSE exams.

NOTE   Not every objective has Necessary Procedures associated with it.

Exam Essentials

In this section, we've put together a concise list of the most crucial topics that you'll need to comprehend fully prior to taking the MCSE exam. These summaries can help you identify subject areas that might require more study on your part.

Key Terms and Concepts

Here you'll find a mini-glossary of the most important terms and concepts related to the specific objective. This list will help you understand what the technical words mean within the context of the related subject matter.

Sample Questions

For each objective, we've included a selection of questions similar to those you'll encounter on the actual MCSE exam. Answers and explanations are provided so you can gain some insight into the test-taking process.

How Do You Become an MCSE?

Attaining MCSE certification has always been a challenge. In the past, people could acquire detailed exam information—even most of the exam questions—from online "brain dumps" and third-party "cram" books or software products. For the new MCSE exams, however, this simply will not be the case.

To avoid the "paper-MCSE syndrome" (a devaluation of the MCSE certification because unqualified individuals manage to pass the exams), Microsoft has taken strong steps to protect the security and integrity of the new MCSE track. Prospective MSCEs will need to complete a course of study that provides not only detailed knowledge of a wide range of topics, but true skills derived from working with Windows 2000 and related software products.

In the new MCSE program, Microsoft is heavily emphasizing hands-on skills. Microsoft has stated that "nearly half of the core required exams' content demands that the candidate have troubleshooting skills acquired through hands-on experience and working knowledge."

Fortunately, if you are willing to dedicate time and effort with Windows 2000, you can prepare for the exams by using the proper tools. If you work through this book and the other books in this series, you should successfully meet the exam requirements.

TIP   This book is part of a series of MCSE Study Guides and Exam Notes published by Sybex that covers the five core requirements as well as the electives you need to complete your MCSE track.

Exam Requirements

Successful candidates must pass a minimum set of exams that measure technical proficiency and expertise.

- Candidates for MCSE certification must pass seven exams, including four core operating system exams, one design exam, and two electives.

- Candidates who have already passed three Windows NT 4 exams (70-067, 70-068, and 70-073) may opt to take an "accelerated" exam plus one core design exam and two electives.

NOTE   If you do not pass the accelerated exam after one attempt, you must pass the five core requirements and two electives.

The following tables show the exams that a new certification candidate must pass. *All* of these exams are required:

Exam #	Title	Requirement Met
70-216	Implementing and Administering a Microsoft® Windows® 2000 Network Infrastructure	Core (Operating System)
70-210	Installing, Configuring, and Administering Microsoft® Windows® 2000 Professional	Core (Operating System)
70-215	Installing, Configuring, and Administering Microsoft® Windows® 2000 Server	Core (Operating System)
70-217	Implementing and Administering a Microsoft® Windows® 2000 Directory Services Infrastructure	Core (Operating System)

One of these exams is required:

Exam #	Title	Requirement Met
70-219	Designing a Microsoft® Windows® 2000 Directory Services Infrastructure	Core (Design)
70-220	Designing Security for a Microsoft® Windows® 2000 Network	Core (Design)
70-221	Designing a Microsoft® Windows® 2000 Network Infrastructure	Core (Design)

Two of these exams are required:

Exam #	Title	Requirement Met
70-219	Designing a Microsoft® Windows® 2000 Directory Services Infrastructure	Elective
70-220	Designing Security for a Microsoft® Windows® 2000 Network	Elective
70-221	Designing a Microsoft® Windows® 2000 Network Infrastructure	Elective
Any current MCSE elective	Exams cover topics such as Exchange Server, SQL Server, Systems Management Server, Internet Explorer Administrators Kit, and Proxy Server (new exams are added regularly)	Elective

NOTE For a more detailed description of the Microsoft certification programs, including a list of current MCSE electives, check Microsoft's Training and Certification Web site at www.microsoft.com/trainingandservices.

Exam Registration

You may take the exams at any of more than 1,000 Authorized Prometric Testing Centers (APTCs) and VUE Testing Centers around the world. For the location of a testing center near you, call Sylvan Prometric at (800) 755-EXAM (755-3926), or call VUE at (888) 837-8616. Outside the United States and Canada, contact your local Sylvan Prometric or VUE registration center.

You should determine the number of the exam you want to take, and then register with the Sylvan Prometric or VUE registration center nearest to you. At this point, you'll be asked for advance payment for the exam. The exams are $100 each. Exams must be taken within one year of payment. You can schedule exams up to six weeks in advance or as late as one working day prior to the date of the exam. You can cancel or reschedule your exam if you contact the center at least two working days prior to the exam. Same-day registration is available in some locations, subject to space availability. Where same-day registration is available, you must register a minimum of two hours before test time.

TIP You may also register for your exams online at www.sylvanprometric.com or www.vue.com.

When you schedule the exam, you'll be provided with instructions regarding appointment and cancellation procedures, ID requirements, and information about the testing center location. In addition, you'll receive a registration and payment confirmation letter from Sylvan Prometric or VUE.

Microsoft requires certification candidates to accept the terms of a nondisclosure agreement before taking certification exams.

What the Windows 2000 Server Exam Measures

As in the past, the Windows 2000 Server exam is key to the rest of the MCSE exams. It's the primary exam for completing your MCSE certification. Your knowledge of Windows 2000 Server operation will help you on all of the other exams in the MCSE track.

This book is designed to help you learn about Windows 2000 Server and to pass Exam 70-215. We begin by covering the installation process, including attended and unattended installations—a favorite topic on the exams. You'll be expected to know how to plan for the installation and how to carry it out. Because Windows 2000 is replacing Windows NT 4.0 on networks, you'll also be tested on your understanding of how to perform upgrades.

No network is complete without resources. Windows 2000 provides many tools for managing critical information and making it easier for your users to find what they need on the network. The Distributed file system (Dfs) is a new way to organize network resources. You'll be tested on your proficiency to implement and use the Windows 2000 Server tools for granting access to resources.

On Windows 2000 Server it's easier to install and upgrade hardware. Through driver signing options, Microsoft helps you ensure that the drivers you use are the proper ones. Plug-and-Play devices, too, make hardware issues less complex. These topics will be covered on the exam.

Monitoring what's going on inside the computer, and then optimizing the computer to run at a peak level of performance will always be primary functions of the network administrator. You'll be tested on your knowledge of the tools used for these functions, as well as the parameters critical to understanding the computer's operation. You'll also be expected to understand how to protect the network's data, both System State and user data. Windows 2000 Server incorporates many ways to handle the data. It includes support for data compression, disk quotas, and dynamic disks and volumes.

The network structure itself is covered on the exam. Virtual Private Networks (VPNs), Terminal Services, and Web services have been added to the core services of Windows 2000. These are in addition to the other network services—DHCP, WINS, and dynamic DNS—and protocols supported in past versions.

Finally, there is the important matter of security. Windows 2000 Server makes it easier for you to put a security policy in place. There are several new tools to assist you, including the Encrypting File System (EFS), Local and System policies, and the Security Configuration Tool Set. This last is a set of tools that helps you analyze your security implementation and ensure that it's adequate to protect your network and its assets. Of course, these security issues will all be covered on the exam.

Tips for Taking Your Exam

Here are some general tips for taking your exam successfully:

- Arrive early at the exam center so you can relax and review your study materials, particularly tables and lists of exam-related information.

- Read the questions carefully. Don't be tempted to jump to an early conclusion. Make sure you know *exactly* what the question is asking.

- When answering multiple-choice questions you're not sure about, use a process of elimination to get rid of the obviously incorrect questions first. This will improve your odds if you need to make an educated guess.

- This test has many exhibits (pictures). It can be difficult, if not impossible, to view both the questions and the exhibit simulation on the 14- and 15-inch screens usually found at the testing centers. Call around to each center and see if they have 17-inch monitors available. If they don't, perhaps you can arrange to bring in your own. Failing this, some have found it useful to quickly draw the diagram on the scratch paper provided by the testing center and use the monitor to view just the question.

- You are allowed to use the Windows calculator during your test. However, it may be better to memorize a table of the subnet addresses and to write it down on the scratch paper supplied by the testing center before you start the test.

Once you've completed an exam, you'll be given immediate, online notification of your pass or fail status. You'll also receive a printed Examination Score Report indicating your pass or fail status and your exam results by section. (The test administrator will give you the printed score report.) Test scores are automatically forwarded to Microsoft within five working days after you take the test. You don't need to send your score to Microsoft. If you pass the exam, you'll receive confirmation from Microsoft, typically within two to four weeks.

Contact Information

To find out more about Microsoft Education and Certification materials and programs, to register with Sylvan Prometric, or to get other useful information, check the following resources. Outside the United States or Canada, contact your local Microsoft office or Sylvan Prometric testing center.

Microsoft Certified Professional Program—(800) 636-7544

Call the MCPP number for information about the Microsoft Certified Professional program and exams, and to order the latest Microsoft Roadmap to Education and Certification.

Sylvan Prometric testing centers—(800) 755-EXAM

Contact Sylvan to register to take a Microsoft Certified Professional exam at any of more than 800 Sylvan Prometric testing centers around the world.

Microsoft Certification Development Team—
Web: http://www.microsoft.com/trainingandservices

Contact the Microsoft Certification Development Team through their Web site to volunteer for participation in one or more exam development phases or to report a problem with an exam. Address written correspondence to the Certification Development Team, Microsoft Education and Certification, One Microsoft Way, Redmond, WA 98052.

Microsoft TechNet Technical Information Network—(800) 344-2121

The is an excellent resource for support professionals and system administrators. Outside the United States and Canada, call your local Microsoft subsidiary for information.

How to Contact the Publisher

Sybex welcomes reader feedback on all of its titles. Visit the Sybex Web site at www.sybex.com for book updates and additional certification information. You'll also find online forms to submit comments or suggestions regarding this or any other Sybex book.

Chapter

1

Installing Windows 2000 Server

MICROSOFT EXAM OBJECTIVES COVERED IN THIS CHAPTER:

▶ **Perform an attended installation of Windows 2000 Server.** *(pages 3 – 32)*

▶ **Perform an unattended installation of Windows 2000 Server.** *(pages 33 – 45)*

- Create unattended answer files by using Setup Manager to automate the installation of Windows 2000 Server.

- Create and configure automated methods for installation of Windows 2000.

▶ **Upgrade a server from Microsoft Windows NT 4.0.** *(pages 45 – 52)*

▶ **Deploy service packs.** *(pages 53 – 56)*

▶ **Troubleshoot failed installations.** *(pages 56 – 60)*

As the Windows 2000 Server product matures, you'll notice the exam changing its focus. Initially, upgrading will be an important topic, but after a while Microsoft will begin to de-emphasize the upgrade process and test more heavily on clean installations. As in the past, Microsoft will try to keep the exam focused on what is happening in the marketplace. Initially, many networks will be doing upgrades of existing systems. After the upgrade process has run its course, the majority of installations will be clean installations. The exams will reflect this activity.

This chapter covers what you need to know about installing the Microsoft Windows 2000 Server. As you'll see, there are many facets to the installation process. We'll look at everything from manually installing the operating system to performing unattended installations to performing upgrades.

The attended installation is the most common and is heavily tested. The section on unattended installations covers how to use the Setup Manager to assist in automating the installation process. The tools and installation methodology for unattended installations are also well covered in the exam. The third method of installation, upgrading the system from Windows NT Server, will receive gradually less emphasis in the exams.

Additionally, this chapter discusses deployment of service packs and the troubleshooting of failed installations. Service packs will be lightly covered on the exam, but troubleshooting failed installations will always remain a hot topic.

Perform an attended installation of Windows 2000 Server.

An *attended installation* of Windows 2000 server is the normal and typical way to install. Since most servers are unique in their function on the network, this work is done on a case-by-case basis. Microsoft has provided many tools to help you complete this task as easily as possible.

As is to be expected, this exam topic carries a lot of weight. Your ability to plan and carry out installation of Windows 2000 Server will be thoroughly tested.

Coverage of this objective includes the basic and advanced features of Windows 2000 Server. You'll need to be familiar with the requirements for installation and the basic configuration options needed to complete the installation. This section's Necessary Procedures section walks you through the attended installation process, which assumes that you are not upgrading from a previous version of Windows 2000. The upgrade is covered later in the chapter.

Critical Information

The Windows 2000 Server operating system provides many powerful features, including the Active Directory (AD), the Microsoft Management Console (MMC), and high levels of security. The Windows 2000 Server family is scalable through three versions: Windows 2000 Server, Windows 2000 Advanced Server, and Windows 2000 Datacenter Server. Before you can do anything with Windows 2000 Server, you must first install the product. This process is actually fairly easy if you have prepared for the installation, know what the requirements are, and have met the prerequisites for a successful installation.

Preparing for an installation involves making sure that your hardware meets the minimum requirements and that Windows 2000 Server supports your hardware. When you install Windows 2000 Server, you should know whether you are upgrading or installing a clean copy on your computer. An upgrade preserves existing settings; a clean install puts a clean copy of the operating system with brand-new settings on your computer. Installation preparation also involves making choices about your system's configuration, such as selecting a file system and a disk partitioning scheme.

Once you've completed all the planning, you're ready to install. This is a straightforward process that includes running a Setup program, running a Setup Wizard, and installing Windows 2000 Networking. If you're installing Windows 2000 as a domain controller, the final part of the process is to upgrade the server to a domain controller (DC).

If you have any problems with the installation, you'll need to troubleshoot them. Some problems that you might encounter are media defects or hardware that doesn't meet the minimum requirements.

When you install Windows 2000 Server, you should consider whether the computer will be used for dual-boot or multi-boot purposes. Dual- or multi-booting allows you to have your computer boot with operating systems other than Windows 2000 Server.

The first section of this chapter provides an overview of the Windows 2000 Server family. Then you'll learn how to prepare for Windows 2000 Server installation, perform the installation, troubleshoot any installation problems, and set up for dual-booting.

An Overview of the Windows 2000 Server Family

Following are some of the primary features of the Windows 2000 Server operating system:

- The *Active Directory,* which is based on Directory Services and provides a scalable network architecture that can be used to support a single server with a few objects, or thousands of servers with millions of objects

- An administrative console called the Microsoft Management Console (MMC), which can be customized by administrators to provide whatever administrative tools are required in a single logical framework

- Improved hardware support, including Plug-and-Play capabilities and hardware Wizards that facilitate new hardware installation

- File management services, which include features such as the Distributed File System (Dfs), increased security through the Encrypting File System (EFS), and the ability to set disk quotas for users of volumes

- High levels of security through utilities such as Security Configuration and Analysis; protocols such as Kerberos (for accessing resources in a Windows 2000 domain) and the IP Security Protocol (for authentication and data encryption); and the use of smart cards

---

NOTE Smart cards provide storage for protecting account numbers, passwords, and private keys.

- Support for remote operating system installations through services such as Remote Installation Server

- Intellimirror services, which include features such as offline files and folders, automatic installation and repair of network applications, and the ability to control users' Desktops by specifying Desktop configurations

- Windows Terminal Services, which enable legacy Desktops to access the network using the server's processing power

- Significant support for Internet connections through Internet Information Server (IIS)

- System recovery options, available through Startup and Recovery Options when Windows 2000 Server is started

The choice of Windows 2000 Server, Windows 2000 Advanced Server, or Windows 2000 Datacenter Server will be based on which version is best suited for your company's needs and budget. It is expected that Windows 2000 Server will be used in small to medium-sized companies, and Windows 2000 Advanced Server and Windows 2000 Datacenter Server by medium-sized to large companies or by Internet service providers (ISPs). The following sections describe the main features of the three versions of Windows 2000 Server.

Windows 2000 Server

Windows 2000 Server contains all the core features of the Windows 2000 Server family. Windows 2000 Server can serve as a file and print server, an applications server, a Web server, and a communications server. Some of the features supported by Windows 2000 Server include the following:

- Active Directory

- Internet and Web services

- High levels of security through Kerberos and a public-key infrastructure

- Windows Terminal Services

- Support for up to 4GB of memory

- Support for two processors on a new installation, or up to four-way symmetrical multiprocessing (SMP) support for servers that are upgraded from Windows NT Server

---

NOTE This book and the associated MCSE exam are based on Windows 2000 Server. All of the features of Windows 2000 Server are included in Windows 2000 Advanced Server and Windows 2000 Datacenter Server.

Windows 2000 Advanced Server

Windows 2000 Advanced Server is a more powerful server designed for medium to large operations. It includes all the features of Windows 2000 Server and more, including the following:

- Network load balancing

- Cluster services for application fault tolerance

- Support for up to 8GB of memory

- Up to eight-way SMP support

Windows 2000 Datacenter Server

Windows 2000 Datacenter Server is the most powerful in the Microsoft server family. Designed for large-scale enterprise networks, this operating system includes all the features of Windows 2000 Advanced Server and adds the following:

- Advanced clustering services

- Support for up to 64GB of memory

- Up to 16-way SMP support (OEM versions can support up to 32-way SMP)

Preparing to Install Windows 2000 Server

Planning and preparation are key to making your Windows 2000 Server installation go smoothly. Before you begin the installation, you should know what is required for a successful installation and have ready all the pieces of information you'll need to supply during the installation process. Make sure you have or know the following:

- The hardware requirements for Windows 2000 Server

- Whether your hardware is supported by Windows 2000 Server

- The difference between a clean installation and an upgrade

- What installation options are suitable for your system, such as the disk-partitioning scheme and file system you'll select for Windows 2000 Server to use

Hardware Requirements

In order to install Windows 2000 Server successfully, your system must meet certain hardware requirements. Table 1.1 lists the minimum requirements as well as the more-realistic recommended requirements.

NOTE The minimum hardware requirements for Windows 2000 Server and Windows 2000 Advanced Server are the same.

The *minimum* requirements specify the minimum hardware necessary before you should even consider installing Windows 2000 Server. These minimums assume that you are just installing the operating system and not running any special services or applications. For example, you may be able to get by with the minimum requirements if you are installing the operating system just to learn the basics of the software.

The *recommended* requirements are what Microsoft recommends in order to achieve what is considered "acceptable performance" for the most common configurations. Since computer technology and the standards for acceptable performance are constantly changing, these recommendations are somewhat subjective. They are based on the standards at the time Windows 2000 Server was released.

NOTE   The hardware requirements listed in Table 1.1 were those specified at the time this book was published. Check Microsoft's Web site at http://www.microsoft.com/windows2000/guide/server/ sysreq/default.asp for the most current information.

TABLE 1.1:   Hardware Requirements for Windows 2000

Component	Minimum	Recommended
Processor	Pentium 133MHz or higher	Pentium 166MHz or higher
Memory	128MB	256MB
Disk space	2GB hard drive with 1GB free disk space (more free space is required if you are installing Windows 2000 Server from over the network)	Depends on the applications and data you'll store on your server

TABLE 1.1: Hardware Requirements for Windows 2000 *(continued)*

Component	Minimum	Recommended
Network	None	Network card and any other hardware required by your network topology (if you want to connect to a network)
Display	Video adapter and monitor with VGA resolution	Video adapter and monitor with VGA resolution or better

TIP Table 1.1 represents the operating system requirements. If you are running any processor- or memory-intensive tasks or applications, factor these in separately. When determining required disk space for add-on software and data, a good rule of thumb is to plan what you need for the next 12 months, then double that number.

Depending on the installation method you choose, other devices may be required:

- If you're installing Windows 2000 Server from the CD, you should have at least a 12X CD-ROM drive.

- To start the installation locally and to create an Emergency Repair Disk, you need a high-density floppy drive.

- If you choose to install Windows 2000 Server from the network, you need a network connection and a server with the distribution files.

The Hardware Compatibility List (HCL)

Along with meeting the minimum requirements, your hardware should appear on the Hardware Compatibility List (HCL). The HCL is an extensive list of computers and peripheral hardware that have been tested with the Windows 2000 Server operating system.

The Windows 2000 Server operating system requires control of the hardware for stability, efficiency, and security. The hardware and supported drivers on the HCL have been put through rigorous tests. Microsoft guarantees that the items on the list meet the requirements for Windows 2000 Server and do not have any incompatibilities that could affect the stability of the operating system.

If you call Microsoft for support, the first thing a Microsoft support engineer will ask about is your configuration. If you have any hardware that is not on the HCL, there is no guarantee of support.

TIP To determine if your computer and peripherals are on the HCL, check the most up-to-date list at www.microsoft.com/hwtest/hcl.

Clean Install or Upgrade?

Once you've determined that your hardware meets the minimum requirements and is on the official HCL, you need to decide whether you want to do a clean install or an upgrade.

If you already have Windows NT installed on your computer, you might want to upgrade that system to Windows 2000 Server. In an *upgrade,* you retain options such as the Desktop, users and groups, and program groups and items. During an upgrade, you point to a prior operating system, and the Windows 2000 Server files are loaded into the same folder that contained the former operating system.

The only operating systems that can be upgraded to Windows 2000 Server are Windows NT Server versions 3.51 and 4. Any other operating systems cannot be upgraded, but they may be able to coexist with Windows 2000 in a multi-boot environment.

If you don't have Windows NT Server, you need to perform a clean install. A *clean install* puts the operating system into a new folder and uses its default settings the first time the operating system is loaded.

Installation Options

You'll make many choices during the Windows 2000 Server installation process. Before you start the installation, you should know which options you'll select. Following are some of the options that you'll configure, as described in the sections coming up:

- How your hard disk space will be partitioned
- The file system your partitions will use
- The licensing method the computer will use
- Whether the computer will be part of a workgroup or a domain
- The language and locale for the computer's settings

Partitioning of Disk Space

Disk partitioning is the act of taking the physical hard drive and creating logical partitions. Creating a *logical drive* is how space is allocated to the drive's primary and logical partitions. Disk partitioning and logical drives are discussed in Chapter 5. Following are some of the major considerations for disk partitioning:

- The amount of space required
- The location of the system and boot partition
- Any special disk configurations you'll use
- The utility you'll use to set up the partitions

SIZE MATTERS

One important consideration in your disk-partitioning scheme is determining the partition size. You need to consider the amount of space taken up by your operating system, the size of applications that will be installed, and the amount of stored data. It's also important to consider future space requirements.

Just for Windows 2000 Server itself, Microsoft recommends that you allocate at least 1 GB of disk space. This allows room for the operating system files and for future growth in terms of upgrades, and for installation files that are placed with the operating system files.

THE SYSTEM AND BOOT PARTITIONS

When you install Windows 2000, files will be stored in two locations: the system partition and the boot partition.

The *system partition* contains the files needed to boot the Windows 2000 Server operating system. The system partition files do not take any significant disk space. By default, the system partition uses the computer's active partition, which is usually the C: drive.

The *boot partition* contains the files that are the Windows operating system. By default, the Windows operating system files are located in a folder named WINNT. You can, however, specify another location for this folder during the installation process. Microsoft recommends that the boot partition be at least 1GB.

TIP   Remember, the system and boot partitions hold files that are the opposite of what their names imply. The system file contains the boot files, and the boot partition holds the operating system files.

SPECIAL DISK CONFIGURATIONS

Windows 2000 Server supports several disk configurations. Options include simple, spanned, striped, mirrored, and RAID-5 volumes.

NOTE   Windows 2000 Professional does not support mirrored and RAID-5 volumes. It does support the simple, spanned, and striped dynamic volumes.

DISK PARTITION CONFIGURATION UTILITIES

If you're partitioning your disk prior to installation, you can use several utilities, including the DOS or Windows FDISK program or a third-party utility such as PowerQuest's Partition Magic. You might want to create only the first partition where Windows 2000 Server will be installed. You can then use the Disk Management utility in Windows 2000 to create any other partitions you need. The Windows 2000 Disk Management utility is discussed in Chapter 5.

TIP   You can get more information about FDISK and other disk utilities from your DOS or Windows documentation. Also, basic DOS functions are covered in *Windows 2000: MCSE JumpStart*, by Lisa Donald (Sybex, 2000).

File System Selection

Another factor that determines your disk-partitioning scheme is the type of file system you use. Windows 2000 Server supports three file systems: the File Allocation Table (FAT16), FAT32, and New Technology File System (NTFS).

FAT16

FAT16 (originally just FAT) is the 16-bit file system widely used by DOS and Windows 3.*x*. FAT16 tracks the storage location of files on a disk using a file allocation table and a directory entry table. With FAT, the table of directory entries keeps track of the location of the file's first block, the filename and extension, the date and time stamps on the file, and any attributes associated with the file.

The disadvantages of FAT16 are that it only supports partitions up to 2GB and does not offer the security features of NTFS.

On the plus side, FAT16 is backward compatible, which is important if the computer will be dual-booted with DOS or any other operating system. DOS, Unix, Linux, OS/2, Windows 3.1, and Windows 9*x* are compatible with FAT16.

FAT32

FAT32 is the 32-bit version of FAT. It was first introduced in 1996 with Windows 95, OEM (original equipment manufacturer) Service Release 2 (OSR2). FAT32's many advantages over FAT16 include the following:

- Disk partitions can be as large as 2TB (terabytes).

- More safeguards were added to provide fault tolerance in the event of disk failure.

- It improves disk-space usage by reducing cluster size.

The disadvantages of FAT32 are that it lacks several of the features offered by NTFS for a Windows 2000 system, such as local security, file encryption, disk quotas, and compression.

If you choose to use FAT, Windows 2000 will automatically format the partition with FAT16 if the partition is under 2GB. Partitions over 2GB will be automatically partitioned as FAT32.

WARNING   Windows NT 4 and earlier releases of NT do not support FAT32.

NTFS

NTFS is a file system designed to provide additional features for Windows NT and Windows 2000 computers. NTFS version 5 ships with Windows 2000. Following are some features of NTFS:

- Local security settings for files and folders

- Data compression to reduce disk storage requirements

- Disk quotas, which can be assigned to limit the amount of disk space a user can use

- File encryption, for an additional level of security

Unless you're planning to dual-boot your computer to an operating system other than Windows NT, Microsoft recommends using NTFS.

Licensing Mode

Licensing pays the good folks at Microsoft for all of the hard work they put into developing the Windows 2000 operating system. There are two main aspects to licensing: You pay for the local operating system, and you pay for client access. So if you're running Windows 2000 Server as your server and Windows 2000 Professional and Windows 98 for your clients, you must license the appropriate operating system for each individual computer. You also license the access of network servers.

When you install Windows 2000 Server, you're given the choice between Per Server or Per Seat licensing. *Per Server licensing* specifies the number of concurrent network connections that can be made to a server. *Per Seat licensing* specifies that each client will be licensed separately and that each client can access as many servers as it needs.

You should choose Per Server licensing if your users access only one server at a time. For example, if you have 10 users and one server, Per Server will be less expensive.

If your users access more than one server concurrently, choose Per Seat licensing. For example, if you have 10 users and two servers with Per Seat licensing, you'll need to buy only 10 client licenses, called *Client Access Licenses (CALs)*. Under Per Server licensing, each server would have to be licensed for 10 connections.

NOTE   Windows 2000 Professional only requires that you license the operating system.

Membership in a Domain or Workgroup

One installation choice for Windows 2000 Server is whether your computer will be installed as a part of a *workgroup* or as part of a *domain*.

You should install as part of a workgroup if you're part of a small, decentralized network or if you're running Windows 2000 Server on a nonnetworked computer. To join a workgroup, you simply choose that workgroup.

Domains are part of larger, centrally administered networks. Install your computer as part of a domain if any Windows 2000 servers on your network are configured as domain controllers with the Active Directory installed. To join a domain, you must specify the name of a valid domain and provide the username and password of a user who has rights to add a computer to the domain. Both a DC for the domain and a DNS server must be available to authenticate the request to join the domain.

Language and Locale

Language and locale settings are used to determine the language the computer will use. Windows 2000 supports many languages for the operating system interface and utilities.

Locale settings are used to configure the *locality* for items such as numbers, currencies, times, and dates. Examples of a locality are that English for United States specifies a short date as *mm/dd/yyyy* (month/day/year), and English for South Africa specifies a short date as *yyyy/mm/dd* (year/month/day).

Choosing Your Installation Method

You can install Windows 2000 Server by using the distribution files on the Windows 2000 Server CD, or by using files that have been copied to a network share point. The following sections describe each installation method.

Installing from the Windows 2000 Server CD

When you install Windows 2000 Server from the product CD, you have three options for starting the installation:

- You can boot to another operating system, access your CD-ROM drive, and run WINNT.EXE or WINNT32.EXE, depending on which operating system you are using.

- If your computer can boot to the CD, you can insert the Windows 2000 Server CD into the computer's CD-ROM drive and restart your computer.

- If your computer has no operating system installed and does not support booting from the CD-ROM drive, you can use the Windows 2000 Server Setup Boot Disks.

Installing from Another OS

If your computer already has an operating system (OS) installed and you want to upgrade your OS or dual-boot your computer, first boot your computer to the currently installed OS, and then start the Window 2000

Server installation process. Depending on which OS you're running, you would use one of the following commands from the I386 folder to start the installation process:

- From Windows *9x* or Windows NT, use WINNT32.EXE.

- From any other operating system, use WINNT.EXE.

Installing by Booting the Windows 2000 CD

If your computer can boot from the CD, then all you need to do to start the installation process is insert the Windows 2000 Server CD and restart your computer. When the computer boots, the Windows 2000 Server installation process will launch automatically.

Installing from Setup Boot Disks

If your computer cannot boot from the CD-ROM drive, you can create floppy disks that boot to the Windows 2000 Server operating system. These disks are called the *Windows 2000 Server Setup Boot Disks*. Using them, you can install or reinstall Windows 2000 Server. The Setup Boot Disks are not specific to a computer; they are general Windows 2000 Server disks that can be used on any computer running Windows 2000 Server.

To create these disks, you need four high-density floppy disks. Label them **Windows 2000 Server Setup Boot Disk, Windows 2000 Server Setup Disk #2, Windows 2000 Server Setup Disk #3,** and **Windows 2000 Server Setup Disk #4.**

The command to create boot disks from Windows 2000, Windows NT, or Windows *9x* is MAKEBT32.EXE. The command to make boot disks from a 16-bit operating system is MAKEBOOT.EXE. These utilities are located on the Windows 2000 Server CD in the BOOTDISK folder.

NOTE The Windows 2000 Server Setup Boot Disks are also used for the Recovery Console and the Emergency Repair Disk disaster-recovery methods. The Recovery Console and the Emergency Repair Disk are discussed in Chapter 4.

Installing over a Network Connection

If you are installing Windows 2000 Server over the network, you need a distribution server and a computer with a network connection. A *distribution server* is a server that has the Windows 2000 Server distribution files in a shared folder. Here are the steps to install Windows 2000 Server over the network:

1. Boot the target computer.

2. Attach to the distribution server and access the share that has the WINNT folder shared.

3. Launch WINNT or WINNT32 (depending on the computer's current operating system).

4. Complete the Windows 2000 Server installation.

Running the Windows 2000 Server Installation Process

As explained in the preceding section, you can run the Windows 2000 Server installation from a CD or over a network. The only difference in the installation procedure is the starting point—from your CD-ROM drive or from a network share.

The installation steps in the following sections assume that the disk drive is clean and that you're starting the installation using the Windows 2000 Server CD.

There are four steps in the Windows 2000 Server installation process:

- Run the Setup program. If you boot from DOS or Windows 9x, the Setup program will be DOS-based. If you boot from Windows NT, the Setup program will be GUI-based.

- Run the Setup Wizard.

- Install Windows 2000 Networking.

- Upgrade the server to a DC (if this is a DC rather than a member server).

Running the Setup Program

The Setup program starts the Windows 2000 Server installation. In this stage, you start the installation program, choose the partition where Windows 2000 will be installed, and then copy files. After you indicate the partition that will be used as the Windows 2000 boot partition, the Windows installation files are copied to the installation folders. Then the computer automatically reboots.

Running the Windows 2000 Setup Wizard

Once your computer finishes with the Setup program and the computer has restarted, the Windows 2000 Setup Wizard starts automatically. The first thing it does is detect and install device drivers. This process takes several minutes, and your screen may flicker in the meantime. Then the Setup Wizard gathers information about your locale, name, product key, licensing mode, computer name, and password.

Installing Windows 2000 Networking

After the Setup Wizard is done, the Network Identification Wizard starts automatically. This Wizard is responsible for the network component installation. Depending on your server's configuration, you may see a dialog box with options for specifying how users will log on to the computer. You have two choices:

- Users Must Enter a User Name and Password to Use This Computer. This option does just what it says—users must enter a username and password to log on to the computer.

- Windows Always Assumes the Following User Has Logged On. This option sets up Windows 2000 so that the user doesn't need to enter a username or password to use the computer. You might choose this option if you are the only person using the computer in a secure, nonnetworked environment. On the other hand, you don't want to allow such a security risk in a networked business environment.

Next, the Network Identification Wizard prompts you to finish the Wizard. If you chose Users Must Enter a User Name and a Password, you need to provide a valid Window 2000 username and password in the Log On to Windows dialog box. At this point, the only users who are enabled are Administrator and the *initial user* (which is the username you entered for identification).

After the installation is complete, you are logged on and greeted by the Windows 2000 Server Getting Started Wizard. This Wizard helps new users navigate the operating system.

Upgrading a Member Server to a Domain Controller

Once a server has been installed with the Windows 2000 OS, you can upgrade the server to a *domain controller (DC)* using the DCPROMO utility. You can specify that the server is the first DC in a new domain or add it to an existing domain. If you already have the Active Directory installed on your network, you can create a new child domain in the existing domain tree or install the domain tree as part of an existing forest (domain trees and forests are explained just below).

The steps for this process, described in the Necessary Procedures section, assume that you are creating the first DC in a new domain and that you are installing the Active Directory for the first time; this is our configuration for the procedures shown in this chapter. These steps also assume that DNS is not yet configured on your network.

The Logical Organization of the Active Directory

The Windows 2000 *Active Directory (AD)* is designed to be a scalable network structure. The logical structure of the Active Directory consists of containers, domains, and organizational units (OUs).

- A *container* is an AD object that holds other AD objects. Domains and OUs are examples of container objects.

- A *domain* is the main logical unit of organization in the Active Directory. The objects in a domain all share common security and account information. Each domain must have at least one domain controller. The DC is a Windows 2000 Server computer that stores the complete domain database.

- Each domain can consist of multiple *organizational units*, logically organized in a hierarchical structure. OUs may contain users, groups, security policies, computers, printers, file shares, and other Active Directory objects.

Domains are connected to one another through logical structure relationships. The relationships are implemented through domain trees and domain forests.

A *domain tree* is a hierarchical organization of domains in a single, contiguous namespace. In the AD, a tree is a hierarchy of domains interconnected through a series of *trust relationships* (logical links that combine two or more domains into a single administrative unit). The advantage of using trust relationships between domains is that they allow users in one domain to access resources in another domain, assuming the users have the proper access rights.

A *domain forest* is a set of domain trees that do not form a contiguous namespace. For example, you might have a forest if your company merged with another company. With a forest, each company could maintain a separate corporate identity through its namespace but share information across the Active Directory.

Supporting Multiple-Boot Options

You may want to install Windows 2000 Server but still be able to run other operating systems. *Dual-booting* or *multi-booting* allows your computer to boot multiple operating systems. Your computer will be automatically configured for dual-booting if there was a supported OS on your computer prior to the Windows 2000 Server installation (and you didn't upgrade from that OS).

One reason for dual-booting is to test various systems. If you have a limited number of computers in your test lab and you want to be able to test multiple configurations, you dual-boot. For example, you might configure one computer to multiple-boot with Windows NT Workstation 4, Windows NT Server 4 configured as a *primary domain controller (PDC)*, Windows 2000 Professional, and Windows 2000 Server.

Another reason to set up dual-booting is for backward compatibility among software. For example, you may have an application that works with Windows 95 but not under Windows 2000 Server. If you want to use Windows 2000 and still be able to access your legacy application, you can configure a dual-boot.

Here are the keys to successful dual-boot configurations:

- Make sure you have plenty of disk space. It's a good idea to put each OS on a separate partition, although this is not required.

- Put the simplest operating systems on the disk first. If you want to support dual-booting between DOS and Windows 2000 Server, DOS must be installed first. If you install Windows 2000 Server first, you cannot install DOS without ruining your Windows 2000 Server configuration. This requirement also applies to Windows 9x.

- *Never, ever, upgrade to Windows 2000 dynamic disks.* Dynamic disks are seen only by Windows 2000 and are not recognized by any other operating system, including Windows NT.

- Do not convert your file system to NTFS if you are planning a dual-boot with any operating system other than Windows NT or Windows 2000. These two operating systems are the only ones that recognize NTFS.

- If you will dual-boot with Windows NT 4, you must turn off disk compression, or Windows 2000 will not be able to read the drive properly.

NOTE   If you're planning to dual-boot with Windows NT 4, you should upgrade it to NT 4 Service Pack 4 (or higher) so that you'll have NTFS version 5 support.

Once you have installed each operating system, you can choose the operating system that you'll boot to during the boot process. You'll see a boot options screen that asks you to choose which operating system you want to boot.

Necessary Procedures

This section contains procedures for running the Setup program, running the Windows 2000 Setup Wizard, and upgrading a member server to a domain controller.

Running the Setup Program

1. On an Intel computer, access your CD-ROM drive and open the
I386 folder. This folder contains all the installation files for an
Intel-based computer.

2. Start the Setup program.

- If you are installing Windows 2000 Server from an operating
  system other than Windows 9*x* or Windows NT, launch
  WINNT.EXE.

- If you are installing Windows 2000 Server from 32-bit mode
  Windows 9*x* or Windows NT, launch WINNT32.EXE.

3. The Windows 2000 Setup dialog box appears. Your first choice is
to specify the location of the distribution files. By default, this is
where you executed the WINNT program. Normally, you just accept
the default path and press Enter.

4. The Setup files are copied to your disk. If the SMARTDRV program is
not loaded on your computer, you'll see a message recommending
that you load SMARTDRV. This is a disk-caching program that
speeds up the process of copying files. SMARTDRV ships with DOS
and Windows.

NOTE With SMARTDRV, it usually takes a few minutes to copy the
files. Without SMARTDRV, it can take more than an hour.

---

5. Once the files have been copied, you are prompted to remove any
floppy disks and to restart the computer.

6. The opening Windows 2000 Setup dialog box appears. At this point,
you can set up Windows by pressing Enter; or repair a Windows 2000
installation by pressing R; or quit the Setup process by pressing F3.

7. The Windows 2000 License Agreement dialog box appears. You can
accept the License Agreement by pressing F8, or you can disagree by
pressing Escape (or F3 if you are in DOS mode). If you press Escape,
the installation program will terminate, and your name and address
will be sent directly to Microsoft for further analysis (just kidding
about that second part).

8. The next dialog box asks you in which partition you want to set up Windows 2000. You can pick a partition that already exists, or choose some free space and let a partition be created for you. Whichever method you choose, the partition must have at least 1GB of free space. The default folder name will be WINNT. At this point, you can create or delete partitions and the file systems the partitions will use (discussed in Chapter 5).

Running the Windows 2000 Setup Wizard

1. The Regional Settings dialog box appears. From this dialog box, you choose your locale and keyboard settings. Locale settings are used to configure international options for numbers, currencies, times, and dates. With keyboard settings, you can configure your keyboard to support specific local characters or keyboard layouts (for example, Danish and United States-Dvorak).

2. In the Personalize Your Software dialog box, fill in the Name and Organization boxes. This information is used to personalize your operating system software and the applications that you install. If you install Windows 2000 Server in a workgroup, the Name entry here is used for the *initial user.*

3. Next up is the Product Key dialog box. In the boxes at the bottom, you type the 25-character product key, found on the back of your Windows 2000 Server CD case.

4. In the Licensing Modes dialog box, choose Per Server licensing or Per Seat licensing.

5. The Computer Name and Administrator Password dialog box appears next. Your computer name can be up to 15 characters. Specify a name that will uniquely identify your computer on the network. The Setup Wizard suggests a name, but you can change it. Also, type and confirm the Administrator password. An account called Administrator will automatically be created as a part of the installation process.

WARNING   Be sure that the computer name is a unique name within your network. If you're part of a corporate network, verify that the computer name follows the naming convention designated by your Information Services (IS) department.

---

6. If you have a Plug-and-Play modem installed, you'll see the Modem Dialing Information dialog box next. Here, you specify your country/region, your area code (or city code), whether you dial a number to get an outside line, and whether the telephone system uses tone dialing or pulse dialing.

7. In the next dialog box, Date and Time Settings, enter your date and time settings and the time zone in which your computer is located. You can also configure the computer to automatically adjust for daylight savings time.

8. Next up is the Network Settings dialog box, where you specify how you want to connect to other computers, networks, and the Internet. You have two choices:

   - Typical Settings installs network connections for Client for Microsoft Networks, as well as File and Print Sharing for Microsoft Networks. This choice also installs the TCP/IP protocol with an automatically assigned address.

   - Custom Settings allows you to customize your network settings. You can choose whether or not you want to use Client for Microsoft Networks, File and Print Sharing for Microsoft Networks, and the TCP/IP protocol. Use the Custom Settings if you need to specify particular network settings, such as a specific IP address and subnet mask.

9. In the next dialog box, Workgroup or Computer Domain, specify whether your computer will be installed as a part of a local workgroup or as a part of a domain.

10. Now the computer will perform some final tasks, including installing Start menu items, registering components, saving settings, and removing any temporary files. This will take several minutes. After

the final tasks are complete, you'll see the Completing the Windows 2000 Setup Wizard dialog box. Remove the CD, and click the Finish button to restart your computer.

Upgrading a Member Server to a Domain Controller

1. Select Start ➢ Run, type **DCPROM** in the Run dialog box, and click the OK button.

2. The Active Directory Installation Wizard starts. Click the Next button.

3. The Domain Controller Type dialog box appears. Select the option Domain Controller for a New Domain, and click Next to continue.

4. The Create Tree or Child Domain dialog box appears. To create a new domain tree, select Create a New Domain Tree and click the Next button.

5. In the Create or Join Forest dialog box, select Create a New Forest of Domain Trees and click Next.

6. The New Domain Name dialog box appears. Specify the full DNS name for the new domain, such as sample.com, and click Next to continue.

NOTE Usually, DNS is configured for the network before you create a domain controller.

---

7. The NetBIOS Domain Name dialog box is next. NetBIOS domain names are used for compatibility with Windows NT clients. By default, the domain NetBIOS name is the same as the DNS name. You can change this to another name or accept the default. Click Next to continue.

8. In the Database and Log Locations dialog box, specify the locations of the Active Directory database and the database log files. You can accept the default locations for these files or select other locations. Then click the Next button.

9. Next up is the Shared System Volume dialog box. This volume must be an NTFS 5 volume. You can accept the default folder location or select another location. Then click the Next button. (If the partition is not NTFS 5, you'll see an error message indicating that the file system must be converted.)

10. If DNS has not been configured, you'll see an informational message stating that the DNS server can't be located. Click the OK button to continue. If DNS has been configured, you'll go directly to the Configure DNS dialog box.

11. The Configure DNS dialog box appears next. To configure DNS, select the option Yes, Install and Configure DNS on This Computer (Recommended). If you want to install DNS manually, select No, I Will Install and Configure DNS Myself. After you have made your selection, click Next to continue.

12. The Permissions dialog box appears. If you want to be able to use server programs on servers that run earlier versions of Windows or that are in a domain operating under a previous version of Windows, select the option for Permissions Compatible with Pre-Windows 2000 Servers. Otherwise, select the Permissions Compatible only with Windows 2000 Servers option. Then click the Next button to continue.

13. Next up is the Directory Services Restore Mode Administrator Password dialog box, in which you can specify a password to be used if the server needs to be restarted in the Directory Services Restore Mode. Enter and confirm this password, then click the Next button.

NOTE   The Directory Services Restore Mode is an option on the Advanced Options menu, which is available at Windows 2000 startup.

---

14. The Summary dialog box appears, letting you confirm all the selections you have made. When this information is correct, click the Next button.

15. You'll see the Configuring Active Directory dialog box, which tells you that the Wizard is configuring the Active Directory and that this process may take several minutes. Then you'll be asked to insert your Windows 2000 Server CD so that additional files can be copied. Insert the CD and click the OK button.

16. The Configuring Active Directory dialog box reappears. When the configuration process is complete, you'll see the Completing the Active Directory Installation Wizard dialog box. Click the Finish button.

17. Finally, you're prompted to restart Windows 2000 so that the changes will be in effect. Click the Restart Now button.

NOTE   Once a server is upgraded to a DC, you can use the Active Directory. Creating domains, designing your DNS structure, and planning the Active Directory are covered in detail in *MCSE: Windows 2000 Directory Services Administration Study Guide*, by Anil Desai with James Chellis (Sybex, 2000).

Exam Essentials

Know the features of Windows 2000 server.   Windows 2000 Server offers support for Active Directory, Internet and Web services, Security, Windows Terminal services, support of 4GB of memory, and support of up to two processors (four if upgrading from Windows NT 4.0).

Know the additional features of Windows 2000 Advanced Server. Beyond the basic support offered by Windows 2000 Server, Windows 2000 Advanced Server offers network load balancing, cluster services for application fault tolerance, support of up to 8GB of memory, and support of up to eight processors.

Know the additional features of Windows 2000 Datacenter Server. In addition to the support offered by Windows 2000 Advanced Server, Windows 2000 Datacenter Server offers advanced clustering services, support for up to 64MB of memory, and support for up to 16 processors.

Know how to determine if your system hardware meets the standards for Windows 2000 Server.   Hardware requirements can be verified by checking the Hardware Compatibility List (HCL). Check the Microsoft Web site for the latest HCL.

Know the minimum hardware requirements for Windows 2000 Server. Windows 2000 Server requires, at a minimum, a Pentium 133MHz processor, 128MB of memory, 1GB of free space on the hard drive, and VGA resolution. In addition, a 12X CD-ROM, a high-density floppy drive, and a network connection are recommended.

Know what file systems are supported by Windows 2000 server. Windows 2000 supports FAT16, FAT32, and NTFS file systems.

Know the difference between the boot partition and the system partition. The boot partition contains the operating system files, contained in the WINNT directory. The system partition contains the boot files.

Know the two licensing modes for Windows 2000 Server. You have a choice between the Per Server and the Per Seat licensing modes. Per Server limits the number of concurrent connections to the server. Per Seat licensing applies the Client Access Licenses to the client systems. This allows for an unlimited number of connections to the server.

Know the difference between a workgroup and a domain. A workgroup is a small, decentralized network. Domains are larger, centrally administered networks.

Know the various methods for installing Windows 2000 Server. There are many ways to install Windows 2000 Server, including installing from the CD; upgrading from another operating system; booting from the Windows 2000 Server CD; and installing over a network connection. Each method offers different advantages.

Know the main steps in the Windows 2000 Server installation. Installation is performed in four major steps: running the Setup program, running the Windows 2000 Setup Wizard, installing Windows 2000 Networking, and upgrading a member server to a domain controller.

Know the multi-boot (dual-boot) options. Multi-booting allows you to boot to more than one OS. This is very useful when you're testing out different configurations or operating systems. Also, it allows backward compatibility for older operating systems.

Key Terms and Concepts

Active Directory (AD)   The Windows 2000 scalable network structure, consisting of containers, domains, and organizational units.

attended installation   The most common method of installing Windows 2000 Server. This method requires manual intervention to answer the many questions required by the installation process to configure the Windows 2000 Server.

boot partition   The partition that contains the Windows 2000 operating system files. These files are located in the WINNT directory.

clean install   A fresh installation of Windows 2000 Server.

Client Access License (CAL)   The license that allows client access to a Windows 2000 Server computer.

container   An Active Directory object that holds other Active Directory objects, such as domains and organizational units.

DCPROMO   The utility that is run to upgrade a member server to a DC.

distribution server   A server that has the Windows 2000 Server installation files in a shared folder; required for over-the-network installations.

domain   The main logical organizational unit in the Active Directory. Objects in a domain all share common security and account information.

domain controller (DC)   The Windows 2000 Server that stores the complete domain database.

domain forest   Set of domain trees that does not form a contiguous namespace, yet is part of the Active Directory.

domain tree   The hierarchical organizations that link domains that have trust relationships.

dual-boot   The ability of a computer to host and boot to multiple operating systems; also called multi-booting.

FAT32   The 32-bit version of File Allocation Table system; one of the file systems supported by Windows 2000 Server.

FAT16   Originally called FAT, the FAT16 file system is used by DOS and Windows 3.*x*. It is one of the file systems supported by Windows 2000 Server.

Hardware Compatibility List (HCL)   Microsoft's listing of all tested hardware for Windows 2000 Server.

NTFS   New Technology File System; the file system designed to provide additional features to Windows 2000, such as security, compression, disk quotas, and encryption.

organization unit (OU)   The hierarchical organization within a domain; contains users, groups, security policies, computers, printers, file shares, and other Active Directory objects.

Per Seat licensing   A licensing mode that applies the CALs to the client machines; allows an unlimited number of connections to the Windows 2000 Server.

Per Server licensing   A licensing mode that applies the CALs to the server; limits the number of connections to the Windows 2000 Server to the number of CALs applied.

system partition   The partition that contains the boot files for Windows 2000.

trust relationships   Logical links that combine two or more domains into a single administrative unit.

upgrade   An installation of Windows 2000 Server that preserves existing settings and applications from a previous version of Windows NT Server.

Windows 2000 Server Setup Boot Disks   The set of four disks that can be used to install Windows 2000 Server; also used for the Recovery Console and the Emergency Repair Process.

workgroup   A small, decentralized network with typically not more than 10 computers.

Sample Questions

1. You are the network administrator. You have just installed Windows 2000 Server on a computer. You want to upgrade the computer to a DC. Which utility do you use?

A. winnt32.exe

B. winnt.exe

C. dcpromo

D. dcupgrade.exe

Answer: C. The dcpromo utility is used to upgrade a member server to a domain controller. Winnt and winnt32 are used to install Windows 2000 Server.

2. Which of the following options can be specified during the installation of Windows 2000 Server? Choose all that apply.

A. Other operating systems that should be presented in a dual-boot or multi-boot configuration

B. The networking components that the server will use

C. The workgroup or domain that the server will join

D. Whether the server will be installed as a DC or member server

Answer: B, C. You can specify which workgroup or domain the server will join. You can't specify the server's role. If you want the server to be a DC, you upgrade the server through the DCPROMO utility. Your computer will be automatically configured for dual- or multi-boot if a supported OS was on your computer prior to the Windows 2000 Server installation.

Perform an unattended installation of Windows 2000 Server.

- **Create unattended answer files by using Setup Manager to automate the installation of Windows 2000 Server.**
- **Create and configure automated methods for installation of Windows 2000.**

The *unattended installation* is more appropriate for the Windows 2000 Professional installation. However, with the ability to cluster servers, the unattended installation is growing in importance to the Windows 2000 Server family. Several handy tools make the unattended installation an easier process, and Microsoft will lightly test your knowledge of these tools.

Although many third-party utilities have been used in the past to perform disk imaging, Microsoft has now included this capability to automatically deploy Windows 2000 Server. The System Preparation Tool allows you create the master image and then copy the image to the target computers. A Mini-Setup Wizard then walks you through the rest of the installation process to configure the unique information for each machine. For automation of the last portion of the installation, the Setup Manager utility helps you create an answer file for the unattended installation.

Critical Information

When you need to install Windows 2000 Server on multiple computers, one option is to manually install the operating system on each computer (as described in Chapter 1 of the *MCSE: Windows 2000 Server Study Guide*, "Getting Started with Windows 2000 Server"). Automated deployment, on the other hand, will make your job easier to do, your work more efficient, and the results more cost-effective.

You can automate the installation of Windows 2000 Server through the use of disk imaging or by using the unattended installation method. You can also use unattended answer files with automated installation, to answer the questions that are normally asked during the installation process. This section explains the use of disk images and unattended answer files, and briefly describes unattended installation.

Extracting the Windows 2000 Deployment Tools

The Windows 2000 Deployment Tools include two utilities that you can use to prepare for automated installations:

- The *System Preparation Tool* (Sysprep) is used for preparing disk images.

- The *Setup Manager* (Setupmgr) is used for creating unattended answer files.

Using Disk Images

Disk imaging, or disk duplication, is the process of creating a *reference computer* for the automated deployment. The reference, or *source,* computer has Windows 2000 Server installed and is configured with the settings and applications intended for the target computers. Disk imaging is a good choice for automatic deployment when you have the hardware that supports disk imaging and you have many computers with similar configuration requirements. For example, education centers that reinstall the same software every week might use this technology. Also, if a computer is having technical difficulties, you can use a disk image to quickly restore it to a baseline configuration.

Once you have your source computer configured with Windows 2000 Server and any applications that you wish to deploy, you use the System Preparation Tool to prepare the disk image. Then you remove the drive with the disk image, and insert the drive into a special piece of hardware called a disk duplicator, to copy the images. The copied disks are inserted into the target computers. After you add the hard drive that contains the disk image to the target computers, you can complete the installation from those computers. You can also copy disk images by using special third-party software.

Preparing for Disk Duplication

In order to use a disk image, the source and target computers must meet the following requirements:

- The mass-storage controllers (SCSI or IDE) must be the same type on the source and destination computers.

- The HAL (Hardware Abstraction Layer) must be the same on the source and destination computers. This means the processor type must be the same.

- The size of the destination computer's hard drive must be at least as large as the source computer's hard drive.

- Plug-and-Play devices on the source and destination computers do not need to match, as long as the drivers for the Plug-and-Play devices are available.

Using the System Preparation Tool

The System Preparation Tool (Sysprep) is included on the Windows 2000 Server CD in the Support\Tools folder, in the Deploy.cab file. After you extract Sysprep, you can run it on the source computer. Sysprep prepares the disk image, stripping from the master copy the information that must be unique for each computer, such as the security ID (SID).

After you install the copied image on the target computer, a Mini-Setup Wizard runs. This Wizard automatically creates a unique computer SID and then prompts the user for computer-specific information, such as the product ID, regional settings, and network configuration. The required information can also be supplied through an unattended answer file.

Table 1.2 list some of the command switches that you can use to customize the tasks Sysprep performs.

TABLE 1.2: Sysprep Command Switches

Switch	Description
-quiet	Runs the installation with no user interaction
-pnp	Forces Setup to run Plug-and-Play detection of hardware

TABLE 1.2: Sysprep Command Switches *(continued)*

Switch	Description
-reboot	Restarts the target computer
-nosidgen	Doesn't create an SID on the destination computer (used with disk cloning)

WARNING After you run the System Preparation Tool on a computer, you need to run the Setup Manager Wizard to reconfigure all the unique information for the computer. You should run this utility only on source (reference) computers that will be used for disk duplication purposes.

Copying and Installing from a Disk Image

After you've run Sysprep on the source computer, you can copy the disk image and then install it on the target computer.

If you're using special hardware (a disk duplicator) to duplicate the disk image, shut down the source computer and remove the disk. Copy the disk and install the copy into the target computer. If you're using special software, copy the disk image per the software vendor's instructions.

After the image is copied, turn on the destination computer. The Mini-Setup Wizard runs and prompts you to do the following (if you have not configured an answer file):

- Accept the End User License Agreement.

- Specify regional settings.

- Enter a name and organization.

- Specify your product key.

- Specify the licensing mode that will be used.

- Specify the computer name and Administrator password.

- Specify dialing information (if a modem is detected).

- Specify date and time settings.

- Specify which networking protocols and services should be installed.

- Join a workgroup or a domain.

If you have created an answer file for use with disk images, as described in the next section, the installation will run without requiring any user input.

Using Setup Manager to Create Answer Files

Answer files are automated installation scripts that answer the questions appearing during a normal Windows 2000 Server installation. You can use answer files with Windows 2000 Server Sysprep (disk image) installations or with unattended installations. Setting up answer files allows you to easily deploy Windows 2000 Server to computers that may not be configured identically, with little or no user intervention.

You create answer files through the Setup Manager (Setupmgr) utility. Using Setup Manager to create answer files has several advantages:

- You work through a graphical interface, which lets you create answer files easily and with fewer syntax errors.

- Addition of user-specific or computer-specific configuration information is simplified.

- You can include application setup scripts within the answer file.

- The utility creates the distribution folder that will be used for installation files.

The Setup Manager is included on the Windows 2000 Server CD in the Support\Tools folder, in the Deploy.cab file. After you extract the Setup Manager utility, you can run it to create a new answer file, create an answer file that duplicates the current computer's configuration, or edit an existing answer file.

NOTE With Remote Installation Services (RIS), the RIS server installs Windows 2000 on RIS clients. The RIS server can be configured with either of two types of images: a CD-based image, which contains only the Windows 2000 operating system; or a Remote Installation Preparation (RIPrep) image, which can contain the Windows 2000 OS and applications. RIS is typically used for remote installation of Windows 2000 Professional, and Microsoft has now introduced support for Windows 2000 Server installation through RIS.

Using Unattended Installation

Unattended installation is a practical method of automatic deployment when you have many servers to install and you don't want to use disk imaging. With an unattended installation, you use a distribution server to install Windows 2000 Server on a target computer.

The distribution server contains the Windows 2000 Server OS files and possibly an answer file to respond to installation configuration queries. The target computer must be able to connect to the distribution server over the network. After the distribution server and target computers are connected, you can initiate the installation process. Figure 1.1 illustrates the unattended installation process.

FIGURE 1.1: Unattended installation uses a distribution server and a target computer.

Distribution Server

Target

Stores:
Windows 2000 Server
operating system files
Answer files (optional)

Requires enough software to
connect to the distribution server

Necessary Procedures

The procedures in this section show you how to extract and install the Windows 2000 Deployment Tools; how to create a disk image using Sysprep; and how to make an answer file.

Installing the Deployment Tools

1. Log on to your Windows 2000 computer as Administrator.

2. Use Windows Explorer to create a folder named **Deployment Tools** on the root folder of drive C:.

3. Insert the Windows 2000 Server CD. Using Windows Explorer, copy the Support\Tools\Deploy file (the .cab extension is hidden) to the new Deployment Tools folder on C:.

4. Double-click the Deploy.cab file to display its contents.

5. In Windows Explorer, select Edit ➢ Select All. Then select File ➢ Extract.

6. The Browse for Folder dialog box appears. Select Local Disk (C:) and then Deployment Tools. Click the OK button to extract the files to the specified folder.

7. Verify that the Deployment Tools were extracted to C:\Deployment Tools. There should be eight items (including the Deploy.cab file).

Creating a Disk Image with *Sysprep*

1. Install Windows 2000 Server on a source computer. (See Chapter 1 of the *Study Guide* for instructions on installing Windows 2000 Server.)

2. Log on to the source computer as Administrator, and if desired, install and configure any other applications that you also want installed on the target computer.

3. Extract the Deploy.cab file from the Windows 2000 Server CD (see the procedure just above).

4. Select Start ➤ Run, and click the Browse button in the Run dialog box. Select Local Drive (C:), then Deployment Tools. Double-click Sysprep and click the OK button.

5. The Windows 2000 System Preparation Tool dialog box appears next, and warns you that the execution of this program will modify some of the computer's security parameters. Click the OK button.

6. You'll be prompted to turn off your computer.

Creating an Unattended Answer File

1. Select Start ➤ Run, and click the Browse button in the Run dialog box. Double-click the Deployment Tools folder, double-click the Setupmgr program, and then click the OK button.

2. When the Windows 2000 Setup Manager Wizard starts, click the Next button to proceed.

3. In the New or Existing Answer File dialog box, select Create a New Answer File and click the Next button.

4. In the Product to Install dialog box, choose Sysprep Install and click the Next button.

5. The Platform dialog box appears next. Select Windows 2000 Server and click the Next button.

6. In the License Agreement dialog box, choose to accept the End User License Agreement (EULA), so that the installation is fully automated. Select the option for Yes, Fully Automate the Installation, and click the Next button. If you don't accept the EULA, the end user will need to accept the license agreement, so the installation will not be fully automated.

7. Next up is the Customize the Software dialog box. Specify the name and organization that will be used for licensing information. After you enter this information, click the Next button.

8. In the Licensing Mode dialog box, specify whether you'll license the server by concurrent connections (Per Server) or by seat (Per Seat). If you choose Per Server, you can also set the number of concurrent connections allowed. (See Chapter 1 of the *Study Guide* for more information about the Per Server and Per Seat licensing modes.) Click Next to continue.

9. In the Computer Name dialog box, type in the name of the destination computer and click the Next button.

10. The Administrator Password dialog box appears next. You can
enter the Administrator password or specify that the user will be
prompted for an Administrator password. You can also specify
that when the computer starts, the Administrator will automatically be logged on for x number of times. Enter and confirm an
Administrator password and click Next to proceed.

11. Now you'll see the Display Settings dialog box. You can configure
the following settings:

   • Colors: Set the display color to the Windows default, 16 colors, 256
   colors, high color (16-bit), true color (24-bit), or true color (32-bit).

   • Screen Area: Set the screen area to the Windows default, or to 640
   × 480, 800 × 600, 1024 × 768, 1280 × 1024, or 1600 × 1200.

   • Refresh Frequency (the number of times the screen is updated):
   Set the refresh frequency to the Windows default, or to 60Hz,
   70Hz, 72Hz, 75Hz, or 85Hz.

   • Custom: This button displays a dialog box that helps you further customize display settings for the color, screen area, and
   refresh frequency.

   Click Next to accept all the default settings and continue.

12. The Network Settings dialog box appears. Typical Settings installs
TCP/IP, enables DHCP, and installs Client for Microsoft Networks. Custom Settings allows you to customize the computer's
network settings. Select the Typical Settings option and click the
Next button.

13. Next up is the Workgroup or Domain dialog box. Select the workgroup or Windows Server domain that the computer will be a part
of, and click the Next button.

14. In the Time Zone dialog box, select your computer's time zone
from the drop-down list. Click Next to continue.

15. The Additional Settings dialog box appears. If you want to edit
additional settings, you can configure the following:

   • Telephony settings

- Regional settings

- Languages

- Install printers

- A command that will run once the first time a user logs on

Click the Next button to accept the default selection of No, Do Not Edit the Additional Settings.

16. In the Sysprep Folder dialog box, you can create a Sysprep folder that will be used during the Sysprep installation to customize the installation. As noted in the dialog box, you might use this option to supply additional language support or third-party device drivers. Make your selection and click the Next button.

17. The Additional Commands dialog box appears next, allowing you to run commands at the end of the automated installation. You can specify any command that does not require a user to be logged on. After you add any additional commands, click the Next button.

18. The OEM Branding dialog box is next. You can configure an optional logo or background that can be used to display Original Equipment Manufacturer (OEM) information, called "OEM branding." If you want to use a logo and/or a background, specify the path to the appropriate files. Then click Next to continue.

19. The Additional Files or Folders dialog box appears. Specify any additional files or folders that should automatically be copied on the destination computers. If you want to copy other files, designate where you want the files to be stored on the destination computers, click the Add Files button, and select the files to include. Click the Next button.

20. A message box appears, asking you to specify the location of the Sysprep.exe file. Click OK, and the Open dialog box appears. By default, this dialog box shows the folder from which the Sysprep.exe command was run (in our example, C:\Deployment Tools). Click the Open button.

21. The OEM Duplicator dialog box appears. This dialog box allows you to configure information about the Sysprep installation that will be

included in the computer's Registry. This information can be used to determine which Sysprep image is installed on a specific computer. After this information is configured, click the Next button.

22. Now the Answer File Name dialog box appears. The Setup Manager Wizard will create a file in the folder from which the Sysprep command was run. This file is named sysprep.inf by default, but you can edit the location and name of this file. Click Next to continue.

23. Finally, you'll see the Completing the Windows 2000 Setup Manager Wizard dialog box, where you click the Finish button to end the Wizard.

Exam Essentials

Know what the System Preparation tool (Sysprep) does.   The System Preparation tool is used for preparing disk images. It also strips from the master copy the information that must be unique for each computer.

Know what the Setup Manager utility (Setupmgr) does.   The Setup Manager utility creates the unattended answer files used in unattended installations.

Know how to extract the Windows 2000 Deployment Tools. Before Sysprep and Setupmgr can be used, they must be extracted from the Deploy.cab file on the CD in the Support\Tools folder.

Know what is required for disk duplication.   To use a disk image, the source and target computer must have the same mass-storage controller and the same HAL; the target computer's hard drive must be at least as large as the source computer's; Plug-and-Play devices need not match, as long as the drivers are available.

Know when to use the Setup Manager Wizard.   The Setup Manager Wizard is run to configure all the unique information on the computer. This is done after the image has been copied.

Know how to create an answer file. The Setup Manager is used to create an unattended answer file. This utility reduces the number of syntax errors when you have to create the answer file manually.

Key Terms and Concepts

answer file   Automated installation scripts that are used to answer the questions that appear during the Windows 2000 Server installation process.

disk imaging   The process of creating a reference (source) computer for automating the deployment of Windows 2000 Server.

Setup Manager (Setupmgr)   A utility used to create unattended answer files.

System Preparation Tool (Sysprep)   A utility used to prepare disk images.

unattended installation   The practical method used to automatically deploy many servers without using disk imaging.

Sample Questions

1. Which of the following is *not* true of the computers involved in disk imaging?

A. The size of the hard drives must be the same.

B. The mass-storage controllers must be the same.

C. Plug-and-Play devices must be the same.

D. The HAL must be the same.

Answer: C. The Plug-and-Play devices need not be the same, as long as the drivers are available. The hard drive on the target computer must be at least as large as the hard drive on the source computer.

2. What is required to perform an unattended installation of Windows 2000 Server? Select all that apply.

A. A distribution server

B. An answer file

C. Setup Manager

D. Network connection

Answer: A, B, and D. With unattended installations, you use a distribution server. The target computer connects to the distribution server over the network. The answer file provides the answers to the installation process's questions. The Setup Manager is used to create the answer file but is not used during the unattended installation.

Upgrade a server from Microsoft Windows NT 4.0.

This section covers what you'll need to know on how to upgrade existing Windows NT Servers to Windows 2000 Servers. Although the upgrade process is much simpler than a clean installation, you do need to know the new hardware requirements. Follow the checklist to ensure that the upgrade can be completed without problems. The key to a successful upgrade lies in the preparation of the previous configuration.

This chapter contains only one Necessary Procedure; performing the upgrade is a relatively straightforward process. Once again, the details in the checklist are the key points to this section.

The topic of upgrading will be tested very heavily on the exam initially. Over time, the exam focus will move away from upgrading to focus on clean installations.

Critical Information

Before you attempt to upgrade Windows 2000 Server, you need to understand the difference between an *upgrade* and a *clean install*. If your existing operating system can be upgraded to Windows 2000 Server and you want to retain your system settings, then you'll choose to perform an upgrade. If your operating system does not support a Windows 2000 upgrade or if you want to start from scratch, then you'll perform a clean install. Client upgrade paths and requirements are used to determine if your operating system can be upgraded to Windows 2000 Server. In order to upgrade, you must be running Windows NT Server 3.51 or 4, and your hardware must meet the minimum requirements. This section explains the requirements for upgrading to Windows 2000 Server.

You'll need to perform several important tasks to prepare your computer before you start the upgrade process. This chapter provides a checklist to help you plan your upgrade strategy. For example, the items in the checklist include deleting any unnecessary files and applications, and taking an inventory of your computer's configuration.

After you've made your preparations, you're ready for the big moment. Here, you'll learn about all of the steps involved in the Windows 2000 Server upgrade process.

NOTE The upgrade process for Windows 2000 Professional and Windows 2000 Server. The primary differences are in the upgrade paths and hardware requirements.

Deciding Whether to Upgrade

An *upgrade* allows you to preserve existing settings. A *clean install* places Windows 2000 in a new folder. After a clean install, you need to reinstall all of your applications and reset your preferences.

You should perform an upgrade if all of the following conditions are true:

- You are running Windows NT Server 3.51 or 4.

- You want to keep your existing applications and preferences.

- You want to preserve local users and groups you've created under Windows NT.

- You want to upgrade your current OS with the Windows 2000 Server OS.

You should perform a clean install if any of the following conditions are true:

- There is no operating system currently installed.

- You have an OS installed that does not support an upgrade to Windows 2000 Server (such as DOS, Windows 3.*x*, Windows 9*x*, or Windows NT Workstation).

- You want to start from scratch, without keeping any existing preferences.

- You want to be able to dual-boot between Windows 2000 Server and your previous OS.

NOTE Performing a clean install and dual-booting are covered in detail in Chapter 1 of the *Study Guide.*

Preparing to Upgrade to Windows 2000 Server

This section describes the steps you need to take to get ready for an upgrade to Windows 2000 Server:

- Making sure that your system meets the operating system and hardware requirements

- Planning for the upgrade with an upgrade checklist

Server Upgrade Paths and Requirements

In order to upgrade to Windows 2000 Server, you must follow a particular path. In addition, the only operating systems that you can upgrade to Windows 2000 Server are Windows NT Server 3.51 and

Windows NT Server 4. If you're running a version of Windows NT Server prior to 3.51, you'll first need to upgrade to Windows NT Server 3.51 or 4 before you can upgrade to Windows 2000 Server.

NOTE There is no upgrade path from Windows NT Workstation to Windows 2000 Server.

The hardware requirements for upgrading to Windows 2000 Server are the same as those for a clean install. Your computer hardware must meet the following requirements:

- Pentium 133MHz or higher processor

- 128MB of RAM (256MB is better)

- 2GB hard drive with at least 1GB of free disk space

- VGA or better resolution monitor

Along with meeting these requirements, your hardware should be listed on the official Microsoft Hardware Compatibility List (HCL). See Chapter 1 of the *Study Guide* for more information about the HCL.

NOTE The foregoing hardware requirements were those specified at the time this book was published. Check Microsoft's Web site at http://www.microsoft.com/windows2000/upgrade/ for the latest information about system requirements, upgrade issues, and hardware and software compatibility.

Upgrade Checklist

Once you've made the decision to upgrade, you should develop a plan of attack. The following checklist will help you plan and implement a successful upgrade strategy.

- Back up all your data and configuration files and verify that you can successfully restore your backup. Before you make any major changes to your computer's configuration, you should always back up your data and configuration files. Chances are, if you have a valid backup, you won't have any problems; if you *don't* have a valid backup, you'll have problems.

- Delete any unnecessary files or applications, and clean up any program groups or program items you don't use. Theoretically, you want to delete all the junk on your computer before you upgrade. Think of this as the spring-cleaning step.

- To prepare your drive for the upgrade, perform a disk scan, a current virus scan, and defragmentation (more "spring-cleaning" chores). Verify that your drive has no errors or problems before you start the upgrade.

- Decompress any partitions that have been compressed with DriveSpace or DoubleSpace. You cannot upgrade compressed partitions.

- Be sure that your computer meets the minimum hardware requirements for Windows 2000 Server and that all of your hardware is on the HCL.

- Take an inventory of your current configuration. This inventory should include documentation of your current network configuration, the applications that are installed, the hardware items and their configuration, the services that are running, and any profile and policy settings.

- Perform the upgrade. In this step, you upgrade from your previous OS to Windows 2000 Server.

- Verify your configuration. After Windows 2000 Server has been installed, use your configuration inventory to verify that the upgrade was successful.

Performing the Windows 2000 Server Upgrade

As you'd expect, the process of upgrading to Windows 2000 is much simpler than performing a clean install. You designate the system from which you're upgrading, and then follow the Setup Wizard's instructions to provide the information the Setup program needs. The final steps in the upgrade process are automatic.

Once the Wizard is run, the computer will copy some files needed for installation and then automatically restart. Then the Windows 2000 Server installation process automatically examines your disk and begins copying files, which takes a few minutes. The installation continues through several phases. When the automated upgrade is complete, Windows 2000 Server will be installed on your computer.

NOTE If you're upgrading from a Windows NT domain controller, you'll also need to run the Active Directory Installation Wizard to complete the installation.

After the upgrade process is complete, verify that everything was upgraded properly. Using the inventory you made before upgrading (see the "Upgrade Checklist" section just above), check that your hardware and software have made it through the transition and are working properly.

Necessary Procedures

The following procedure tells you how to use the Windows 2000 Setup Wizard to perform a server upgrade.

Using the Setup Wizard to Perform an Upgrade

1. Start your current operating system and insert the Windows 2000 Server CD into your CD-ROM drive. If auto-play is turned on, you'll see an Upgrade dialog box. Click Yes to upgrade. If your computer doesn't automatically bring up the Upgrade dialog box, select Start ➤ Run ➤ Browse ➤ My Computer ➤ *your CD-ROM drive* ➤ I386 ➤ WINNT32.

2. When you see the Welcome to the Windows 2000 Setup Wizard dialog box, click the Upgrade to Windows 2000 (Recommended) option. Click the Next button to proceed.

3. In the License Agreement dialog box, click the option to accept the agreement.

NOTE   The upgrade will terminate if you do not accept the agreement.

4. The Product Key dialog box appears next. Type in the valid 25-character product key, which you can find on the back of the Windows 2000 Server jewel case. Click Next to proceed.

5. If your computer has FAT16 or FAT32 partitions, the next dialog box will be the Upgrading to the Windows 2000 NTFS File System dialog box. This dialog box allows you to convert your existing file system to NTFS. Make your selection and click the Next button.

The computer will copy some files needed for installation and then automatically restarts. After the restart, file copying begins. When the automated upgrade is complete, Windows 2000 Server will be installed.

Exam Essentials

Know when to perform an upgrade.   You should upgrade when you're running Windows NT Server 3.51 or Windows NT Server 4.0, when you want to preserve local users and groups that have been created, and when you want to preserve existing applications.

Know when to perform a clean installation.   Do a clean installation when you want to start from scratch, when you want to dual-boot, or when the current operating system does not support an upgrade.

Know the upgrade path.   You can only upgrade from Windows NT Server 3.51 or Windows NT Server 4.0.

Know how to prepare for an upgrade.   Before you upgrade, it's important to delete unnecessary files and applications, back up your data, do a disk scan, decompress any partitions, verify hardware requirements, and take inventory of the current configuration.

Know how to start an upgrade.   Run the `Winnt32` utility to begin the upgrade. After the Windows 2000 Setup Wizard dialog box appears, click the Upgrade to Windows 2000 option.

Key Terms and Concepts

There are no new terms for this section.

Sample Questions

1. You are currently running Windows NT Workstation 3.51. You want to upgrade to Windows 2000 Server. Which command do you use?

A. Winnt32.exe

B. Setup.exe

C. Winnt.exe

D. You cannot upgrade

Answer: D. You cannot upgrade Windows NT Workstation to Windows 2000 Server.

2. You are ready to upgrade from Windows NT 4.0 Server to Windows 2000 Server. What should you do before proceeding?

A. Decompress all compressed partitions.

B. Back up all your data.

C. Delete all applications.

D. Verify hardware requirements.

Answer: A, B, and D. Upgrade preparation includes deleting unnecessary files and applications, backing up your data, performing a disk scan, decompressing any partitions, verifying hardware requirements, and taking inventory of the current configuration. You don't need to delete all applications—only the ones that are no longer used or are unnecessary.

Deploy service packs.

Service packs are a necessary part of the Windows 2000 Server product. As new features are released and bugs are fixed, you'll want to incorporate the changes into Windows 2000 Server. This section describes the Windows Update utility and tells you how to work with service packs.

This topic will be covered only lightly on the exam. The Windows Update utility is so easy to use that not much testing is needed to see if you know how to use it.

Critical Information

One way to make sure that your Windows 2000 system is working at its best is to keep it up-to-date. The Windows Update utility helps you install Windows 2000 Server service packs as they become available, to fix bugs and (sometimes) add new features. You can also use the utility to check for and download the latest software (such as new drivers).

Using the Windows Update Utility

The *Windows Update utility* connects your computer to Microsoft's Web site and checks your files to make sure that you have all the latest and greatest updates.

To use Windows Update, you must first have a valid Internet connection. Then simply choose Start ➢ Windows Update to go to the correct URL for updates. For product updates, click the Product Updates link on the home page and follow the directions to choose which files you want to update. The files in the update section are arranged in the following categories:

- Critical updates

- Picks of the month

- Recommended updates

- Additional Windows features

- Device drivers

Within each category, you'll see the available updates, along with a description, file size, and estimated download time for each update. Just check the files you want to update and click the Download icon to download your selections.

Using Windows Service Packs

Service packs are used to deliver bug fixes (and sometimes new features) to Windows operating systems. Windows 2000 offers a new technology for service packs called *slipstream*. With slipstream technology, service packs are applied once and they are not overwritten as new services are added to the computer. This means you shouldn't need to reapply service packs after new services are added, as was sometimes required when Windows NT 4 service packs were applied.

To determine whether any service packs have been installed on your computer by using the winver command, select Start ➢ Programs ➢ Accessories ➢ Command Prompt. In the Command Prompt dialog box, type **winver** and press Enter. You'll see a dialog box that shows which service packs are currently installed.

Necessary Procedures

There are no necessary procedures for this objective.

Exam Essentials

Know how to get updates to Windows 2000 Server.   Updates are performed over the Internet, by connecting to the Microsoft Web site.

Know what the Windows Update utility can do.   The Windows Update utility checks the Microsoft Web site for critical updates, picks of the month, recommended updates, additional Windows features, and device drivers.

Know the purpose of service packs. Service packs are used to deliver bug fixes and sometimes new features to Windows operating systems.

Know how to determine which service packs are installed. The winver command is used to determine which service packs have been installed on a computer.

Key Terms and Concepts

service pack   A collection of bug fixes and (possibly) new features for a Windows operating system.

slipstream technology   A new technology used to deliver service packs from Microsoft. It allows you to install a service once. The service pack is not overwritten as new services are applied.

Windows Update utility   A utility that will connect your computer to the Microsoft Web site to ensure that you have the latest files and updates.

Sample Questions

1. You are the network administrator. You have applied the latest service pack to your Windows 2000 Server. You then add an additional service to the computer. What must you do to accommodate the new service?

A. Reapply the service pack.

B. Run the Windows Update utility.

C. Run the winnt32 command.

D. Nothing.

Answer: D. With slipstream technology, the service pack does not need to be applied more than once.

2. You are the network administrator and you're ready to run the Windows Update utility. What will be downloaded?

A. Picks of the month

B. Additional Windows features

C. Device drivers

D. Critical updates

Answer: A, B, C, and D. All of the answers are correct. In addition, you'll receive recommended updates.

Troubleshoot failed installations.

Troubleshooting is always a very critical skill needed to keep a network operating. Coverage of this objective includes the most common troubleshooting errors that you may encounter. Additionally, you'll need to know about the Setup Log files that you can use to help pinpoint the problems encountered.

Microsoft always focuses on troubleshooting as an important aspect of MCSE skills. Be prepared to demonstrate your knowledge of the investigative process and what to do with the information gathered during installation. Be sure that you have a thorough understanding of all of the installation principles covered in the sections of this chapter.

Critical Information

The Windows 2000 installation process is designed to be as simple as possible. The chances of installation errors are greatly minimized through the use of Wizards and the step-by-step process. Nevertheless, it is possible that errors may occur. Following are some possible installation errors you might encounter.

Media errors	Media errors are caused by defective or damaged CDs. To check the CD, put it into another computer and see if you can read it. Also check for scratches or dirt— the CD may just need to be cleaned.
Insufficient disk space	Windows 2000 Server needs at least 1GB free space, or the installation program won't run properly. If the Setup program cannot verify that this space exists, the program will not let you continue.
Not enough memory	Make sure your computer has the minimum amount of memory required by Windows 2000 Server (128MB). Insufficient memory may cause the installation to fail or blue-screen errors to occur after installation.
Not enough processing power	Make sure your computer has the minimum processing power required by Windows 2000 Server (Pentium 133MHz). Insufficient processing power may cause the installation to fail or blue-screen errors to occur after installation.
Hardware that is not on the HCL	If your hardware is not on Microsoft's Hardware Compatibility List, Windows 2000 may not recognize the hardware or a device may not work properly.
Hardware with no driver support	Windows 2000 does not recognize hardware that doesn't have driver support.
Hardware that is not configured properly	If your hardware is Plug-and-Play compatible, Windows should configure it automatically. Otherwise, you'll need to manually configure the hardware per the manufacturer's instructions.

Incorrect CD key	Without a valid CD key, the installation won't go beyond the Product Key dialog box. Make sure you haven't typed in an incorrect key by mistake (look on the back of your CD case for this key).
Failure to access TCP/IP network resources	If you install Windows 2000 with typical settings, the computer is configured as a DHCP client. If no DHCP server exists to provide IP configuration information, the client won't be able to access network resources through TCP/IP.
Failure to connect to a domain controller when joining a domain	Make sure you have specified the correct domain name. If your domain name is correct, verify that your network settings have been set properly and that a domain controller and DNS server are available. If you're still unable to join a domain, install the computer in a workgroup and then join the domain after installation.

Helpful Setup Log Files

When you install Windows 2000 Server, several log files are created by the Setup program. You can view these logs to check for any problems during the installation process. Two log files are particularly useful for troubleshooting:

- The action log (stored as *Windir*\setupact.log) includes all actions performed during the Setup process, in chronological order, with a description of each action. (*Windir* is the directory that stores the system files.)

- The error log (stored as *Windir*\setuperr.log) includes any errors that occurred during the installation, with a description of the error and an indication of its severity. (*Windir* is the directory that stores the system files.)

Necessary Procedures

Here are the steps for troubleshooting failed Windows 2000 Server installations using the Setup logs.

1. Select Start ➢ Programs ➢ Accessories ➢ Windows Explorer.

2. In Windows Explorer, double-click My Computer, double-click Local Disk (C:), and double-click WINNT (this is the default name of the system files folder, set up earlier in the procedure "Running the Setup Program").

3. Since this is the first time you have opened the WINNT folder, click the Show All Files option to display all the files that it contains.

4. In the WINNT folder, double-click the `setupact` file to view your action log in Notepad. When you are finished viewing this file, close Notepad.

5. Double-click the `setuperr` file to view your error file in Notepad. If no errors occurred during installation, this file will be empty. When you are finished viewing this file, close Notepad.

6. Close Windows Explorer.

Exam Essentials

Know the possible installation errors.   Be prepared to recognize problems with the installation media, insufficient disk space, not enough memory, not enough CPU power, unsupported hardware, no driver support, and failed connections.

Know where to check the Setup process.   The Setup process is recorded in the `\winnt\setupact.log` file. It records each action and a description of each action.

Know where to check for errors during the Setup process.   Errors and their severity are recorded in the `\winnt\setuperr.log` file.

Key Terms and Concepts

setupact.log   The log file that contains the Windows 2000 Server installation process activities and a description of the activities.

setuperr.log   The log file that contains any errors recorded during the Windows 2000 Server installation process, with indications of their severity.

Sample Questions

1. You have just installed Windows 2000 Server, but you failed in your attempt to connect to the domain controller. What is a possible reason? Select all that apply.

A. Domain name spelled incorrectly

B. Network setting not correct

C. No DNS server available

D. Domain Controller not online

Answer: A, B, C, and D. All of the above reasons may cause failure to connect to the domain controller.

Chapter

2

Installing, Configuring, and Troubleshooting Access to Resources

Access to resources is the reason why we create and manage networks. Your major role as a network administrator is to ensure that the network's users can get to the resources they need, while preventing those same users from having access to restricted or sensitive resources.

The objectives in this chapter concern your knowledge of managing access to resources on networks that use various protocols and network operating systems, such as NetWare and AppleTalk. You're expected to know how to control access to files, folders, and shared folders that exist on Windows 2000 servers. This includes resources listed in Dfs, and files and folders on NTFS partitions. And there's an objective on governing access to resources located on a Web site.

In addition to files, folders, and shared folders, you'll need to be able to manage access to print resources. This topic includes the nomenclature that is important to printing. As usual, Windows 2000 Server offers great flexibility when it comes to configuring printers. Access to these printers and the print devices they control is handled in the printer's security properties.

Your knowledge of how to manage resources is always a top priority in the Windows 2000 Server exam. The Necessary Procedures in this chapter will walk you through the steps of resource management. You may want to practice these procedures thoroughly, until you are comfortable with them. In many cases, your success on the exam will depend on your ability to make distinctions between the many terms used to describe what's going on in the system. So spend some time learning the proper terms.

Install and configure network services for interoperability.

One of the strengths of Windows 2000 Server is its ability to operate in concert with a variety of other operating systems, including Novell's NetWare networks and Apple's Macintosh networks. This exam objective ensures that you understand the tools that Microsoft has provided to manage this interoperability. You'll also need to know what it takes to optimize these tools, in order to provide adequate network connectivity to your users.

Here's what you'll need to know: what's required to connect to resources on a Novell server, how to provide and control gateways to the resources on a Novell server, and how to provide connectivity to an AppleTalk network.

The Necessary Procedures for this objective will step you through installation and configuration of Gateway Service for NetWare, and connecting to the resources on a NetWare server. There are also procedures for providing access to AppleTalk networks and giving Macintosh users access to resources on the Windows 2000 server. By performing these procedures, you'll master the mechanics behind the principles. Notice that a majority of the Exam Essentials are concerned with making the interoperability happen.

Critical Information

Windows 2000 Server and Windows 2000 Professional provide several services that enable computers running Windows 2000 to coexist and cooperate with Novell NetWare networks and servers, and with Apple's AppleTalk networks. Most of these services are included in Windows 2000 Server; others are available as separate products.

NWLink

The NWLink IPX/SPX/NetBIOS Compatible Transport Protocol (*NWLink*) is an implementation of Novell's Internetwork Packet Exchange/Sequenced Packet Exchange (IPX/SPX) and NetBIOS protocols. Windows 2000 clients can use NWLink to access client and server applications running on Novell NetWare servers, and vice versa for NetWare clients accessing applications on Windows 2000 servers. With NWLink, Windows 2000 servers can communicate with printers and other network devices using IPX/SPX.

NWLink is a Network Driver Interface Specification (NDIS)–compliant implementation of Novell's IPX/SPX protocol. NWLink supports two networking APIs (application programming interfaces): NetBIOS and Windows Sockets. These APIs support communication among Windows 2000 servers and between computers running Windows 2000 and NetWare servers.

Cooperating with Microsoft Resources

By default, the file and print sharing components of Windows 2000 use NetBIOS over IPX to send messages related to file and print sharing.

Alternatively, you can disable NetBIOS so that the file and print sharing messages are sent directly over IPX. This is known as *direct hosting.* Although direct hosting may be more efficient, it causes an interoperability issue: A direct hosting client can only connect to a direct hosting server.

NOTE You cannot use direct hosting of IPX to gain access to resources on any computer acting as a direct host server from a Windows 2000 server. Computers running Windows 2000 do not include a direct hosting client for NWLink.

Setting the Frame Type

The frame type defines the way in which the network adapter in a Windows 2000 server formats data to be sent over a network. To enable communication between a Windows 2000 server and

NetWare servers, you need to configure NWLink on the Windows 2000 computer with the same frame type as the one used by the NetWare servers.

NOTE   On Ethernet networks, the standard frame type for NetWare 2.2 and NetWare 3.11 is 802.3. Starting with NetWare 3.12, the default frame type was changed to 802.2.

You can choose to automatically detect or manually configure the frame type. However, the frame type is automatically detected when NWLink is loaded. If multiple frame types are detected in addition to the 802.2 frame type, NWLink defaults to the 802.2 frame type.

If the frame type is manually configured, a Windows 2000 server can use multiple frame types simultaneously.

Setting the External and Internal Network Numbers

NWLink uses two types of IPX network numbers for routing purposes: external network numbers and internal network numbers.

The *external network number* ("Network number" in the Manual Frame Detection dialog box) is associated with physical network adapters and networks. To communicate with each other, all computers on the same network that use a given frame type must have the same external network number. If you don't set this number, it is automatically detected by the Windows 2000 OS. However, if your computer has multiple network adapters that are connected to various networks, you must assign an external network number to each configured frame type and network adapter combination on your computer.

The *internal network number,* also called a virtual network number, identifies a virtual network inside a computer. (This number is referred to as the "Internal network number" in the NWLink IPX/SPX/Net-BIOS Compatible Transport Protocol Properties dialog box.) On a Windows 2000 server, programs advertise themselves as being located on the virtual network, not a physical network. When you assign internal network numbers, you gain more efficient routing to the programs in a computer with multiple network adapters that are connected to multiple, interconnected networks. By default, the internal network number is 00000000.

Gateway Service for NetWare

With *Gateway Service for NetWare (GSNW)*, you can create a gateway through which Microsoft client computers without Novell NetWare client software can still access NetWare file and print resources. You can make gateways for resources located on Novell Directory Services (NDS) trees, as well as for resources on servers with bindery security. These resources include volumes, directories, directory map objects, printers, and print queues. When a gateway is enabled, network clients running Microsoft client software can access NetWare files and printers without having to run NetWare client software locally.

For file access, the gateway server redirects one of its own drives to the NetWare volume and then shares that drive to other Microsoft clients. The file gateway uses a NetWare account on the computer running Windows 2000 Server to create a validated connection to the NetWare server. This connection appears as a redirected drive on the Windows 2000 server. When you share the redirected drive, it becomes like any other shared resource on the Windows 2000 server.

NOTE   Because requests from Microsoft networking clients are processed through the gateway, access is slower than direct access from the client to the NetWare network. Clients that require frequent access to NetWare resources should run Windows 2000 Professional with Client Service for NetWare, or Windows 95 and Windows 98 with their NetWare client software, to achieve higher performance.

A user who works locally at a Windows 2000 server can use GSNW to gain direct access to NetWare file and print resources, on NDS trees as well as servers with bindery security.

GSNW does not support the IP protocol to operate with NetWare version 5.*x*. To do this, you must run the IP/IPX gateway in NetWare 5.*x*, or use a redirector that is compatible with NetWare Core Protocol (NCP) and supports native IP.

NOTE   Windows 2000 includes an upgrade for NetWare client software for cooperating with Windows. This upgrade only applies to computers running NetWare client software and a version of Windows that was upgraded to Windows 2000.

Configuring Gateway Service for NetWare

When you first log on after GSNW is installed, you are prompted to set your default tree and context, or your preferred server. The tree and context define the position of the user object for the username with which you log on to an NDS tree. A preferred server is the NetWare server to which you are automatically connected when you log on, if your network does not use NDS.

You can have either a default tree and context or a preferred server, but not both. (In NDS environments, you set a default tree and context.) If you select a default tree and context, you can still access NetWare servers that use bindery security.

Creating a Gateway

The following conditions must be in place before you can create a gateway to NetWare resources on a computer running Windows 2000 Server:

- The NetWare server must have a group named NTGATEWAY with the necessary rights for the resources that you want to access.

- You must have a user account on the NetWare network with the necessary rights for the resources that you want to access.

- The NetWare user account you use must be a member of the NTGATEWAY group.

The NetWare user account you use to enable gateways can be either a Novell Directory Services (NDS) account or a bindery account. If the server will have gateways to NDS resources as well as resources on servers running bindery security, the user account must be a bindery account. (This account can connect to NDS resources through bindery emulation.) If you create gateways only to NDS resources, the account can be an NDS account.

After installing GSNW, creating a gateway is a two-step process:

1. First, you enable gateways on the computer running Windows 2000 Server. When you enable a gateway, you must type the name and password of the user account that has access to the NetWare server and is a member of the NTGATEWAY group on that NetWare server. You need to do this only once for each server that will act as a gateway.

2. For each volume or printer to which you want to create a gateway, you activate a gateway. When you activate a gateway, you specify the NetWare resource and a share name that Microsoft client users will use to connect to the resource.

Security for gateway resources is provided on two levels:

- On the computer running Windows 2000 Server and acting as a gateway, you can set share-level permissions for each resource made available through the gateway.

- On the NetWare file server, the NetWare administrator can assign trustee rights to the user account that is used for the gateway or to the NTGATEWAY group. These rights are enforced for all Microsoft client users who access the resource through the gateway. There is no auditing of gateway access.

Connecting Directly to NetWare Resources

In addition to providing gateway technology, GSNW enables users working locally at a Windows 2000 Server computer to access NetWare resources directly, just as Client Service for NetWare provides this service to Windows 2000 Professional users.

NDS trees (as well as NetWare servers running bindery security) appear in the NetWare or Compatible Network list in Windows Explorer. You can double-click a tree name to expand it, and then double-click any container object to expand its contents and structure. You can connect to and assign a local drive to any volume, folder, or directory map object anywhere in the tree hierarchy (for which you have credentials).

To connect to an NDS printer, you can use the Add Printer wizard, just as you would to connect to any network printer.

If you have a default tree and context, once you've logged on, you don't need to log on again or supply another password to access any volume in your default tree. If you access another tree, you are prompted to supply a full context (including username) for that tree.

Changing the NetWare Password

Users who use either Gateway Service for NetWare or Client Service for NetWare to directly access NetWare resources can change their passwords on NDS trees on the network. To do this, you can use the standard password-changing procedure for Windows 2000 Server: Press Ctrl+Alt+Del, click Change Password, and in Log On To, click NetWare or Compatible Network.

To change the password on a NetWare server running bindery security, you can use the setpass command on the NetWare server.

Running NetWare Utilities and NetWare-Aware Programs

With Windows 2000 Server and GSNW, you can run some standard NetWare utilities from a command prompt, and many NetWare-aware programs. GSNW does not support NetWare 4.*x* or 5.*x* utilities. In addition, you must use Windows 2000 Server management tools for some administrative functions.

AppleTalk Concepts

You can use Microsoft Windows 2000 Server AppleTalk network integration to share files and printers between Intel-based and Apple Macintosh clients.

After AppleTalk protocol is set up, a computer running Windows 2000 Server can also function as an AppleTalk router. Routing capability is supported for AppleTalk Phase 2.

With AppleTalk network integration, Macintosh computers need only the Macintosh operating system software to function as clients; no additional software is required. You can, however, set up and distribute the optional user authentication module, which lets Macintosh clients securely log on to the Windows 2000 Server computer using the same logon method as Windows clients.

AppleTalk network integration simplifies administration by maintaining just one set of user accounts instead of separate user accounts (one on the Macintosh server and another on the Windows 2000 server).

Understanding AppleTalk Network Integration

Windows 2000 Server AppleTalk network integration is made up of three parts:

- *File Server for Macintosh* (also called MacFile) lets you designate a folder as a Macintosh-accessible volume, ensures Macintosh file names are legal NTFS names, and handles permissions.

- *Print Server for Macintosh* (also called MacPrint) lets all network users send print jobs to a spooler on the Windows 2000 Server and continue working; they don't have to wait for their print jobs to finish.

- *AppleTalk* is the layer of AppleTalk Phase 2 protocols that delivers data to its destination on the network.

Necessary Procedures

You'll need to be familiar with the following procedures for installing and configuring the services that provide access to the resources on other operating systems.

To Install NWLink

1. From Control Panel, open Network and Dial-up Connections.

2. Right-click a local area connection, and select Properties.

3. On the General tab, click Install.

4. In the Select Network Component Type dialog box, click Protocol and then Add.

5. In the Select Network Protocol dialog box, click NWLink IPX/SPX/ NetBIOS Compatible Transport Protocol and then click OK.

To Install Gateway Services for NetWare

1. From Control Panel, open Network and Dial-up Connections.

2. Right-click a local area connection, and select Properties.

3. On the General tab, click Install.

4. In the Select Network Component Type dialog box, click Client and then Add.

5. In the Select Network Client dialog box, click Gateway (and Client) Services for NetWare and then click OK.

To Connect to a NetWare Volume through My Network Places

1. On the desktop, double-click My Network Places.

2. Do one of the following:

- Double-click NetWare or Compatible Network.

- Double-click Entire Network, view the entire contents, and then double-click NetWare or Compatible Network.

- Double-click a tree or volume to see the contents. You can then double-click those contents to see other computers or volumes.

3. Do one of the following:

- When you find the volume or folder that you want to access, double-click to expand it.

- To map a local drive to the volume or folder, click the volume or folder, and select Tools ➢ Map Network Drive.

To Activate a Gateway to a NetWare Resource

1. Open Gateway Service for NetWare.

2. Click Gateway, and then select the Enable Gateway check box.

3. Click Add, and in Share Name, type a share name that Microsoft clients will use to access the NetWare resource.

4. In Network Path, type the network path of the NetWare volume or directory you want to share.

5. In Use Drive, enter the default drive you want to use, if necessary.

6. Click Unlimited and then OK; or you can click Allow, enter a maximum number of concurrent users, and then click OK.

To Change a Password on a NetWare NDS Tree

1. Press Ctrl+Alt+Delete.

2. Click Change Password.

3. In Log On To, click NetWare or Compatible Network.

4. In Old Password, type your current password.

5. In New Password, type your new password and type it again in Confirm New Password.

To Install AppleTalk Protocol and Routing

1. From Control Panel, open Network and Dial-up Connections.

2. Right-click any network connection icon (Local Area Connection is the default) and select Properties.

3. On the General tab, click Install.

4. In Select Network Component Type, click Protocol and then Add.

5. In Select Network Protocol, click AppleTalk Protocol and then OK.

To Create a Macintosh-Accessible Volume

1. From Administrative Tools, select Computer Management.

2. In the console tree, double-click Shared Folders, right-click Shares, and then click New File Share.

3. In Folder To Share, type the drive and path to the folder that you want to make Macintosh-accessible. Or you can click Browse to find the folder.

4. In Share name, type the name and, optionally, in Share description, type a description of the Windows 2000 Server share.

5. Select the Apple Macintosh check box, click Next, and then follow the instructions in the Create Shared Folder Wizard.

To Capture/Release an AppleTalk Printing Device

1. From Control Panel, open Printers.

2. Right-click a printer and select Properties.

3. On the Ports tab, click the port, and then click Configure Port.

4. Either select or clear the check box for Capture This AppleTalk Printing Device, and then click OK.

Exam Essentials

Know the requirements to allow connectivity between a Windows 2000 server and a NetWare server.   To access file and printer resources on a NetWare server, you need to install both GSNW and NWLink on a Windows 2000 server. If you are only running a client/server application, you will need to install NWLink only.

Know how to create a gateway to resources on a NetWare server. After you have installed GSNW and NWLink, you need to enable the gateway. Once it's enabled, you need to activate the gateway for each resource by specifying the resource and the providing it with a share name.

Know why to create a gateway to resources on a NetWare server. Installing GSNW and NWLink will provide access to resources on a NetWare server for a Windows 2000 server. Microsoft clients, too, can gain access to NetWare resources by using the gateway on the Windows 2000 server; they need not install NetWare client software.

Know how to control the security for gateway resources.   Security for gateway resources can be set on the Windows 2000 servers by applying share-level permissions. Security can also be handled on the

NetWare file servers by assigning trustee rights to the user account in the NTGATEWAY group.

Know how to change a NetWare password.   On NetWare 3.*x* servers, you can change your password by using the `setpass` command. On NetWare 4.*x* servers, you change passwords by using the Change Password utility.

Know what is required to allow connectivity between a Windows 2000 server and an AppleTalk network.   Windows 2000 server can implement AppleTalk network integration by installing the AppleTalk protocol and the File Server for Macintosh or Print Server for Macintosh services.

Key Terms and Concepts

AppleTalk protocol   The protocol used by Macintosh computers to network. Can be installed on Windows 2000 servers to allow network integration between Windows 2000 and Apple Macintosh clients.

direct hosting   A method of communicating directly to file and print share messages by disabling NetBIOS.

external network number   The unique number that associates physical network adapters with networks. This number must be the same for all network adapters on a physical segment.

File Server for Macintosh   Allows you to designate folders as Macintosh-accessible volumes.

GSNW   Gateway Services for NetWare (GSNW) is a network service that allows connectivity between Windows 2000 and NetWare servers. GSNW can also be used to provide gateway services for Microsoft clients needing access to NetWare resources.

internal network number   The internal number assigned to network adapters inside a single computer to gain efficiency in routing between the adapters. This creates a virtual network inside the computer.

NWLink   An IPX/SPX/NetBIOS-compatible transport protocol that supports two networking APIs: NetBIOS and Windows Sockets.

Print Server for Macintosh   Allows Macintosh users to send print jobs to a spooler on the Windows 2000 server.

Sample Questions

1. You are the network administrator. You have installed GSNW and NWLink on the Windows 2000 server. You have several Microsoft clients that need access to resources on a NetWare server. What is the next step in providing gateway services for these clients?

A. Enable the gateway.

B. Share the resources on the NetWare server.

C. Share the resources on the Windows 2000 server.

D. Install NWLink and CSNW on all clients that need access to resources on the NetWare server.

Answer: A. The gateway needs to be enabled before you can share the resources to the Microsoft clients. Windows 2000 can provide gateway services, so you need not install NWLink and GSNW on all of the Microsoft clients.

2. You are the network administrator. You are using a SQL server to host your database. NetWare clients need access to the database. What has to be installed to support this?

A. GSNW and NWLink

B. NWLink only

C. NWLink, and File and Print Services for NetWare

D. Windows Sockets

Answer: B. When running a client/server application, you only need to install NWLink.

Monitor, configure, troubleshoot, and control access to printers.

This objective applies to your knowledge of the basics of Windows 2000 Server printing. This includes how to set up and configure printers, how to manage printers and print jobs, and how to manage print servers. The exam focuses on the configuration and troubleshooting of printers and print devices. Perhaps the most difficult issue to master is the printing terminology itself. There is some confusion between interpretation of what a printer is and what a print device is. When we hear "printer," we think of the device that produces paper copies. The technical term "printer," however, refers to the software that controls the print device. This section shows you how to configure and manage the printers, and some information about how to best manage print devices.

Microsoft has made printing a highly configurable and controllable function. You are expected to know how to take advantage of this flexibility. Specifically, the exams will test your knowledge of controlling access to print devices by configuring multiple printers, and of using multiple print devices controlled by a single printer. For example, let's say you have two user groups that print to a single print device. One group has small jobs that have a high priority to print immediately. The other group prints large jobs that typically don't have an immediate priority. You have the flexibility of creating a different printer for each group, with each printer configured with the options that best suit the group. You can then give each group the permissions for the printer that is appropriate to their work.

The exam also focuses on how to configure and manage printers. This objective covers the general configuration of a printer, to include settings for creating printer pools, redirecting jobs, and security. It also covers management of print jobs once they've been sent to the print server. As stated earlier, Microsoft will test your ability to perform these important network functions.

Critical Information

Before you can access your physical *print device* under Windows 2000 Server, you must first create a logical *printer*. The logical printer is what controls access to the physical print device. Logical printers can be configured to give users various levels of access, or different options on the same print device. After you've created printers, you may need to delete or rename them.

To create a logical printer, use the Add Printer Wizard, which guides you through all of the steps. (To start it, double-click the Add Printer Wizard in the Printers folder, available from My Computer or Control Panel.) Before you can create a new printer in Windows 2000 Server, you must be logged on as a member of the Administrators or Power Users group.

The computer on which you run the Add Printer Wizard and create the printer automatically becomes the *print server* for that printer. As the print server, this computer must have enough processing power to support incoming print jobs and enough disk space to hold the queue of print jobs.

Printer properties include options such as the printer name, whether or not the printer is shared, and printer security. To access the printer Properties dialog box, open the Printers folder, right-click the printer you want to manage, and choose Properties from the pop-up menu. The printer Properties dialog box has six tabs: General, Sharing, Ports, Advanced, Security, and Device Settings.

NOTE   The Properties dialog boxes for some printers will contain additional tabs to allow other configurations of the printer. For example, if you install an HP DeskJet 970Cse printer, its Properties dialog box will have tabs for Color Management and Services.

General Printer Information

You'll find information about the printer—including the name of the printer, the location of the printer, and comments about the printer—in the General tab of the printer Properties dialog box. This tab reflects the entries made when you set up the printer. You can add to or change the information in the text boxes. Beneath the tab's Comment box, you'll see the model of the printer. The items listed in the Features section of will depend on the model and driver you are using. At the bottom of the dialog box, you can set printing preferences and print test pages.

Setting Printing Preferences

The Printing Preferences button in the General tab of the printer Properties dialog box brings up the Printing Preferences dialog box, which has Layout and Paper/Quality tabs, as well as an Advanced button that presents more configuration options.

Layout Tab

Your choices for the Orientation setting are Portrait (vertical) or Landscape (horizontal).

The Page Order setting is new to Windows 2000. You can specify whether you want page 1 of the document to be on the top of the stack (Front to Back) or on the bottom of the stack (Back to Front).

The Pages Per Sheet setting designates how many pages should be printed on a single page. You might use this feature if you were printing a book and wanted two pages to be printed side-by-side on a single page.

Paper/Quality Tab

The Paper/Quality settings are for the paper type and quality of a print job. The options available will depend on the features of your printer.

Advanced Settings

Clicking the Advanced button in the lower-right corner of the Printing Preferences dialog box brings up the Advanced Options dialog box. Here, you can configure printer options such as Paper/Output, Graphic, Document Options, and Printer Features. Once again, the availability of these options depends on the print driver you are using.

Printing a Test Page

The option to print a *test page* is especially useful in troubleshooting printing problems. For example, you might use this option in a situation where no print driver is available for a print device and you want to try to use a compatible print driver. If the print job doesn't print or doesn't print correctly (it might print just one character per page, for example), you'll know that the print driver isn't an acceptable alternative.

To print a test page, go to the General tab in printer Properties and click the Print Test Page button at the bottom of the tab.

Configuring Sharing Properties

Use the Sharing tab of the printer Properties dialog box to specify whether the computer will be configured as a *local printer* or as a shared *network printer*. If you choose to share the printer, you also need to specify a share name that will be seen by the network users.

The Sharing tab also lets you configure driver support for print clients other than Windows 2000 clients. This is a significant feature of Windows 2000 Server print support, because it allows you to specify automatic download of print drivers for other clients. The only driver that is loaded by default is the Intel driver for Windows 2000.

To provide the additional drivers for the clients, click the Additional Drivers button at the bottom of the Sharing tab. This brings up the Additional Drivers dialog box. Windows 2000 Server supports adding print drivers for the following platforms:

- Windows 95 or Windows 98 Intel
- Windows NT 3.1 Alpha, Intel, and MIPS
- Windows NT 3.5 or 3.51 Alpha, Intel, MIPS, and PowerPC
- Windows NT 4.0 Alpha, Intel, MIPS, and PowerPC

Configuring Print Ports

The interface that allows the computer to communicate with the print device is known as a port. Windows 2000 Server supports local ports (or *physical ports*) and standard TCP/IP ports (or *logical ports*).

Local ports are used when the printer attaches directly to the computer. If you're running Windows 2000 Server in a small workgroup, you are very likely running printers attached to local port LPT1 on some machines.

Standard TCP/IP ports are used when the printer is attached to the network by installing a network card in the printer. Network printers are faster than local printers and can be located anywhere on the network. When you specify a TCP/IP port, you must know the IP address of the network printer.

You configure all ports that have been defined for a particular printer's use in the Ports tab of the printer's Properties dialog box. Along with deleting and configuring existing ports, you can also set up printer pooling and redirect print jobs to another printer.

NOTE The Enable Bidirectional Support option on the Ports tab will be available if your printer supports this feature. It allows the printer to communicate with the computer. For example, your printer may be able to send more informative printer errors to the computer.

Printer Pooling

Printer pools are used to associate multiple physical print devices with a single logical printer. You use a printer pool if you have multiple physical printers in the same location that are the same type and can use a single print driver. The advantage of using a printer pool is that the first available print device will print your job—useful in situations where print devices are shared by a group of users, such as a secretarial pool.

To configure a printer pool, go to the Ports tab of the printer Properties dialog box, click the Enable Printer Pooling check box at the bottom, and then check all the ports to which the print devices in the printer pool will attach. If you don't turn on the Enable Printer Pooling option, you can select only one port per printer.

NOTE   All of the print devices within a printer pool must be able to use the same print driver.

Redirecting Print Jobs to Another Printer

If your print device fails, you can redirect all of its scheduled jobs to another print device that has been configured as a printer on the print server. For this redirection to work, the new print device must be able to use the same print driver as the old print device.

To redirect print jobs, click the Add Port button in the Ports tab, highlight New Port, and choose New Port Type. In the Port Name dialog box, type the UNC (Universal Naming Convention) name of the printer to which you want the jobs redirected. Use the format *computername\printer*.

Configuring Advanced Properties

This section describes the options available in the Advanced tab of a printer's Properties dialog box.

Printer Availability

Availability, or scheduling, specifies when a printer will service jobs. Usually, availability is an issue when you have multiple printers that use a single print device. The Always Available radio button in the Advanced tab is selected by default, so that users can use the printer 24 hours a day. To control the printer's availability, select the Available From radio button and specify a range of time for the printer to be available.

Printer Priority

Priority is another printer attribute that you might configure if you have multiple printers that use a single print device. When you set priority, you specify the order in which jobs are sent to the print device. This is done by setting the priority value for the printer. You can set the Priority value to a number from 1 to 99, with 1 as the lowest priority and 99 as the highest priority. Jobs from a printer with a higher priority are placed in the print queue before jobs from a printer with a lower priority.

Print Driver

The Driver setting in the Advanced tab indicates the *print driver* (printer software) associated with this printer. If you have configured multiple printers on the computer, you can select any of the installed drivers to use. Clicking the New Driver button starts the Add Printer Driver Wizard, which allows you to update or add new print drivers.

Spooling

When you configure spooling options, you specify whether print jobs are spooled or sent directly to the printer. *Spooling* means print jobs are saved to disk in a queue before they are sent to the printer. Think of spooling as the printing traffic controller—it keeps the print jobs from trying to print all at the same time.

By default, spooling is enabled, with printing beginning immediately. Your other option is to wait until the last page is spooled before printing (the Start Printing After Last Page Is Spooled option). If you choose the latter option, a smaller print job that finishes spooling first will print before your print jobs, even if a job starts spooling before the smaller job. With Start Printing Immediately option, the smaller job waits until your print job is complete.

NOTE   The Print Directly to the Printer option bypasses spooling altogether. This option doesn't work well in a multiuser environment, where many print jobs are sent to the same device; however, the setting is useful in troubleshooting printer problems. If you can print to a print device directly, but you can't print through the spooler, then you know your spooler is corrupt or malfunctioning.

Print Options

The Advanced tab contains check boxes for four print options:

- Hold Mismatched Documents is useful when you're using multiple forms with a printer. This feature is disabled by default. Jobs are printed on a first-in-first-out (FIFO) basis, and all the jobs with the same form will print first.

- The Print Spooled Documents First option tells the spooler to print jobs that have completed spooling before large jobs that are still spooling, even if the large print job has a higher priority. This setting, which increases printer efficiency, is enabled by default.

- The Keep Printed Documents option specifies that print jobs should not be deleted from the *print spooler* (queue) when they are finished printing. You normally want to delete the print jobs as they print, because saving print jobs can take up a lot of disk space. This option is disabled by default.

TIP   Enabling the Keep Printed Documents option is useful if you need to identify the source or other attributes of a finished print job.

- The Enable Advanced Printing Features option specifies that any advanced features supported by your printer, such as Page Order and Pages Per Sheet, are to be enabled. This setting is turned on by default. Disable the advanced printing features when you use a print driver on a similar print device that doesn't have all of the same features.

Printing Defaults

The Printing Defaults button in the lower-left corner of the Advanced tab calls up the Printing Preferences dialog box. This is the same dialog box that appears when you click the Printing Preferences button in the General tab of the printer Properties dialog box.

Print Processor

Print processors are used to specify whether Windows 2000 Server needs to do additional processing of print jobs. These programs interpret what type of data is being passed from the spooler to the print device. Each print device is capable of understanding a specific type of data. The five print processors supported by Windows 2000 Server are listed in Table 2.1.

To modify your Print Processor settings, click the Print Processor button at the bottom of the Advanced tab; this opens the Print Processor dialog box. You should generally leave the default settings as is,

TABLE 2.1: Print Processors Supported by Windows 2000

Print Processor	Description
RAW	Makes no changes to the print document
RAW (FF appended)	Makes no changes to the print document except to always add a form-feed character
RAW (FF Auto)	Makes no changes to the print document except to try to detect if a form-feed character needs to be added
NT EMF	Generally spools documents that are sent from other Windows 2000 clients
TEXT	Interprets all data as plain text, and the printer will print the data using standard text commands

unless otherwise directed by the print device manufacturer. This will only be done if the print device needs a specific type of data to print the information correctly.

Separator Pages

Separator pages are used at the beginning of each document to identify the user that submitted the print job. If your printer is not shared, a separator page is generally a waste of paper. If the printer is shared by many users, the separator page can be useful for distributing finished print jobs.

To add a separator page, click the Separator Page button in the lower-right corner of the Advanced tab. In the Separator Page dialog box, click the Browse button to locate and select the separator page file that you want to use. Windows 2000 Server supplies the Separator files listed in Table 2.2, which are stored in \%*systemroot*%\System32.

TIP You can also create custom separator pages. For more information about creating separator pages, refer to the Windows 2000 Resource Kit.

TABLE 2.2: Separator Page Files

Separator Page File	Description
pcl.sep	Sends a separator page on a dual-language HP printer after switching the printer to PCL (Printer Control Language), which is a common printing standard
pscript.sep	Does not send a separator page, but switches the computer to PostScript printing mode
sysprint.sep	On PostScript printers, sends a separator page
Sysprintj.sep	Same as sysprint.sep, but with support for Japanese characters

Configuring Security Properties

As a network administrator, you can control user and group access to Windows 2000 printers by configuring the print permissions of the printer. In Windows 2000 Server, you can allow or deny access to a printer. If you deny access, the user or group will not be able to use the printer, even if their user or group permissions allow such access.

You assign print permissions, defined in Table 2.3, to users and groups through the Security tab of the printer's Properties.

TABLE 2.3: Print Permissions

Print Permission	Description
Print	Allows a user or group to connect to a printer and can send print jobs to the printer.
Manage Printers	Allows administrative control of the printer. With this permission, a user or group can pause and restart the printer, change the spooler settings, share or unshare a printer, change print permissions, and manage printer properties.

TABLE 2.3: Print Permissions *(continued)*

Print Permission	Description
Manage Documents	Allows users to manage documents by pausing, restarting, resuming, and deleting queued documents. Users cannot control the status of the printer.

Whenever a printer is created, default print permissions are assigned. The default permissions, defined in Table 2.4, are appropriate for most network environments.

TABLE 2.4: Default Print Permissions

Group	Print	Manage Printers	Manage Documents
Administrators	✓	✓	✓
Power Users	✓	✓	✓
Creator Owner		✓	
Everyone	✓		

Advanced Security Settings

The advanced settings accessed from the Security tab allow you to configure permissions, auditing, and owner properties. Clicking the Advanced button in the lower-left corner of the Security tab brings up the Access Control Settings dialog box, with three tabs that you use to add, remove, or edit print permissions:

- The Permissions tab lists all the users, computers, and groups that have been given permission to the printer. It also lists the permission that has been granted, and whether the permission applies to documents or to the printer.

- The Auditing tab helps you keep track of who is using the printer and with what type of access. You can track the success or failure of the six events: Print, Manage Printers, Manage Documents, Read Permissions, Change Permissions, and Take Ownership.

- The Owner tab shows the owner of the printer (the user or group who created the printer), which you can change if you have the proper permissions. For example, if the print permissions exclude the Administrator from using or managing the printer, and the print permissions need to be reassigned, an Administrator can take ownership of the printer and then reapply print permissions.

Configuring Device Settings

The properties that you see on the Device Settings tab of the printer's Properties dialog box will depend on the printer and print driver installed. You might configure these properties if you want to designate the forms (types of paper) associated with tray assignments. For example, you could configure the upper tray to use letterhead and the lower tray to use regular paper.

Managing Printers and Print Documents

Administrators, or users with the Manage Printers permission, can manage the parameters of a printer's print jobs and the print documents in a *print queue*. When you manage a printer, you manage all the documents in a queue. When you manage print documents, you manage specific documents.

Managing Printers

To manage a printer, open the Printers folder and right-click the printer you want to manage. From this pop-up menu, select the option for the area you want to manage (see Table 2.5):

TABLE 2.5: Printer Management Options

Option	Description
Set as Default Printer	Specifies that this is the default printer, which will be used when the user does not send a job to an explicit printer (if the computer is configured to access multiple printers).
Printing Preferences	Brings up the Printing Preferences dialog box, containing printer settings for page layout and paper quality. You can also access this dialog box through the General tab of the printer's Properties, as described earlier in this chapter.
Pause Printing	Pauses the printer. Print jobs can be submitted to the printer, but they will not be forwarded to the print device until you resume printing (by unchecking this option). You might use this option if you need to troubleshoot the printer or maintain the print device.

TABLE 2.5:   Printer Management Options *(continued)*

Option	Description
Cancel All Documents	Deletes any jobs that are currently in the queue. You might use this option if the print queue contains jobs that are no longer needed.
Sharing	Allows the printer to be shared or unshared.
Use Printer Offline	Pauses the printer. Print documents will remain in the print queue, even if you restart the computer.
Delete	Removes the printer from the network. You might use this option if you no longer need the printer, if you want to move the printer to another print server, or if you suspect the printer is corrupt and you want to delete and re-create it.
Rename	Allows you to rename the printer. You might use this option to give a printer a more descriptive name or a name that follows naming conventions.

Managing Print Documents

An Administrator, or a user with the Manage Printers or Manage Documents permission, can manage print documents within a print queue. You can view the print queue when you open the Printers folder and double-click the printer you want to manage. The document management options are described in Table 2.6.

TABLE 2.6:   Document Management Options

Option	Description
Pause	Places the printing of this document on hold
Resume	Allows the document to print normally (after it has been paused)
Restart	Resends the job from the beginning, even if it has already partially printed
Cancel	Deletes the job from the print spooler

TABLE 2.6: Document Management Options *(continued)*

Option	Description
Properties	Brings up the document's Properties, where you can set options such as user notification of job completion, document priority, document printing time, page layout, and paper quality

Managing Print Servers

A print server is the computer on which printers have been defined. When you send a job to a network printer, you are actually sending it to the print server first. You manage print servers by configuring their properties in the Printer Server Properties dialog box, reached by right-clicking on the print server's icon and selecting Properties in the pop-up menu.

FORM PROPERTIES

If your printer has support for multiple trays and you use a different kind of paper in each tray, you will want to configure *forms* and assign them to specific trays. The Forms tab of the Printer Server Properties dialog box allows you to create and manage forms for a printer. Forms can be given any description and are configured primarily based on size.

You *associate* a form with a specific printer tray through the printer's Properties dialog box, rather than through the Printer Server Properties dialog box. Open the Device Settings tab and, under Form To Tray Assignment, select the paper tray that you will associate with the form. Then choose the form that will be used with the paper tray from the drop-down list.

PRINT SERVER PORT PROPERTIES

The Ports tab of the Printer Server Properties dialog box is very similar to the Ports tab of the printer's Properties (discussed earlier). The difference is that the Printer Server Properties dialog box is used to manage all of the ports for the print server, rather than the ports for a particular print device.

DRIVER PROPERTIES

The Drivers tab of the Printer Server Properties dialog box allows you to manage the print drivers installed on the print server. For each print driver, the tab shows the name, the environment (such as Intel or Alpha) for which the driver was written, and the operating system platform that the driver supports. You can add, remove, and update print drivers.

To see a print driver's properties, select the driver and click the Properties button. A print driver's properties include the following:

- Name

- Version

- Environment

- Language monitor

- Default data type

- Driver path

PRINT SERVER ADVANCED PROPERTIES

The Advanced tab of the Printer Server Properties dialog box allows you to configure the spool file, spooler event logging, and notifications about remote documents. You can set the following options:

- The spool file, or hard disk location, where the print files wait until they can be serviced by the print device

- Whether Error, Warning, and Information events are logged in Event Viewer

- Whether the print server will beep if there are errors when remote documents are printed

- Whether notification should be sent to the print server when remote documents are printed

- Whether the computer, as opposed to the user, should be notified when remote documents are printed

Necessary Procedures

The following procedure is for adding a local or network printer. Remember that you can add as many printers as are needed for a single print device, to allow access to different groups with different printer needs.

1. Select Start ➤ Settings ➤ Printers to open the Printers folder. Double-click the Add Printer icon to start the Add Printer Wizard. Click the Next button to proceed.

2. The Local or Network Printer dialog box appears next. Choose Local Printer if you are creating a printer directly attached to computer, or choose Network Printer for a printer attached to a network. Click Next to continue.

NOTE If you have a Plug-and-Play print device attached to the computer, it should be automatically detected and you can skip to step 6. If your print device is not attached or recognized, turn off the option to Automatically Detect and Install My Plug and Play Printer, and continue with the following steps to manually specify the print device configuration.

---

3. If you chose to manually configure a print device, the Select the Printer Port dialog box appears. Specify the port to be used by the print device, and click the Next button.

4. Now you'll see a dialog box that lists printer manufacturers and models. Specify the print device manufacturer and model and click the Next button. If the print device is not listed, click the Have Disk button and insert the disk that contains the driver that came with your print device.

NOTE If you've already installed this driver on your computer, the dialog box listing printer manufacturers and models will include a Windows Update button next to the Have Disk button.

---

5. In the Name Your Printer dialog box, accept the default name or enter another name for your printer and click the Next button.

6. In the Printer Sharing dialog box, indicate whether the printer is to be shared or not shared. If you choose to share the printer, specify a share name. Then click the Next button.

7. If you designated a shared printer in step 6, the Location and Comment dialog box appears. Specify location information and a comment. Network users can use this information to search for a description of the printer's location, configuration, and capabilities. Click Next to continue.

8. Next up is the Print Test Page dialog box. If the print device is attached to your computer, you should print a test page to verify that everything is configured properly. Otherwise, skip this step. Click Next to continue.

9. The Completing the Add Printer Wizard dialog box appears next, giving you a chance to verify that all of the printer settings are correct. If you see any problems, click the Back button to make the necessary corrections. When everything is configured properly, click the Finish button.

To complete the setup process for the new printer, the Add Printer Wizard will copy files (if necessary) and create your printer. An icon for the printer will appear in the Printers folder.

Exam Essentials

Know the difference between a printer and a print device.
Microsoft calls the device that makes paper copies of electronic information a print device. A printer is the software interface that controls the print device. You can have multiple printers controlling a single print device, and a single printer controlling multiple print devices.

Know what platforms can be supported by Windows 2000 Server print support.   Windows 2000 Server supports print drivers for Windows 95 or Windows 98, Windows NT 3.1, Windows NT 3.5 or 3.51, and Windows NT 4.0.

Know what options are available when configuring printer properties. Windows 2000 Server offers a wide range of options in the printer's Properties, including settings for printer pooling, printer availability, printing priorities, spooling options, preferences, and other options.

Know what printer pooling is. Printer pools are used to configure multiple print devices with a single logical printer.

Know how to redirect print jobs. You can redirect print jobs by adding a new port to an existing printer, and specifying the UNC name of the new print device.

Know how to configure spooling. Spooling can be used to control traffic to a print device. You can set the following options: Start Printing Immediately, Start Printing After Last Page Is Spooled, and Print Directly to the Printer.

Know when to use separator pages. Separator pages can be used to identify the originator of the print job, and to switch the computer to Post-Script or PCL printing modes. They can be used to give support for Japanese characters as well.

Key Terms and Concepts

form Printing term to describe the paper in a printer's paper trays. Most often associated with the size of the paper.

local printer A printer created on the local machine. The print device can either be connected to a physical or to a logical port. This printer can be shared to allow others access to the print device.

logical port A port that is not physically connected to the local machine but can be used when the print device is physically attached to the network and not to another computer.

network printer A printer that is available on the network, not on the local machine.

physical port A port that is physically connected to the local machine, used when the print device is directly attached to the computer.

print device   A physical, peripheral device that makes paper copies of computer generated data.

print driver   Software that controls a print device.

print processor   A program that performs any modifications to the print job before it is sent to the print monitor.

print queue   The location where documents are stored until they are processed by a print device.

print server   The computer that supports one or more printers.

print spooler   Accepts documents from each client, stores them, and then sends them to the print device when it is ready.

printer pool   Two or more identical print devices associated with one printer.

separator page   Used to identify the owner of a print job; also to identify the format of the print job, such as PCL or PostScript.

test page   A printed page of material used to test the configuration of a printer.

Sample Questions

1. You are the network administrator. Your print device has just crashed, and you notice that there are still several jobs in the printer queue. What, if anything, can be done to print the remaining jobs?

    A. Nothing, the jobs will be lost.

    B. Add a new port for the existing printer that points to a similar print device.

    C. Create a new printer and manually move the print queue to the new device.

    D. Tell your users to reprint their jobs and select another printer.

    Answer: B. The jobs can be redirected to another print device by adding a new port for the existing printer.

2. What default permissions do Power Users have for printers?

A. Print

B. Manage Printers

C. Manage Documents

D. None; they must manually add permissions

Answer: A, B, C. Power Users get Print, Manage Printers, and Manage Documents permissions by default.

Monitor, configure, troubleshoot, and control access to files, folders, and shared folders.

- Configure, manage, and troubleshoot a stand-alone Distributed file system (Dfs).
- Configure, manage, and troubleshoot a domain-based Distributed file system (Dfs).
- Monitor, configure, troubleshoot, and control local security on files and folders.
- Monitor, configure, troubleshoot, and control access to files and folders in a shared folder.
- Monitor, configure, troubleshoot, and control access to files and folders via Web services.

For this objective, you'll learn the basics of how Windows 2000 Server controls access to its files, folders, and shared folders. You'll review the flow of access to resources and how that access can be controlled through the use of permissions and share permissions.

Microsoft has added functionality to help users access the files and folders they need on a network. Dfs gives network administrators a centralized database of the links that point to the shares across the domain, which simplifies the user's access. Your knowledge of Dfs concepts and terms added to Windows 2000 Server will, of course, be tested on the exam.

You're expected to know how to manage access to the critical resources that support and sustain your enterprise. You'll be tested on your familiarity with how and when to apply available security measures. Specifically, Microsoft expects you to know how to determine effective permissions for file access locally and over the network. The Exam Essentials for this objective will help you focus on what is important.

Critical Information

When networks grow large, users often find themselves searching through a seemingly endless array of shares trying to find specific files. Once they've found the files, the server storing those files may go down, and users are out of luck. They have to wait for the server to be restored in order to use shared files. Managing access to resources is a critical function of any network administrator.

The Distributed File System (Dfs)

Administrators can use Windows 2000's *Distributed file system* (Dfs) to create a central database of links that point to shares across the network. This makes it much easier for users to quickly find the files they need. If your network has domains, the Dfs is particularly useful because you can replicate this central database across multiple domain member servers. Even if one server goes down, users will still have access to their files.

The Dfs gives users a central point of access to files and folders that are physically distributed across a network. For example, if users in your sales department need to access files that are stored on several computers in the Sales domain, you can use the Dfs to make it appear as though all of the files reside in the same network share. When you use the Dfs, users won't need to search through several computers to find the files or folders they need.

Before you set up and manage the Dfs, you should understand how it is implemented. The Dfs uses a simple topology similar to that used by the Windows file system. The following sections describe the main benefits of the Dfs, its topology, and its architecture.

Benefits of the Dfs

Using the Dfs has three primary benefits for network users.

Easier file access: The Dfs simplifies access to files. Users need to know about only one location on the network to access files that might actually be distributed across several physical computers. Even if you change the physical location of a folder that is part of the Dfs, users will not be affected. The folder still appears to be in the central Dfs location.

Increased file availability: The Dfs increases the availability of network files and folders. Windows 2000 Server automatically publishes all Dfs information to the Active Directory, thus ensuring that users on every server in the domain have access to the files in the Dfs. Administrators can also replicate the contents of the Dfs to multiple servers across the domain. If one of your servers goes down or must be taken offline for maintenance, the files and folders contained in the Dfs can be accessed from other member servers in the domain. This process is transparent to the user, who always sees the same files and folders regardless of their physical storage location.

Server load balancing: Sometimes multiple users in a domain need access to a single file simultaneously. This can present a significant network load to the server that contains the file. The Dfs helps to ease this load by supporting multiple shared folders that are physically distributed across the network. Again, to users the file appears to reside in only one network location.

The Dfs Topology

A Dfs topology consists of three main components: a *Dfs root*, one or more *Dfs links*, and one or more *Dfs shared folders*, or *replicas*. Each Dfs link points to one shared folder and all of its replicas. You can replicate the Dfs root by creating *root shares* on other member servers in the domain. When you create a Dfs root, you can specify whether it is a stand-alone Dfs root or a domain-based Dfs root.

A *stand-alone Dfs root* offers no replication or backup capabilities, so it is not fault tolerant. The following rules apply to a stand-alone Dfs root:

- It cannot use the Active Directory.
- It cannot have root-level Dfs shared folders.
- It can have only a single level of Dfs links in its hierarchy.

A *domain-based Dfs root* automatically publishes its Dfs topology to the Active Directory. The following rules apply to a domain-based Dfs root:

- It can be hosted only on a domain member server.
- It can have root-level Dfs shared folders.
- It can have multiple levels of Dfs links in its hierarchy.
- It must have fault-tolerant roots located on NTFS version 5 (or higher) partitions

The domain server that contains the Dfs root is known as the *host server*. The host server automatically publishes the Dfs topology to the Active Directory and provides synchronization of the topology across the domain member servers.

You can replicate the Dfs root by creating root shares on other member servers in the domain. To administrators, the Dfs topology appears as a single DNS namespace. The DNS names for the Dfs root shares resolve to the host servers for the Dfs root.

The Dfs Architecture

The Dfs consists of a server-based component, administered through the Distributed File System utility, and a client-based component. Table 2.7 summarizes the Dfs clients and servers available for the various Windows platforms.

NOTE In order to integrate Dfs with Windows 95, Windows 98, and Windows NT Workstation clients, you must add the DFS Services for Microsoft Network Client service to the client. This client software can be downloaded from www.microsoft.com.

TABLE 2.7: Dfs Client and Server Platforms

Platform	Dfs Client	Dfs Server
DOS, Windows 3.x, Windows for Work-groups, NetWare servers	No	No
Windows 95	Client version 4.x and 5.0 available for download	No
Windows 98	Client version 4.x and 5.0 (stand-alone) included; client version 5.0 (domain-based) available for download	No
Windows NT 4.0	Client version 4.x and 5.0 (stand-alone) included	Stand-alone server only on Server version
Windows 2000	Client version 5.0 included	Stand-alone and domain-based server on Server version only

Adding a Dfs Link

A Dfs link is a link from the Dfs root to one or more shared folders. Dfs links are added at the root of the Dfs topology. You can have up to 1,000 Dfs links assigned to a Dfs root.

To create a Dfs link, right-click the Dfs root and select New Dfs Link from the pop-up menu. In the Create a New Dfs Link dialog box (Figure 2.1), specify the link name, the path to the shared folder that will be used as the Dfs link, and an optional comment to provide additional information about the Dfs link. The Dfs path can be up to 260 characters.

You can also set a value for how long clients will cache the referral. The client cache option allows you to specify the number of seconds that client systems will store information about the location of the requested Dfs shared folder.

FIGURE 2.1: Creating DFs links

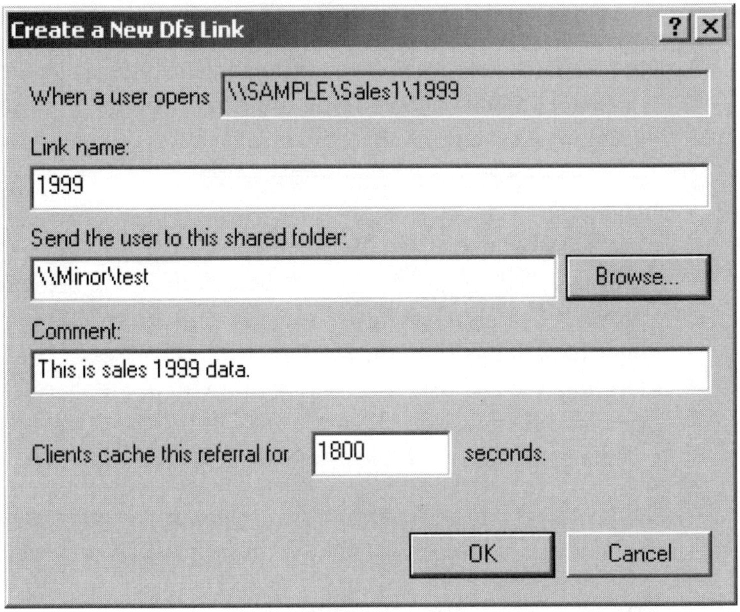

After you supply the Dfs link information and close the dialog box, you'll see the new Dfs link listed under the Dfs root in the Dfs console window.

Configuring Replication

Replication ensures that if the host server goes down, the files and folders that are part of the Dfs will still be available. Automatic replication can be used only in conjunction with NTFS volumes. If you don't specify automatic replication, you'll have to replicate your Dfs shared folders manually.

You can enable the Dfs to automatically replicate the contents of one or more shared folders. The Dfs uses the *File Replication Service (FRS)* for this task. When changes are made to one shared folder, FRS updates the other shared folders to reflect the changes (by default, this happens every 15 minutes). You should specify that all of the shared folders in a Dfs link are replicated automatically, if possible. This ensures proper synchronization of all the shared folders in a Dfs link. You select one of your shared folders to be the initial master, which replicates its contents to the other shared folders in the Dfs link the first time the replication policy is set.

WARNING Do not mix and match manual replication with automatic replication. If you do, you take the risk that all your shared folders may be synchronized incorrectly.

Checking Dfs Shared Folder Status

You can check to see if your Dfs shared folders are being referenced properly by right-clicking any element in the Dfs topology and selecting Check Status from the pop-up menu. If you check the status of a Dfs link, the Dfs will verify the status of all of the shared folders in that link. If you check the status of a Dfs root, the Dfs will verify the status of every shared folder in every Dfs link.

A link that is properly configured will appear with a green check mark. A link that is not properly configured will be marked with a red ×.

Configuring Dfs Security

Permissions that apply to folders and files still apply in the Dfs. If a user has access to a specific shared folder, that user also has access to that folder when using the appropriate Dfs share. If users have access to one Dfs shared folder, they can also see all the other Dfs shared folders, but they won't be able to use them without having the appropriate permissions.

In the Security tab, you can specify who has access to the Dfs object and what access has been allowed or denied. Permissions include Full Control, Read, and Write. By default, the Administrators group is allowed Read and Write permissions. The Authenticated Users group is allowed Read permission by default.

Troubleshooting Dfs

If you are unable to access a Dfs shared folder, check the following:

- Is the server that hosts the Dfs root available?

- Does the user have appropriate permissions on the NTFS folder that they are trying to access through Dfs?

- Does the user have appropriate permissions assigned from the Distribute File System utility for the resource they are trying to access?

- Use the Distributed File System utility to check the status of your Dfs shared folders.

Managing Local Access

The two common types of file systems used by local partitions are FAT (which includes FAT16 and FAT32) and NTFS. FAT partitions do not support local security; NTFS partitions do support it. Therefore, if users access a file system on a FAT partition, you cannot specify any security for the file system once a user has logged on. However, if the partition is NTFS, you can specify each user's access to specific folders on the partition, based on the user's logon name and group associations.

NTFS Permissions

NTFS permissions control access to NTFS folders and files. You configure access by allowing or denying NTFS permissions to users and groups. Normally, NTFS permissions are cumulative, based on group memberships if the user has been allowed access. However, if the user had been denied access through user or group membership, that limitation overrides allowed permissions.

Windows 2000 Server offers six levels of NTFS permissions: Full Control, Modify, Read & Execute, List Folder Contents, Read, and Write, as defined in Table 2.8. Any user with Full Control access can manage the security of a folder. By default, the Everyone group has Full Control permission for the entire NTFS partition. However, in order to access folders, a user must have physical access to the computer as well as a valid logon name and password. By default, regular users can't access folders over the network unless the folders have been shared.

TABLE 2.8: NTFS Permissions

Permission	List of Rights
Full Control	Traverse folders and execute files (programs) in the folders List the contents of a folder and read the data in a folder's files See a folder's or file's attributes Change a folder's or file's attributes Create new files and write data to the files Create new folders and append data to files Delete subfolders and files Delete files Change permissions for files and folders Take ownership of files and folders
Modify	Traverse folders and execute files in the folders List the contents of a folder and read the data in a folder's files See a folder's or file's attributes Change a folder's or file's attributes Create new files and write data to the files Create new folders and append data to files Delete files
Read & Execute	Traverse folders and execute files in the folders List the contents of a folder and read the data in a folder's files See a folder's or file's attributes
List Folder Contents	Traverse folders List the contents of a folder and read the data in a folder's files See a folder's or file's attributes
Read	List the contents of a folder and read the data in a folder's files See a folder's or file's attributes
Write	Change a folder's or file's attributes Create new files and write data to the files Create new folders and append data to files

Applying NTFS Permissions

You apply NTFS permissions through Windows Explorer. Right-click the file or folder for which you want to control access. Select Properties from the pop-up menu to bring up the related Properties dialog box.

NOTE   The process for configuring NTFS permissions for folders is the same as for folders. NTFS permissions are most commonly applied at the folder level.

The tabs in the Properties dialog box depend on the options that have been configured for your computer. For files and folders on NTFS partitions, the dialog box will contain a Security tab, which is where you configure NTFS permissions. The Security tab lists the users and groups who have been assigned permissions to the file or folder or file. (The Security tab is not present for files or folders on FAT partitions because FAT partitions do not support local security.)

NOTE   Through the Advanced button of the Security tab, you can configure more granular NTFS permissions, such as Traverse Folder/Execute File and Read Attributes permissions.

To remove the NTFS permissions for a user, computer, or group, highlight that user, computer, or group in the Security tab and click the Remove button. Note that if the permissions are being inherited, before removing the NTFS permissions you must first uncheck the Allow Inheritable Permissions from Parent to Propagate to This Object check box.

WARNING   Be careful when you remove NTFS permissions. You won't be asked to confirm this action, as you are for deleting most other types of items in Windows 2000 Server.

Controlling Permissions Inheritance

Normally, the directory structure is organized hierarchically. This means you are likely to have subfolders in the folders to which you apply permissions. In Windows 2000 Server, parent folder permissions are by default applied to any files or subfolders in that folder. These are called *inherited permissions*.

NOTE   In Windows NT 4.0, files in a folder automatically inherited permissions from the parent folder, but subfolders did not inherit parent permissions. In Windows 2000 Server, the default is for the permissions to be inherited by subfolders.

In the Security tab of the folder's Properties, you can specify that permissions should not be inherited. If you deselect the Allow Inheritable Permissions from Parent to Propagate to This Object check box at the bottom of the dialog box, you have disabled inherited permissions at this folder level. You are then given a choice of either copying the permissions or removing them from the parent folder.

If an Allow or a Deny check box in the Permission list has a shaded check mark, this means the permission was inherited from an upper-level folder. If the check mark is not shaded, the permission was applied at the selected folder. This is known as an *explicitly assigned permission*.

TIP   Because of the complexities of permissions on files and folders, it's useful to view inherited permissions so that you can more easily troubleshoot user access to the files and folders.

Determining Effective Permissions

To determine a user's *effective rights* (the rights the user actually has to a file or folder), add up all the permissions allowed through the user's assignments based on username and group associations. Then subtract any permissions that have been denied the user through the username or group associations.

TIP   You may want to remove permissions from the Everyone group in order to test the combinations of permissions for other groups. If you decide to do this, adding the Administrators group with Full Control permission will make it easier to troubleshoot any problems that arise.

Determining NTFS Permissions for Copied or Moved Files

When you copy or move NTFS files, the permissions that have been set for those files might change. The following guidelines can be used to predict what will happen:

- If you move a file from one folder to another folder on the same volume, the file will retain the original NTFS permissions.

- If you move a file from one folder to another folder between different NTFS volumes, the file is treated as a copy and will have the same permissions as the destination folder.

- If you copy a file from one folder to another folder on the same volume or on a different volume, the file will have the same permissions as the destination folder.

- If you copy or move a folder or file to a FAT partition, it will not retain any NTFS permissions.

Managing Network Access

Sharing is the process of allowing network users to access a folder, called a *shared folder,* located on a Windows 2000 Server computer. A network share provides a single location to manage shared data used by many users. Sharing also allows an administrator to install an application once only, as opposed to installing it locally at each computer, and to manage the application from a single location.

Creating Shared Folders

To share a folder on a Windows 2000 member server, you must be logged on as a member of the Administrators or Power Users group. To share a folder on a Windows 2000 domain controller, you must be logged on as a member of the Administrators or Server Operators group. You enable and configure sharing through the Sharing tab of the folder's Properties dialog box. If you share a folder and then decide that you don't want to share it, just select the Do Not Share This Folder radio button in the Sharing tab.

TIP In Windows Explorer, you can easily see that a folder has been shared because of the hand icon under the folder.

When you share a folder, you can configure the options listed in Table 2.9.

TABLE 2.9: Folder Share Options

Option	Description
Do Not Share This Folder	The folder is only available through local access
Share This Folder	The folder is available through local access and network access
Share Name	A descriptive name by which users will access the folder
Comment	Additional descriptive information about the share (optional)
User Limit	The maximum number of connections to the share allowed at any one time
Permissions	How users will access the folder over the network
Caching	How folders are cached when the folder is offline

Configuring Share Permissions

You can control users' access to *shared folders* by assigning *share permissions*. Share permissions are less complex than NTFS permissions and can be applied to folders only (unlike NTFS permissions, which can be applied to folders and files).

To assign share permissions, click the Permissions button in the Sharing tab of the folder's Properties dialog box. This brings up the Share Permissions dialog box. You can assign three types of share permissions:

- The Full Control share permission allows full access to the shared folder.

- The Change share permission allows users to change data in a file or to delete files.

- The Read share permission allows a user to view and execute files in the shared folder.

Full Control is the default permission on shared folders for the Everyone group. When the Full Control permission is assigned, the Change and Read permissions are checked as well.

NOTE   Shared folders do not use the same concept of inheritance as NTFS folders. If you share a folder, there is no way to block access to lower-level resources through share permissions.

Managing Shares with the Shared Folders Utility

Shared Folders is a Computer Management utility for creating and managing shared folders on the computer. The Shared Folders window displays all shares that have been created on the computer, the user sessions that are open on each share, and the files that are currently open, listed by user.

TIP   You can add the Shared Folders utility as an MMC snap-in.

Viewing Shares

When you select Shares in the Shared Folders utility, you see all shares that have been configured on the computer.

Along with the shares that you have specifically configured, you also see the Windows 2000 administrative shares, which are shares created by the system automatically to facilitate system administration. A share name followed by a dollar sign ($) indicates that the share is hidden from view when users access utilities such as My Network Places and browse network resources. The following special shares may appear on your Windows 2000 Server computer, depending on how the computer is configured:

- The *drive_letter*$ share is the share for the root of the drive; for example, the C drive is shared as C$. By default, the root of every drive is shared.

NOTE   On Windows 2000 member servers and Windows Professional computers, only members of the Administrators and Backup Operators groups can access the *drive_letter*$ share. On Windows 2000 domain controllers, members of the Administrators, Backup Operators, and Server Operators groups can access this share.

- The ADMIN$ share points to the Windows 2000 system root (for example, C:\WINNT).

- The IPC$ share allows remote administration of a computer and is used to view a computer's shared resources. (IPC stands for interprocess communication.)

- The PRINT$ share is used for remote printer administration.

- The FAX$ share is used by fax clients to cache fax cover sheets and documents that are in the process of being faxed.

Viewing Share Sessions

When you select Sessions in the Shared Folders utility, you see a listing of all users who are currently accessing shared folders on the computer. Figure 2.2 shows an example of a Sessions listing in Shared Folders. The listing includes the following information:

- The username that has connected to the share

- The name of the computer from which the user has connected

- The client operating system used by the connecting computer

- The number of files the user has open

- The amount of time the user has been connected

- The amount of idle time for the connection

- Whether the user has connected through Guest access

FIGURE 2.2: The Sessions listing in the Shared Folders window

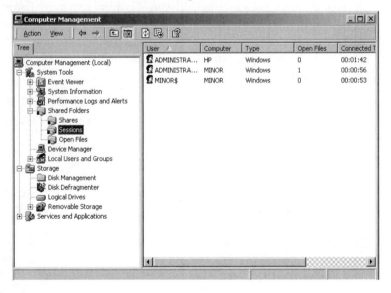

Viewing Open Files in Shared Folders

When you select Open Files in the Shared Folders utility, you see a list of all the currently open files in shared folders. The listing includes the following information:

- The path and files that are currently open

- The username accessing the file

- The operating system of the user who is accessing the file

- Whether any file locks have been applied (file locks are used to prevent two users from opening the same file and editing it at the same time)

- The current open mode (such as read or write)

Providing Access to Shared Resources

A user can access a shared resource in many ways. Let's look at three common methods.

- **Through My Network Places:** The advantage of mapping a network location through My Network Places is that you do not use a drive letter. This is useful if you have already exceeded the limit of 26 drive letters.

- **By mapping a network drive in Windows Explorer:** Through Windows Explorer, you can map a network drive to a drive letter that users perceive as a local connection on their computer. Once you create a *mapped drive,* it can be accessed through a drive letter using My Computer.

- **Through the NET USE command-line utility:** The NET USE command-line utility provides a quick and easy way to map a network drive. This command has the following syntax:

    NET USE *x*: *computername**sharename*

TIP You can get more information about the NET USE command by typing **NET USE /?** at a command prompt.

Reviewing the Flow of Resource Access

Understanding the resource-flow process will help you troubleshoot access problems. As you've learned, a user account must have appropriate permissions to access a resource. Resource access is determined through the following steps:

1. At logon, an *access token* is created for the logon account.

2. When a resource is accessed, Windows 2000 Server Security Accounts Manager (SAM) checks the *Access Control List (ACL)* to see if the user can be granted access.

3. If the user is on the List, the SAM then checks the *Access Control Entries (ACEs)* to see what type of access the user is given.

Access tokens, ACLs, and ACEs are defined in the following sections.

Access Tokens

Each time a user account logs on, an access token is created. The access token contains the security identifier (SID) of the user currently logged on, as well as for any of the user's associated groups. Once an access token is created, it is not updated until the next logon.

WARNING Access tokens are only updated during the logon sequence. They are not updated on the fly. Therefore, if you add a user to a group, that user must log off and then log on for their access token to be updated.

ACLs and ACEs

Each object in Windows 2000 Server has an ACL. An *object* is defined as a set of data that can be used by the system, or a set of actions that can be used to manipulate system data. Examples of objects include folders, files, network shares, and printers.

The ACL is a list of user accounts and groups that are allowed to access the resource. Figure 2.3 shows how ACLs are associated with each object. For each ACL, there is an ACE that defines what a user or a group can actually do at the resource. Deny permissions are always listed first. This means that if users have Deny permissions through user or group membership, they will not be allowed to access the object, even if they have explicit Allow permissions through other user or group permissions.

FIGURE 2.3: Access control lists (ACLs) for network shares

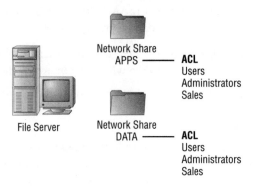

Local vs. Network Access

Local vs. Network Access

Local and network security work together. The most restrictive access will determine what a user can do. For example, if the local folder is formatted with NTFS and the default permissions have not been changed, the Everyone group has the Full Control permission. If that local folder is shared and the permissions are set so that only the Sales group is assigned the Read permission, then only the Sales group can access that shared folder. Conversely, if the local NTFS permissions allow only the Managers group the Read permission on a local folder, and that folder has been shared with default permissions allowing the Everyone group Full Control permission, only the Managers group can access the folder with Read permissions, because Read is the more restrictive permission.

Necessary Procedures

These procedures will help you apply permissions and access network resources. You can count on the certification exam's focusing strongly on these topics.

Creating a Dfs Root

There can only be one Dfs root per server, although there may be unlimited Dfs roots per domain. You should create the Dfs root on an NTFS partition, because automatic replication is available only on the NTFS system. In addition, you can take advantage of the security features offered by NTFS to control access to Dfs shared folders.

1. Select Start ➤ Programs ➤ Administrative Tools ➤ Distributed File System. This opens the Dfs console.

2. Highlight Distributed File System and select Action ➤ New Dfs Root from the menu bar.

3. When the New Dfs Root Wizard starts, click the Next button.

4. The Select the Dfs Root Type dialog box appears. Here, you choose whether to create a domain Dfs root or a stand-alone Dfs root. As explained earlier in the chapter, in a domain environment you can create a domain Dfs root, which uses the Active Directory and supports automatic replication. In a workgroup environment, you can only create a stand-alone Dfs root, which does not use the Active Directory or support automatic replication. In this procedure, you'll create a domain Dfs root. Click the Next button to continue.

5. In the Select the Host Domain for the Dfs Root dialog box, specify the host domain that will be used. Click Next to proceed.

6. In the Specify the Host Server for the Dfs Root dialog box, specify the name of the host server. Click Next to proceed.

7. The Specify the DFS Root Share dialog box appears next. Here you specify that your DFS root share will use an existing share or that you will create a new share. Make your selection and click the Next button. If you choose to create a new share, you'll be prompted to confirm the creation of the new folder.

8. Next up is the Name the Dfs Root dialog box. You can accept the default Dfs root name (which is the share name), or enter another name. Also, if needed, you can enter a comment. Then click the Next button.

9. The Completing the New Dfs Root Wizard dialog box appears next, showing the settings you have specified. If the information is correct, click the Finish button.

Configuring Shared Folder Replication

1. Create and share the folder that will be used to hold the replicated folder.

2. Select Start ➤ Programs ➤ Administrative Tools ➤ Distributed File System to open the Dfs console.

3. In the Dfs console window, right-click the Dfs link you will replicate and select New Replica from the pop-up menu.

4. The Add a New Replica dialog box appears. In the Send the User to This Shared Folder text box, specify the shared folder that will hold the replica. In the Replication Policy section, choose Manual Replication or Automatic Replication. Then click the OK button.

5. Repeat steps 3 and 4 to add other replicas.

6. To configure the replication policy, right-click the Dfs link to which you added the replica and select Replication Policy from the pop-up menu.

7. In the Replication Policy dialog box, highlight the master Dfs link and click the Set Master button. Select the shared folder that will be used for replication and click the Enable button. Then click the OK button.

Applying NTFS Permissions

1. In Windows Explorer, right-click the file or folder on which you want to control access, select Properties from the pop-up menu, and click the Security tab of the Properties dialog box.

2. Click the Add button to open the Select Users, Computers, or Groups dialog box. From the list box at the top, select users in the computer's local database or in your domain (or trusted domains). The list box at the bottom of the dialog box lists all the groups and users for the location you specified in the top list box.

3. Click the user, computer, or group that you wish to add. Use Ctrl+click to select noncontiguous users, computers, or groups, or

Shift+click to select contiguous users, computers, or groups. Click the Add button, and your selected user, computer, or group appears in the bottom list box.

4. Click OK to return to the Security tab of the Properties dialog box. Highlight each user, computer, or group in the top list box individually and specify the NTFS permissions that should be applied. When you're finished, click the OK button.

NOTE Through the Advanced button of the Security tab, you can configure more granular NTFS permissions, such as Traverse Folder/ Execute File and Read Attributes permissions.

Creating New Shares

Here are the steps to create new shares in shared folders, using the Create Shared Folder Wizard.

1. In Computer Management, right-click the Shares folder and select New File Share from the pop-up menu.

2. The Create Shared Folder Wizard starts. Specify the folder that will be shared (you can use the Browse button to select the folder), and provide a share name and description. Click the Next button to continue.

3. Next up is the Create Shared Folder Wizard dialog box for assigning share permissions. You can select from one of the predefined permissions assignments, or you can customize the share permissions. After you specify the permissions that will be assigned, click the Finish button.

4. The Create Shared Folder dialog box appears. This dialog box verifies that the folder has been shared successfully. Click the Yes button to create another shared folder or the No button if you're finished creating shared folders.

NOTE To stop sharing a folder, right-click the share and select Stop Sharing from the pop-up menu. You will be asked to confirm that you want to stop sharing the folder.

Applying Share Permissions

1. Select Start ➤ Programs ➤ Accessories ➤ Windows Explorer. Expand My Computer and then expand Local Disk (D:).

2. Right-click the Share Me folder, select Sharing, and click the Permissions button.

3. In the Share Permissions dialog box, highlight the Everyone group and click the Remove button. Then click the Add button.

4. In the Select Users, Computers, and Groups dialog box, select the users that need access to the file, click the Add button, and then click the OK button.

5. Click OK again to close the dialog box.

Accessing a Shared Resource through My Network Places

1. Double-click the My Network Places icon on the Desktop.

2. Double-click Add Network Place to start the Add Network Place Wizard.

3. Type in the location of the Network Place. This can be a UNC path to a shared network folder, an HTTP path to a Web folder, or an FTP path to an FTP site. If you're unsure of the path, you can use the Browse button to search for your path. Click the Next button to continue.

4. Enter the name that you want to use for the network location. This name will appear in the computer's My Network Places listing.

Mapping a Network Drive through Windows Explorer

1. Select Start ➤ Programs ➤ Accessories ➤ Windows Explorer to open Windows Explorer.

2. Select Tools ➤ Map Network Drive.

3. In the Map Network Drive dialog box, choose the drive letter that will be associated with the network drive.

4. From the Folder drop-down list, choose the shared network folder to which you will map the drive.

5. If you want this connection to be persistent (you want to save the connection and use it every time you log on), make sure that the Reconnect at Logon check box is checked.

6. If you will connect to the share using a different username, click the underlined part of Connect Using a Different User Name. This brings up the Connect As dialog box; click OK.

7. If you want to create a shortcut to a Web folder, click the underlined part of Create a Shortcut to a Web Folder or FTP Site. This starts the Add Network Place Wizard, which was described in the procedure just above.

Exam Essentials

Know the benefits of Dfs. Dfs provides easier file access, increased file availability, and server load balancing.

Know the components of the Dfs topology. The Dfs consists of three main components: a Dfs root, one or more Dfs links, and one or more Dfs shared folders.

Know the difference between a stand-alone Dfs root and a domain-based Dfs root. A stand-alone Dfs root doesn't use the Active Directory. It is not fault tolerant, so no replication occurs. And it can only have a single level of Dfs links. A domain-based root uses the Active Directory, is fault tolerant, and can have multiple levels of Dfs links. Its fault-tolerant roots must be located on NTFS 5 or higher partitions.

Know how Dfs provides fault tolerance. Fault tolerance is provided by the File Replication Service, which automatically checks and makes updates to the shared folders every 15 minutes. This is available on NTFS partitions only.

Know how to check the status of Dfs folders. The status of a Dfs folder can be checked by right-clicking on any element in the folder and selecting Check Status from the pop-up menu. A green check mark indicates that the link is working properly. A red X indicates a broken link.

Understand how security works in Dfs. The Security tab in the Dfs Properties allows you to specify user and group access to the Dfs folders. Once a user has been granted access to one Dfs object, that user will be able to see all of the objects, but will only be able to access the objects to which they have been granted access.

Know the levels of NTFS permissions. The levels of NTFS permissions are Full Control, Modify, Read & Execute, List Folder Contents, Read, and Write.

Know how to apply NTFS permissions. NTFS permissions are granted from Windows Explorer. Right-click on a folder or file and select Properties, and open the Security tab to grant permissions.

Know how inherited permissions work. A subdirectory or file inherits its permissions from its parent directory by default.

Know how to determine effective permissions. Effective permissions are determined by combining the permissions assigned to user and group associations.

Know what happens to permissions when files are moved or copied. The basic rule is that a file, when copied or moved, inherits the permissions of the target directory; the only exception is when a file is moved within the same partition.

Know the levels of share permissions. The levels of share permissions are Full Control, Change, and Read.

Know what to use to manage shares. Shares can be managed using the Shared Folder utility in Computer Management.

Understand how hidden and administrative shares are configured. Administrative shares are created automatically by the system to facilitate system administration. They are hidden by default, by using the $ character at the end of the share name. The $ can be used to hide other shares as needed.

Know when an access token is created. The access token is created during the logon process. It contains the user's SID and any group SIDs associated with the user. The access token does not get updated while the user is logged on.

Understand how NTFS and share permissions are combined.
NTFS and share permissions work together to establish network
security. The most restrictive one of the two is applied when accessing
resources over the network.

Key Terms and Concepts

Access Control List (ACL)   A list of user accounts and groups that
are allowed access to the resource.

Access Control Entry (ACE)   An entry on the ACL that defines
what a user or a group can do at the resource.

access token   Generated during the logon process, the access token
contains the user and group SIDs associated with the user. The access
token also contains the user's rights.

administrative share   Shares automatically created by the system to
facilitate administration. They have limited access. The administrative
shares are root shares, such as C$, ADMIN$, IPC$, PRINT$, and FAX$.

Dfs link   A pointer to a shared folder or one of its replicas.

Dfs replicas   A copy of the files and folders in a Dfs, to ensure that
the files and folders are available if the host is not.

Dfs root   A Dfs root is a local share that serves as the starting point
and host to other shares. Any shared resource can be published into
the Dfs namespace.

Dfs shared folders   Files or folders in the Dfs namespace that are
shared by users with proper permissions. Shared folders can exist at
the root level (domain-based Dfs only) or be referred to by Dfs links.

Distributed file system (Dfs)   A central database of links that point
to shares across the network.

domain-based Dfs root   Domain-based Dfs stores its configuration
information in Active Directory. Because this information is made
available on multiple domain controllers in the domain, domain-
based Dfs provides high availability for any distributed file system in
the domain.

effective rights   The rights actually used by a user when accessing files or folders.

File Replication Service (FRS)   A utility that automatically replicates shared folders in a Dfs.

inherited permissions   Permissions applied to any file or subfolder from its parent folder.

host server   The domain server that contains the Dfs root.

mapped drive   A network resource that has been assigned a local drive letter, making it available for use on the local machine.

My Network Places   A utility that allows you to map network resources without using a drive letter.

NET USE   A command-line utility that connects users to network resources.

NTFS permissions   Security applied to folders or files, controlling the level of users' access.

root share   The share at the top of the Dfs topology that is the starting point for the links and shared files. A Dfs root share can be defined for either domain-based or stand-alone operations. Domain-based Dfs can have multiple root shares in the domain but only one on each member server.

share permissions   Security applied to shared folders, controlling the level of users' access.

Shared Folders   A utility in Computer Management for creating and managing shared folders on the computer.

shared folders   Folders that are available through local and network access.

stand-alone Dfs root   Stand-alone Dfs stores its configuration in the registry of the local computer. It is intended for backward-compatibility with previous versions of Dfs.

Sample Questions

1. You are the network administrator. A user calls up and requests access to a folder. You add this user to a group that has the appropriate rights to the folder. A few minutes later the user calls again and complains that she is still unable to access the resource. What do you need to do?

   A. Redo the permissions. You must apply the changes before you exit.

   B. Add the user individually in order to gain access to the resource.

   C. Tell the user to log off and log on again.

   D. Nothing. The user will eventually figure out the problem.

   Answer: C. The user needs to log off and then log back on to create a new access token that has the updated information.

2. Nancy and Frank both need access to a folder on Nancy's computer. Both Nancy and Frank belong to the Accts, Managers, and Supervisors groups. Nancy has shared the folder and assigned the permissions shown just below. In these circumstances, what are the *effective* permissions for Nancy and Frank?

	NTFS	**Share**
Accts:	List Folder Contents	Read
Managers:	Write	Change
Supervisors:	Read & Execute	Change

   In these circumstances, what are the *effective* permissions for Nancy and Frank?

   A. Nancy has Change permission, and Frank has Change permission.

   B. Nancy has Read permission, and Frank has Read permission.

   C. Nancy has List and Add permissions, and Frank has Read permission.

D. Nancy has Write and Read & Execute permissions, and Frank has Write and Read & Execute permissions.

Answer: D. Nancy's effective permissions are determined by taking the least restrictive permissions on the NTFS, because she is accessing the file locally. So, Nancy gets Add and Read. Frank's effective permissions are determined based on the least restrictive NTFS and the least restrictive Share permissions, and then taking the more restrictive of the two. Frank would get Add and Read.

3. You need to simultaneously connect to 27 different network shares. Where can you make all of the connections?

A. You cannot make that many simultaneous network connections.

B. My Network Places.

C. Windows Explorer.

D. Use the NET USE command.

Answer: B. My Network Places allows you to connect to as many resources as needed. No drive letter is needed, so you can exceed the limitation of 26 drive letters.

4. Which component of the Dfs points to files?

A. Dfs root

B. Dfs shared folders

C. Dfs links

D. Replicas

Answer: C. Dfs links are pointers to the shared folders that will be accessed by the end user.

Monitor, configure, troubleshoot, and control access to Web sites.

This objective covers Web management and troubleshooting. Microsoft has added this functionality as part of the core Windows

2000 Server, and you will be expected to know Web site administration. The material is covered here in the chapter on managing access to resources because Microsoft has made Web site administration an extension of file and application support. You manage the Web site by using the Internet Service Manager (ISM) located in Administrative Tools. ISM lets you manage your Web, FTP, mail, and network news sites. Here we focus on the Web site properties because that is the main focus on the exam. The other sites' management functions are nearly identical to those of the Web site.

FTP, SMTP, and NNTP site properties don't differ dramatically from those of the Web site. The biggest difference is that the Web site properties are more robust than the rest of the services offered in IIS. (The others are scaled-down versions of the Web site.) The principles that govern a Web site apply to the others. The procedure for creating a new Web site is the same for creating a new FTP site.

The exam will focus on your ability to configure the Web site; manage access; tune performance of the processor, memory, and bandwidth; implement security; and troubleshoot IIS.

Critical Information

When Internet Information Services (IIS) are installed, you see the Internet Services Manager program item in Administrative Tools. This is the primary utility used to manage the services and components of IIS.

The following protocols are installed as a part of IIS:

- *File Transfer Protocol (FTP),* used to transfer files between two computers using the TCP/IP protocol

- *Hypertext Transfer Protocol (HTTP),* used to navigate and to create content for Web sites

- *Simple Mail Transfer Protocol (SMTP),* used to transfer mail between two SMTP mail systems

- *Network News Transfer Protocol (NNTP),* used to provide newsgroup services between NNTP servers and NNTP clients

To access Internet Services Manager, select Start ➤ Programs ➤ Administrative Tools ➤ Internet Services Manager. As shown in Figure 2.4, five items are defined by default in the IIS: Default FTP Site, Default Web Site, Administration Web Site, Default SMTP Virtual Server, and Default NNTP Virtual Server. These default sites and virtual servers are provided to help you get IIS up and running as quickly as possible.

FIGURE 2.4: The Internet Services Window

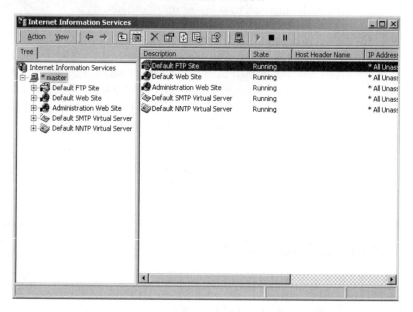

Managing a Web Site

Through Internet Services Manager, you can configure many options for your Web site, such as the number of connections allowed, performance settings, and access controls. To access a Web site's properties, right-click the Web site you want to manage in the left side of the IIS window and select Properties from the pop-up menu. This brings up the Web site Properties dialog box, shown in Figure 2.5. There are ten tabs with options for configuring and managing your Web site, described briefly in Table 2.10 and in more detail in the following sections.

FIGURE 2.5: The Default Web Site Properties

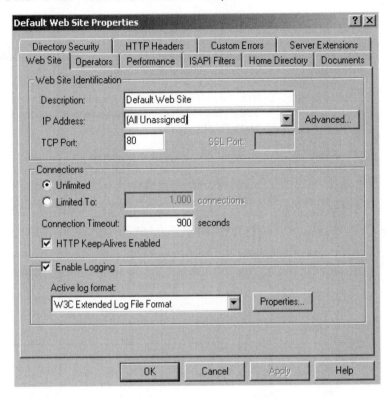

TABLE 2.10: Web Site Properties Dialog Box

Tab	Description of Options
Web Site	Web site identification, connections, and logging
Operators	Users and groups designated to manage the Web site
Performance	Settings for performance tuning, bandwidth throttling, and process throttling
ISAPI Filters	ISAPI (Internet Server Application Programming Interface) filters

TABLE 2.10: Web Site Properties Dialog Box *(continued)*

Tab	Description of Options
Home Directory	Settings for content location, access permissions, content control, and application
Documents	Your specification of the default document users will see if they access your Web site without specifying a specific document
Directory Security	Settings for anonymous access and authentication control, IP address and domain name restrictions, and secure communications
HTTP Headers	Values that will be returned to Web browsers in the Hypertext Markup Language (HTML) headers of the Web pages
Custom Errors	Your customized error message that will appear when there is a Web browser error
Server Extensions	Publishing controls for FrontPage options

Setting Web Site Properties

The Web Site tab (see Figure 2.5) includes options for identifying the Web site, controlling connections, and enabling logging.

WEB SITE IDENTIFICATION

This description of the Web site appears in the IIS window. It defaults to the same name as the Web site, but you can enter another description in the Description text box.

You also configure the IP address associated with the site. This IP address must already be configured for the computer.

Multiple Sites: You can host multiple IP addresses on a single computer, by binding multiple IP addresses to a single network card, or by adding an additional network card for each IP address. To use multiple IP addresses, you must also add the host name and its corresponding IP address to your name resolution system. Then clients need only type the text name in a browser to reach your Web site.

NOTE   If you are using this method of hosting multiple sites on the Internet, you will also need to register the text names with InterNIC.

To host multiple sites, you can use different host header names with a single static IP address. With support for host headers, an organization can host multiple Web sites on a single computer running Microsoft Windows 2000 Server with only one IP address. This lets ISPs and corporate intranets host multiple Web sites on a single server while offering separate user domains for each site. You'll need to add the host names to your name resolution system. The difference is that once a request reaches the computer, IIS 5 uses the host name passed in the HTTP header to determine which site a client is requesting.

The last entry for Web Site Identification, TCP Port, is the port that will be used to respond to HTTP requests. The default port is TCP port 80. If you change this value, clients attempting to connect to the Web site will have to specify the correct port value. This option can be used for additional security.

CONNECTIONS

You can allow unlimited connections to the Web site, or you can control the number of connections. To specify a connection limit, select the Limited To option and enter the maximum number of connections allowed.

The Connection Timeout is used to specify how long an inactive user can remain connected to the Web site before the connection is automatically terminated.

If you turn on the HTTP Keep-Alives Enabled option, the client will maintain an open connection with the server, as opposed to opening a new connection for each client request. This enhances client performance but may degrade server performance.

LOGGING

Logging features record details of Web site access. If you enable logging, you can select from several log formats for collecting information. If you want to log user access to the Web site, be sure the Log Visits check box on the Home Directory tab is also checked (which is the default setting).

Specifying Operators

In the Operators tab of the Web site's Properties dialog, you can configure which users and groups are able to manage the site. No operators are assigned by default. You can add or remove operators from this list.

Setting Performance Options

The Performance tab offers settings for configuring performance tuning, enabling bandwidth throttling, and enabling process throttling.

PERFORMANCE TUNING

Performance tuning allows you to tune your Web site based on the number of hits your Web site is expected to receive each day. Based on the number you specify, server memory is allocated to the Web site to maximize user access. You can configure hits per day at fewer than 10,000, fewer than 100,000 (the default setting), or more than 100,000.

BANDWIDTH THROTTLING

Bandwidth is defined as the total capacity of your transmission media. This can be expressed as bits per second (bps) or as Hertz (frequency). IIS allows you to specify how much bandwidth can be used in terms of kilobytes per second (KB/S).

If the server is used to host other Web sites or for other purposes, such as hosting an e-mail server, you might want to limit the maximum amount of bandwidth your Web server can use. This is called *bandwidth throttling*. If bandwidth throttling is not enabled, the server can use the maximum amount of bandwidth available.

PROCESS THROTTLING

When you enable *process throttling,* you can specify the percentage of CPU processing that can be used by the Web site. If you select the Enforce Limits option, whatever value is set for process throttling will be enforced. If this option is not selected, the Web site will be able to exceed the process throttling settings, and an event will be written to the event log.

Setting ISAPI Filters

ISAPI filters direct Web browser requests for specific URLs to specific *ISAPI (Internet Server Application Programming Interface)* applications, which are then run. ISAPI filters are commonly used to manage customized logon authentication. These filters work by monitoring HTTP requests and responding to specific events that are defined through the filter. The filters are loaded into the Web site's memory. Through the ISAPI Filters tab, you can add ISAPI filters for your Web site. The filters are applied in the order they are listed in the list box; use the up- and down-arrow buttons to the left of the list box to change the order of the filters.

Configuring Home Directory Options

The Home Directory tab includes settings for the Web site's content location, access permissions, content control, and application settings.

CONTENT LOCATION

The home directory is used to provide Web content. The default directory is called inetpub\wwwroot. You have three choices for the location of the home directory:

- A directory on the local computer
- A share on another computer (stored on the local network and identified by a UNC name)
- A redirection to a resource using a URL

ACCESS PERMISSIONS AND CONTENT CONTROL

Access permissions define user access to the Web site. Content control specifies whether logging and indexing are enabled. By default, users have only Read access, and logging and indexing are enabled. The Access Permissions and Content Control options are described in Table 2.11.

NOTE Web service access permissions and NTFS permissions work together. The more restrictive of the two permissions will be the effective permission.

TABLE 2.11: Access Permissions and Content Control Options

Option	Description
Script Source Access	Allows users with Read or Write permissions to access source code for scripts, such as ASP (Active Server Pages) applications.
Read	Allows users to read or download files located in your home folder. This is used if your folder contains HTML files. If your home folder contains CGI applications or ISAPI applications, you should disable this option so that users can't download your application files.
Write	Allows users to modify or add to your Web content. *Note: This access should be granted with extreme caution because it allows any user to upload information to your Web site.*
Directory Browsing	Allows users to view Web site directories; not commonly enabled because it exposes your directory structure to users who access your Web site without specifying a specific HTML file.
Log Visits	Allows you to log access to your Web site. The Enable Logging box in the Web Site tab of the Properties dialog box also must be checked.
Index This Resource	Allows you to index your home folder for use with the Microsoft Indexing Service.

APPLICATION SETTINGS

"Application" in this context is the starting point of a specific folder (and its subfolder and files) that has been defined as an application. For example, if you specify that your home folder is an application, every folder in your content location can participate in the application.

The Execute Permissions setting indicates how applications can be accessed within this folder. If you select None, no applications or scripts can be executed from this folder. The Scripts Only setting lets you run script engines even if no execute permissions have been set.

This permission is used for folders that contain ASP (Active Server Pages) scripts. The other option is Scripts and Executables, which allows all file types (including binary files with .EXE and .DLL extensions) to be executed.

The Application Protection setting specifies how applications will be run: Low (IIS Process) means that the application runs in the same process as the Web service. Medium (Pooled) means that the application is run in an isolated pooled process with other applications. High (Isolated) means that each application runs as a separate isolated application.

Setting a Default Document

In the Documents tab of the Web site's Properties, you can designate a document users will see by default if they access your Web site without specifying a specific document. You normally set your default document as your Web site's home page. You can specify multiple documents in the order you prefer. This way, if a document is unavailable, the Web server will access the next default document that has been defined. You can also specify a document footer—an HTML document that will appear at the bottom of each Web page sent to Web clients.

Setting Directory Security

The Directory Security tab includes options for anonymous access and authentication control, IP address and domain name restrictions, and secure communications.

ANONYMOUS ACCESS AND AUTHENTICATION CONTROL

To enable anonymous access and specify authentication control methods, click the Edit button in the Anonymous Access and Authentication Control section of the dialog box. This brings up the Authentication Methods dialog box.

If your Web site is available for public use, you will most likely allow *anonymous access,* under which your computer will use the IUSR_ *computername* user account. You can also limit the access granted to the Anonymous user account by applying NTFS permissions to your Web content.

There are three Authenticated Access levels in the Authentication Methods dialog box:

- Basic Authentication requires a Windows 2000 user account. If anonymous access is disabled or the anonymous account tries to access data that the account does not have permission to access, the system will prompt the user for a valid Windows 2000 user account. With this method, all passwords are sent as clear text. *You should use this option with caution because it poses a security risk.*

- Digest Authentication for Windows Domain Servers works only for Windows 2000 domain accounts. This method requires accounts to store passwords as encrypted clear text.

- Integrated Windows Authentication uses secure authentication to transmit the Windows 2000 username and password.

IP ADDRESS AND DOMAIN NAME RESTRICTIONS

To control access to the Web site based on IP addresses or domain names, click the Edit button in the IP Address and Domain Name Restrictions section of the dialog box. In the IP Address and Domain Name Restrictions dialog box, you can specify that all computers will be granted or denied access, and then specify exceptions. The exceptions can be based on their IP address, IP network address and subnet mask, or domain name (this requires DNS reverse lookup capabilities, which are described in Chapter 10, "Managing Network Interoperability," of the *Study Guide*).

SECURE COMMUNICATIONS

You can increase the security of your Web site by using secure communications. With secure communications, you are able to create and manage key requests and key certificates, to be used in conjunction with Certificate Server. This lets you specify that you will require secure channel services (using certificates) when accessing your Web site.

Configuring HTTP Headers

The HTTP Headers tab of the Web site's Properties helps you set up values that will be returned to Web browsers in the HTML headers of the Web pages. You can configure four options:

- If your Web site contains information that is timesensitive, you can specify that you want to use content expiration. You can set content to expire immediately, after a specified number of minutes, or on a specific date. This helps the Web browser determine whether it should use a cached copy of a requested page, or request an updated copy of the Web page from the Web site.

- Custom HTTP headers are used to send customized HTTP headers from your Web server to the client browser. For example, you may want to specify a custom HTTP header to send instructions that may not be supported by the HTML specification that is currently in use.

- Content ratings allow you to specify appropriate restrictions if a site contains violence, sex, nudity, or adult language. Most Web browsers can then be configured to block objectionable material based on how the content rating has been defined.

- MIME (Multipurpose Internet Mail Extensions) maps are used to configure Web browsers so that they can view files that have been configured with different formats.

Specifying Custom Error Messages

If the Web browser encounters an error, it will display an error message. By default, predefined error messages are displayed. Through the Custom Errors tab you can set up the error message that the user will see. To generate a custom error message, you create an .HTM file that can then be mapped to a specific HTML error.

Setting Server Extensions

In the Server Extensions tab, you configure publishing controls for FrontPage options. FrontPage is used to create and edit HTML pages for your Web site through a What You See Is What You Get (WYSIWYG) editor. This tab includes the following options:

- The Enable Authoring option specifies whether authors can modify the content of the Web site. If this option is selected, you can specify version control, performance based on how many pages the Web site hosts, and the client scripting method that will be used.

- The Options section includes Settings and Administer buttons, through which you specify how mail should be sent, and Office Collaboration features (this option is enabled only if Office is configured).

- The Don't Inherit Security Settings option overrides the global security settings for the Web site.

Troubleshooting Web Site Access

If users are unable to access your Web site, the problem may be caused by improper access permissions, an improperly configured home folder or default document, or use of the wrong TCP port. Here are some tips for troubleshooting Web site access problems:

- Determine if anonymous access is allowed. If so, verify that the username and password that have been configured through Internet Services Manager match the name of the user account and password that are in the Windows 2000 user database.

- Confirm that access has not been denied based on the IP address or domain name.

- Make sure that the proper access permissions have been configured.

- Confirm that the home folder is properly configured and that the default document has been properly configured.

- Make sure that the TCP port is set to port 80 or that you are accessing the Web site using the proper TCP port.

- Make sure that the NTFS permissions on the home folder have not been set so that they deny access to Web site users.

Necessary Procedures

Testing of your understanding of Web site operations has been added to the requirements for passing the Windows 2000 server exam. The following steps walk you through creating a new Web site and configuring its properties, and will help you learn to answer the questions on the exam.

Creating a New Web Site

IIS allows you to host multiple Web sites on a single computer. To create a new Web site, take the following steps:

1. Select Start ➤ Programs ➤ Administration Tools ➤ Internet Services Manager.

2. In the Internet Information Services window, right-click the computer that is running IIS. Select New ➤ Web Site from the pop-up menu.

3. The Welcome to the Web Site Creation Wizard starts. Click the Next button to proceed.

4. The Web Site Description dialog box appears. Type in a descriptive name for your site, and click the Next button to continue.

5. Next up is the IP Address and Port Settings dialog box. You can specify the IP address, TCP port, and host header for the Web site. After you've configured this information, click the Next button.

6. In the Web Site Home Directory dialog box, enter the path to be used for the home directory. You can also specify whether anonymous access will be allowed for the Web site. Click the Next button to continue.

7. The Web Site Access Permissions dialog box appears. Select the check boxes for the access you want to allow, and then click the Next button.

8. When you see the message that you've successfully completed the Web Site Creation Wizard, click the Finish button.

Exam Essentials

Know how to configure Web site identification, connections, and logging.   Use the Web Site Identification tab of the Web site's Properties to set the name of the Web site, the IP address, and TCP port used by the Web site. You can also configure the number of simultaneous connections allowed and the type of log file used to collect information about the site.

Know how to designate which users and groups can manage Web sites. The Operators tab has settings for designating users allowed to manage the site.

Know how to configure performance tuning, bandwidth throttling, and process throttling. Performance tuning sets the server memory allocated to the Web site based on the number of hits expected in a day. Bandwidth throttling controls the amount of bandwidth available to the Web site. Process throttling controls the amount of CPU processing available to the Web site.

Know how to set ISAPI filters. ISAPI filters are commonly used to manage customized logon authentication. You set them in the ISAPI Filters tab of the Web Site Properties dialog box. Click on the Add button and browse for the location of the filter. Use the arrow buttons to change the order. The ISAPI Filters are executed in the order they appear in the dialog box.

Know how to configure anonymous users access, IP address and domain name restrictions, and secure communications. The Directory Security tab of the Web site's Properties allows you to control user access, IP address, and domain name restrictions, and set up secure communications using Certificate Server.

Know how to configure the values returned to Web browsers in the HTTP headers. HTTP headers contain information that Web browsers use to view Web pages. Specifically, you can control Content Expiration, Customized HTTP Headers, Content Ratings, and MIME settings.

Know how to troubleshoot Web site access. Web access problems are generally due to improper access permissions, an improperly configured home folder, or the use of the wrong TCP port.

Key Terms and Concepts

anonymous access   Access granted to public users. By default, the computer will use the *IUSR_computername* user account.

bandwidth throttling   An option that lets you control the amount of bandwidth available to a Web site.

File Transfer Protocol (FTP)   A TCP/IP protocol used to transfer files between two computers.

Hypertext Transfer Protocol (HTTP)   A TCP/IP protocol used to navigate and create content for Web sites.

Internet Information Services (IIS)   Internet Information Services (IIS) is the standards-based Web application server integrated with the Microsoft Windows 2000 Server operating system. IIS makes it easier to bring business information and applications to the Web.

ISAPI filters   ISAPI (Internet Server Application Programming Interface) filters direct Web browsers to specific ISAPI applications, which are then run.

Internet Services Manager   The tool used to manage and configure Web sites.

Network News Transfer Protocol (NNTP)   A TCP/IP protocol that is used to provide newsgroup services between newsgroup servers and NNTP clients.

process throttling   An option that allows you to control the amount of CPU processing available to a Web site.

Simple Mail Transfer Protocol (SMTP)   A TCP/IP protocol that is used to transfer mail between two SMTP mail servers.

Sample Questions

1. Which utility is used to manage IIS on a Windows 2000 Server computer?

   A. Internet Services Manager

   B. IIS Manager

   C. Internet Service Administrator

   D. Web Site Manager

Answer: A. Internet Services Manager is the primary utility that is used to manage IIS.

2. You are the network administrator and want to control the bandwidth available to a Web site. Which Web site performance option is used for this setting?

A. Bandwidth management

B. Bandwidth allocation

C. Bandwidth pipeline

D. Bandwidth throttling

Answer: D. Bandwidth throttling is used to specify the maximum kilobytes per second (KB/S) that the Web site can consume.

Chapter

3

Managing Hardware Devices and Drivers

MICROSOFT EXAM OBJECTIVES COVERED IN THIS CHAPTER:

After you've installed Windows 2000 Server, you'll need to install and configure your hardware. To help you configure and manage your devices, Microsoft has added Plug-and-Play functionality to the configuration process, as well as several new configuration tools. Windows 2000's consolidated management features help organize these tools so you can use them to their best advantage: the Computer Management utility, Control Panel, and the Microsoft Management Console (MMC). To configure your hardware, you generally use the Computer Management utility or Control Panel. You can also create custom administrative consoles through the MMC.

This chapter shows you how to configure the Windows 2000 Server environment, beginning with an overview of the main configuration utilities. It also discusses how to manage driver signing and how to update drivers. Because of the new tools and the new environment, Microsoft will test your knowledge of the functions of the management tools as well as how to configure devices. You will be expected to understand how to use these tools to recognize and troubleshoot hardware problems. You'll also be tested on the MMC's use and functionality.

NOTE   The utilities and procedures for managing Windows 2000 Server devices and drivers are the same as those for managing Windows 2000 Professional devices and drivers.

Configure hardware devices.

Windows 2000 Server is designed to simplify the process of installing and configuring devices. You need to understand how to configure devices correctly in order to avoid many problems that occur in the real world—and on the exam. When problems do occur, it's important that you know how to reconfigure or update your system's hardware devices and device drivers. In Windows 2000, the Control Panel still is the main location for setting up most devices. The new Computer Management utility consolidates the management tools.

Critical Information

Windows 2000 Server includes several utilities for managing various aspects of the operating system configuration:

- Control Panel helps you configure a wide range of options, including the display, mouse, and system properties.

- The Computer Management utility provides tools for managing common system functions, the computer's storage facilities, and the computer's services.

- The Microsoft Management Console (MMC) is a common environment for administrative tools.

- The Registry Editor allows you to edit the Registry for advanced system configuration.

Control Panel

Control Panel is the main utility for configuring your computer's setup. The Control Panel window contains icons for its options, as described in Table 3.1.

TABLE 3.1: Control Panel Options

Option	Description
Accessibility Options	Configures options that make Windows 2000 more accessible to users with limited sight, hearing, or mobility
Add/Remove Hardware	Options for installing, removing, and troubleshooting your hardware (primarily used for non-Plug-and-Play hardware)
Add/Remove Programs	Options for changing or removing programs that are currently installed on your computer, adding new programs, and adding or removing Windows 2000 components
Administrative Tools	Provides access to Windows 2000 administrative utilities, including Component Services, Computer Management, Data Sources (ODBC), Event Viewer, Local Security Policy, Performance, Services, and Telnet Server Administration
Date/Time	Sets the date, time, and time zone for your computer
Display	Configures your computer's display, including background, screen saver, appearance, Active Desktop, and visual effects
Folder Options	Configures folder options such as general folder properties, file associations, and offline files and folders
Fonts	Helps you to manage the fonts installed on your computer
Game Controllers	Options for adding, removing, and configuring game controllers, including joysticks and game pads
Internet Options	Sets up Internet connection properties, including security, content settings, and Internet programs

TABLE 3.1:   Control Panel Options *(continued)*

Option	Description
Keyboard	Configures keyboard settings, including speed, input locales (language and keyboard layout), and the keyboard driver
Mouse	Configures mouse settings, including button configuration, mouse pointers, motion settings, and the mouse driver
Network and Dial-up Connections	Contains settings for network and dial-up connections and a Wizard to create new connections
Phone and Modem Options	Sets up telephone dialing options and modem properties
Power Options	Configures power schemes, hibernation, APM, and UPS options
Printers	Installs and manages printers
Regional Options	Sets regional options, including numbers, currency, time, date, and input locales
Scanners and Cameras	Configures cameras and scanners
Scheduled Tasks	Configures tasks to be run at specific times or intervals
Sounds and Multimedia	Configures sound devices and assigns sounds to system events
System	Configures system properties, including network identification, hardware, user profiles, and advanced settings
Users and Passwords	For Windows 2000 member servers, provides a simple tool for managing users and passwords.

Computer Management

Computer Management provides a single, consolidated tool for handling common management tasks. The interface is organized into three areas, as shown in Figure 3.1:

- System Tools are utilities for managing the computer, such as Event Viewer and System Information.

- Storage provides utilities for managing the computer's storage, such as Disk Management and Disk Defragmenter.

- Services and Applications are utilities for managing the computer's services, such as WMI (Windows Management Instrumentation) Control, and the Indexing Service.

To access Computer Management, right-click the My Computer icon on your Desktop and select Manage from the pop-up menu.

FIGURE 3.1: The Computer Management window

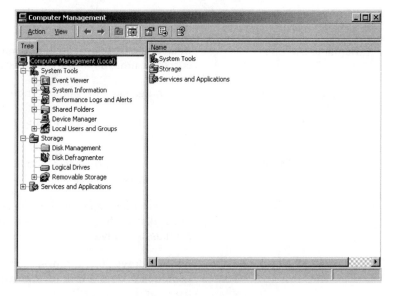

System Tools

System Tools includes six utilities that are used to manage common system functions: Event Viewer, System Information, Performance Logs and Alerts, Shared Folders, Device Manager, and Local Users and Groups.

EVENT VIEWER

The Event Viewer utility tracks information about your hardware and software. You can also monitor Windows 2000 – related security events. Event Viewer tracks information through three log files:

- The Application log shows you events related to applications that are running on the computer, such as errors occurring in SQL Server or Outlook Express applications.

- The Security log lists events related to security, such as the success or failure of actions monitored through auditing.

- The System log tracks events related to the operating system, such as failure to load a device driver.

In addition, Event Viewer creates the following logs on Windows 2000 domain controllers:

- The Directory Service log includes events related to directory services, such as directory database replication.

- The DNS Server log lists events related to the DNS service, such as the DNS server startup.

- The File Replication Service log includes events related to file replication, such as when connections have been established with other computers that will participate in file replication.

SYSTEM INFORMATION

The System Information utility is used to collect and display information about the computer's current configuration. This information can be used to troubleshoot your computer's configuration. It can also be printed and used for reference.

System Information is organized into five categories: System Summary, Hardware Resources, Components, Software Environment, and Internet Explorer 5.

PERFORMANCE LOGS AND ALERTS

Through the Performance Logs and Alerts utility, you can configure logs of performance-related data (called *counter logs* and *trace logs*) and generate alerts based on performance-related data. You can view the logs through the Windows 2000 System Monitor utility and through database or spreadsheet applications.

SHARED FOLDERS

Use the Shared Folders utility to create and manage shared folders on the computer. This utility displays the following information:

- All the shares that have been created on the computer

- The user sessions that are open on each share

- The files that are currently open, listed by user

DEVICE MANAGER

The Device Manager utility provides information about all the devices currently recognized by your computer. The Windows 2000 *device tree* is a record of the devices currently loaded, based on the configuration information in the Registry. The tree is created in random access memory (RAM) each time the system is started or whenever a dynamic change occurs to the system configuration. Each branch in the tree defines a device node. Under each node, the actual devices configured for your system are listed; double-clicking a device node exposes its device list.

For each device, Device Manager shows the following information:

- Whether or not the hardware on your computer is working properly

- Settings for the device

- Resources used by the device

From Device Manager, you can load, unload, and update device drivers. You also can print a summary of all the device information for your computer.

Device Manager does not display all devices by default. Non-Plug-and-Play devices are hidden, but you can view these hidden devices whenever you need to, for troubleshooting problems with devices installed on your computer. Phantom devices, too, are hidden. These are devices not currently attached to the computer.

TIP You can set Device Manager to always show phantom devices. In Control Panel, double-click **System**, click the **Advanced** tab, and then in the Environment Variables dialog box, create the variable set `DEVMGR_SHOW_NONPRESENT_DEVICES=1`.

NOTE You can also see the device tree information in the Registry.

LOCAL USERS AND GROUPS

The Local Users and Groups utility is used to manage users and groups on a Windows 2000 Server running as a member server.

NOTE On Windows 2000 domain controllers, user accounts are managed through the Active Directory Users and Computers utility.

Storage

Storage contains four utilities that are used to manage the computer's storage facilities: Disk Management, Disk Defragmenter, Logical Drives, and Removable Storage.

DISK MANAGEMENT

Disk Management is the Windows 2000 graphical interface for managing disks, volumes, partitions, logical drives, and dynamic volumes.

DISK DEFRAGMENTER

The Disk Defragmenter utility is used to analyze and defragment your disk. The purpose of disk defragmentation is to optimize disk access by rearranging existing files so that they are stored contiguously.

LOGICAL DRIVES

The Logical Drives utility lists all the logical drives that exist on your computer. Through this utility, you can manage the properties of each logical drive.

REMOVABLE STORAGE

The Removable Storage utility provides information about your computer's removable storage media, including CD-ROMs, DVDs, tapes, and jukeboxes containing optical discs.

Services and Applications

Through the Services and Applications utility, you can manage the services installed on your computer. Services are grouped in three categories: WMI Control, Services, and Indexing Service. You may see additional services, depending on your computer's configuration.

WMI CONTROL

WMI (Windows Management Instrumentation) Control provides an interface for monitoring and controlling system resources. Through WMI Control, you can view the status of the WMI interface itself and manage Windows 2000 operations and configuration settings.

SERVICES

In Services you'll find listed all the services on your computer. Through Services, you can manage general service properties, the logon account used by the service, and the computer's recovery response if the service fails. This utility also shows any dependencies that the service requires.

INDEXING SERVICE

The Indexing Service is used to create an index based on the contents and properties of files stored on your local hard drive. A user can then use the Windows 2000 Search function to search through or query the index for specific keywords.

NOTE By default, the Indexing Service is not started on a Windows 2000 Server computer. It can be started manually through the Services icon in Control Panel, or in the MMC. This service is required for successful indexing and query support.

Microsoft Management Console

The *Microsoft Management Console (MMC)* is the console framework for management applications. The MMC provides a common environment for *snap-ins,* which are administrative tools developed by Microsoft or third-party vendors.

The MMC offers many benefits, including the following:

- MMC is highly customizable—you add only the snap-ins you need.

- Snap-ins use a standard, intuitive interface, so they are easier to use than previous versions of administrative utilities.

- MMC consoles can be saved and shared with other administrators.

- You can configure permissions so that the MMC runs in authoring mode, which an administrator can manage, or in user mode, which limits what users can access.

- Most snap-ins can be used for remote computer management.

The console tree lists the hierarchical structure of all snap-ins that have been loaded into the console. The details pane contains a list of properties or other items for the snap-in that is highlighted in the console tree.

On a Windows 2000 Server computer, an item for the MMC isn't created by default. The MMC does not have any administrative functionality per se. It is simply a framework that is used to organize administrative tools through the addition of snap-in utilities.

Configuring MMC Modes

You can configure MMC to run in author mode, for full access to the MMC functions, or in one of three more limited user modes. In the Console Mode dialog box, you can select from the modes listed in Table 3.2.

TABLE 3.2: MMC Modes

Console Mode	Description
Author mode	Allows use of all the MMC functions
User mode–full access	Gives users full access to window management commands, but they cannot add or remove snap-ins
User mode–limited access, multiple window	Users can create new windows, but they can access only the areas of the console tree that were visible when the console was last saved
User mode–limited access, single window	Gives users access to only areas of the console tree that were visible when the console was last saved; and they cannot create new windows

Registry Editor

The Registry is a database that the operating system uses to store configuration information. The *Registry Editor* program is used to edit the Registry. This utility is designed for advanced configuration of the system. When you make other, more typical changes to your configuration, you use other utilities such as Control Panel.

WARNING Only experienced administrators should use the Registry Editor. It is intended for making configuration changes that can only be made directly through the Registry. It can also be used to view information about your system. Improper changes to the Registry can cause the computer to fail to boot, so use the Registry Editor with extreme caution.

Windows 2000 ships with two Registry Editor utilities:

- The REGEDT32 program is the primary utility that you should use in Windows 2000. It supports full editing of the Registry.

- The REGEDIT program is included with Windows 2000 because it has better search capabilities than REGEDT32. However, it lacks some of the options available with REGEDT32.

The Registry is organized in a hierarchical tree format of subtrees, keys, and subkeys that represent logical areas of computer configuration. When you open the Registry Editor, you initially see five Registry key windows. The Registry section pertinent to devices is found in the Hardware key of the HKEY_LOCAL_MACHINE subtree. This key contains the description of your hardware, the device mapping of your computer, and its resource mapping. When you need to view information about your devices, you can see it here. When you need to change the information, you'll use other tools such as Control Panel.

Installing Plug-and-Play Devices

Plug and Play technology uses a combination of hardware and software that lets the operating system automatically recognize and configure new hardware without any user intervention. Windows 2000 Plug-and-Play support includes the following features:

- Automatic and dynamic recognition of installed hardware
- Automatic resource allocation (or reallocation, if necessary)
- Determination of the correct driver to be loaded for hardware support
- Support for interaction with the Plug-and-Play system
- Support for power management features

Installing Non-Plug-and-Play Hardware

Windows 2000 Server also supports legacy or older hardware. When you install this type of hardware, you have to configure it as you did before Plug-and-Play technology was introduced.

First, configure the hardware device's resources manually on the device or through a software configuration program. Hardware resources include the interrupt request (IRQ), I/O port address, memory address, and Direct Memory Access (DMA) settings. Before you configure the resources for the new device, you should determine which resources are available. To view a listing of the currently allocated resources, use the Device Manager utility.

After you've configured the hardware resources, you can use the Add/ Remove Hardware utility in Control Panel to add the new device to Windows 2000 Server and install the device driver. If the device isn't listed in Control Panel, you'll need to use a driver provided by the manufacturer. Insert the disk that contains the driver, and click the Have Disk button in Add/Remove Hardware.

Configuring Hardware Devices

You can manage hardware devices through the Device Manager utility and through Control Panel, depending on the device you wish to configure. Both utilities present Properties dialog boxes for the hardware that is connected to your computer.

Managing Devices through Device Manager

When it displays information about your hardware devices, the Device Manager utility provides some configuration options for these devices. It also offers help for troubleshooting problems with devices that are not working properly.

To manage a device, double-click on the device category, then double-click the device. This brings up the device Properties dialog box, which has at least the following three tabs. (Other, additional tabs are specific to the device.)

- The General tab lists the device type, manufacturer, and location. It also shows the device status, which indicates whether the device is working properly. If it's not, you can click the Troubleshooter button at the lower-right of the dialog box to get some help with resolving the problem.

- The Properties tab allows you to set options such as volume and playback settings.

- The Driver tab shows information about the currently loaded driver, as well as buttons for accessing driver details, uninstalling the driver, or updating the driver.

Necessary Procedures

Understanding how to configure devices correctly can help you avoid many problems. The following procedures give you the steps for displaying current resource information, managing hardware using the Device Manager utility, and adding snap-ins.

Displaying Current Resource Information

You can view a listing of the currently allocated resources in the Device Manager utility as follows:

1. Right-click My Computer and select Manage. In the Computer Management window, select System Tools ➢ Device Manager.

2. Select View ➢ Resources by Connection.

3. Device Manager displays a list of the current resources. Click a resource to see all of the resources of that type that have been allocated.

Managing Hardware with Device Manager

To manage a device, use the Device Manager utility as follows:

1. From the Desktop, right-click My Computer and select Manage. In Computer Management, select System Tools, then Device Manager.

2. Double-click the device you wish to manage.

3. In the General tab of the device Properties dialog box, verify that your device is working properly. If it isn't, click the Troubleshooter button. The Troubleshooter Wizard will ask you a series of questions to help you resolve the problem.

4. Click the Properties tab and configure the options to suit your personal preferences.

5. Click the Driver tab. Note the information about the currently loaded driver.

6. Click the OK button to save your settings and close the dialog box.

Adding Snap-Ins

To add snap-ins to MMC and save your console, follow these steps:

1. From the main console window, select Console ➢ Add/Remove Snap-in to open the Add/Remove Snap-in dialog box.

2. Click the Add button to open the Add Standalone Snap-in dialog box.

3. Highlight the snap-in you wish to add and click the Add button.

4. If prompted, specify whether the snap-in will be used to manage the local computer or a remote computer. Click the Close button, and then click the Finish button.

5. Repeat steps 3 and 4 to add each snap-in you want to include in your console.

6. When you're finished adding snap-ins, click the Close button.

7. Click the OK button to return to the main console screen.

8. After you've added snap-ins to create a console, you can save the console by selecting Console ➢ Save As and entering a name for your console. You can save the console to a variety of locations, including in a program group or on the Desktop. By default, custom consoles have an `.msc` extension.

Exam Essentials

Know how the Computer Management tool is used. The Computer Management tool is organized into three main areas: System Tools, Storage, and Services and Applications. It is a consolidated tool that provides a single interface to manage your system.

Know which utilities are included with the system tools. The six system tools are Event Viewer, System Information, Performance Logs and Alerts, Shared Folders, Device Manager, and Local Users and Groups.

Know how to configure hardware devices. You can manage hardware devices through the Control Panel or the Device Manager. Both utilities present Properties dialog boxes for the hardware that is connected to the computer. The Device Manager also offers help for troubleshooting device problems.

Know how the Microsoft Management Console is used. The MMC provides a common environment that can be used for administration tools. By itself, it has no administrative function. It is simply a framework used to organize your administrative tools, through snap-ins.

Know how to view the devices installed in your computer. Use the device tree to view the devices installed in your computer and to troubleshoot problems and update devices and drivers. You can also use the device tree to view devices that have been configured on your computer but are not currently attached.

Understand how Windows 2000 Server implements Plug and Play. Windows 2000 Server supports the use of Plug-and-Play devices. Plug and Play is an independent set of computer architecture specifications used by hardware manufacturers to produce computer devices that can be configured with no user intervention. When you install a device, you don't need to know its Plug-and-Play requirements because they are set automatically.

Know how to install new hardware devices and update device drivers. Install Plug-and-Play devices by simply plugging them in and turning them on. Use the Wizards included with Windows 2000 Server to install non-Plug-and-Play devices. Review update and installation options for device drivers.

Know how to troubleshoot problems with hardware devices and device drivers. Some problems are caused by outdated device drivers or by incorrectly configured device settings. The Troubleshooter Wizard will help you solve some of the most commonly encountered problems.

Know where to find hardware device entries in the Registry. The HKEY_LOCAL_MACHINE subtree contains the Hardware key. This key stores the description, device map, owner map, and resource map for your system.

Key Terms and Concepts

Computer Management   A single, consolidated tool for managing common management tasks.

Control Panel   The main utility for configuring your computer's setup.

Device Manager   A utility that provides information about all the devices that your computer currently recognizes.

Event Viewer   A utility for tracking information about your hardware and software through the System, Security, and Application logs. Domain controllers also have the Directory Services, DNS Server, and File Replication logs.

Local Users and Groups   A utility for managing users and groups on a Windows 2000 Server running as a member server.

Microsoft Management Console (MMC)   The console framework for management applications.

Performance Logs and Alerts   A utility that allows you to collect logs of performance-related data. Alerts can be generated from the logs to notify you when certain conditions exist on the computer.

Plug and Play   A technology that uses a combination of hardware and software to help the operating system automatically recognize and configure new hardware without user intervention.

Registry Editor   A program that can view and edit the information in the Registry hives. It can be used for advanced configuration changes.

Shared Folders   A utility for creating and managing shared folders on the computer.

snap-in   Administrative tools from Microsoft or third-party vendors, added to and accessed from a common management console.

System Information   A utility for collecting and displaying information about the computer's current configuration.

WMI (Windows Management Instrumentation) Control   An interface for monitoring and controlling system resources.

Sample Questions

1. You have recently added a sound card to your computer. You want to verify that Windows 2000 has properly recognized the device. Which utility will let you see if the device is working properly?

   A. Device Manager

   B. Windows 2000 Diagnostics

   C. System Information

   D. Device Diagnostics

   Answer: A. You can use Device Manager to determine whether devices are working properly.

2. You have a user who needs full access to Windows 2000 management commands. Also, you want to prohibit this user from changing the MMC. Which MMC mode should you give the user?

   A. Author mode

   B. User mode–full access

   C. User mode–limited access

   D. Management mode

   Answer: B. The MMC's user mode–full access allows users full access to Windows 2000 management commands, but does not allow users to add or remove snap-ins.

3. You have added a controller for a scanner. The controller does not support Plug and Play. When you look for the controller in Device Manager, the controller isn't recognized. Which utility should you use to install the device?

   A. Device Manager

   B. System Information

   C. Control Panel ➢ Sound Cards

   D. Control Panel ➢ Add/Remove Hardware

Answer: D. Use Control Panel ≻ Add/Remove Hardware to add any hardware that does not support Plug and Play. Any device that you install should have a device driver compatible with Windows 2000.

Configure driver signing options.

In the past, poorly written device drivers have caused problems with Windows operating systems. Microsoft is now promoting a mechanism called *driver signing* as a way of ensuring that drivers are properly tested before they are released to the public. The Microsoft exam will most likely include a question about driver signing to help reinforce the concept.

Critical Information

Driver signing is included in Windows to help promote driver quality by allowing Windows 2000 to notify users if a driver has passed all Windows Hardware Quality Labs (WHQL) tests. WHQL tests drivers that run on Windows 2000. The *digital signature* is associated with individual driver packages and is recognized by Windows 2000. This certification proves to users that a driver is identical to those Microsoft has tested, and notifies users when a driver file has been changed since its inclusion on the Microsoft Hardware Compatibility List (HCL).

Configuring Driver Signing Options

You can specify how Windows 2000 Server will respond when you select to install an unsigned driver. These options are set through the Driver Signing Options dialog box (Figure 3.2). In the Driver Signing Options dialog box, you can select from three options for file system verification:

- **Ignore** tells Windows 2000 to install all the files, whether or not they are signed. You won't see any type of message about driver signing.

- **Warn** tells Windows 2000 to display a warning message before installing an unsigned file. You can then choose to continue with the installation or cancel it. This is the default setting.

- **Block** tells Windows 2000 to prevent the installation of any unsigned file. You'll see an error message if you attempt to install the unsigned driver, and you won't be able to continue.

If you check the Apply Setting as System Default option, all users who log on to that computer will use the settings that you apply.

FIGURE 3.2: The Driver Signing Options dialog box

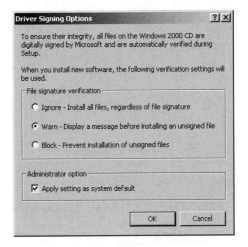

Verifying File Signature

Windows 2000 includes a File Signature Verification utility that you can use to verify that system files have been digitally signed. The sigverif command from the Command Prompt window starts the File Signature Verification utility.

If you want to configure advanced verification options, such as additional search options or logging options, click the Advanced button. When you're ready to check that your files have been digitally signed, click the Start button. The utility will scan all of your system files, and when it's finished will display the signature verification results.

Necessary Procedures

Driver signing is a way to verify if the drivers are the same as those that passed Microsoft's testing. The following procedures show you how to access the driver signing options and run the File Signature Verification utility.

Accessing the Driver Signing Options

To access the Driver Signing Options dialog box, take the following steps:

1. Right-click My Computer and select Properties from the pop-up menu.

2. In the System Properties dialog box, click the Hardware tab.

3. Click the Driver Signing button in the Device Manager section to open the Driver Signing Options dialog box.

Running the File Signature Verification utility

To run the File Signature Verification utility, use the following steps:

1. From the Command Prompt window, type the **sigverif** command. This brings up the File Signature Verification utility (Figure 3.3).

FIGURE 3.3: The File Signature Verification utility

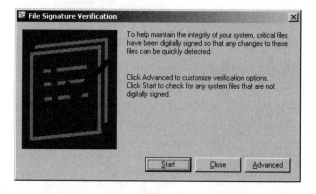

2. Click the Advanced button.

3. In the next screen, click the Start button. The utility will scan all your system files and then display the signature verification results.

Exam Essentials

Know when to use the various options for file verification. The Ignore option tells Windows 2000 to install all the files, whether or not they are signed. The Warn option tells Windows 2000 to display a warning message before installing an unsigned file. The Block option tells Windows 2000 to prevent the installation of any unsigned file.

Know when to use the File Signature Verification utility. The File Signature Verification utility is used to verify that the system files have been digitally signed.

Key Term and Concept

driver signing   A Microsoft mechanism for ensuring that drivers are properly tested before they are released to the public.

Sample Questions

1. You have found updated drivers for a device. You are about to install them, but you want to receive a warning before installing any unsigned files. Which option should you set to give you a warning and then wait for you to decide to continue the install or cancel it?

A. Ignore

B. Override

C. Warn

D. Notice

Answer: C. If you configure driver signing with the Warn option, you can still install an unsigned driver, but you'll see a warning message before the unsigned driver is are installed.

2. You want to verify that all of the system files have been digitally signed. After verification, you want a display of the verification results. Which Windows 2000 command-line utility can you use?

A. sigverify

B. digsig

C. digmanage

D. sigverif

Answer: D. Windows 2000 includes the sigverif command-line utility, which verifies that system files have been digitally signed.

Update device drivers.

A *device driver* is software that allows a specific piece of hardware to communicate with the Windows 2000 operating system. Most of the devices on the Microsoft HCL have drivers that are included on the Windows 2000 Server distribution CD. Managing device drivers involves updating them when necessary. This concept is very simple, and may not even appear on the exam. If it does, Microsoft will want you to know how to use the Device Manger and how to use the Windows Update Web site.

Critical Information

Device manufacturers periodically update their drivers to add functionality or to enhance driver performance. The updated drivers are typically posted on the manufacturer's Web site. Check these sites periodically to look for newer drivers available for your devices.

Updating Drivers

Windows 2000 Server users can install or update drivers from the Windows Update Web site. When a user accesses the Windows Update Web site, Microsoft ActiveX controls compare the drivers installed on the user's system with the latest updates available. If newer drivers are found, Windows Update downloads and installs them automatically.

Drivers, including third-party drivers, are included on the Windows Update site only if they are digitally signed, meet certain Web publishing standards, and have passed the testing requirements for the Windows Logo Program. These controls ensure that the drivers offered to users from Windows Update are of the highest quality. You can access Windows Update directly through your browser, from the Start menu, from Device Manager, or from the Add Printer wizard.

Using the Device Manager, you can manually compare the driver's date with the date of the most recent driver available. You then need to determine if an update is required. Updating a device driver is a simple process in Windows 2000 Server.

Necessary Procedures

Device drivers are updated periodically to enhance their features or to correct problems. As an administrator (and possibly for the exam), you'll have to know the process of updating these drivers.

Updating a Device Driver

When you have acquired a newer device driver, follow these steps to update the existing driver:

1. From the Desktop, right-click My Computer and select Manage. In Computer Management, select System Tools, then Device Manager.

2. In the Device Manager listing, select the device for which you have an updated driver.

3. In the device Properties dialog box, click the Driver tab. Then click the Update Driver button.

4. In the opening dialog box of the Upgrade Device Driver Wizard, click the Next button.

5. In the Install Hardware Device Drivers dialog box, select the option to Search for a Suitable Driver for My Device (Recommended) and click the Next button.

6. In the Locate Driver Files dialog box, select the option that describes where you want the Wizard to look for the driver files. Click the Next button.

7. In the Driver Files Search Results dialog box, select the driver you wish to install and click the Next button.

8. When the Completing the Upgrade Device Driver Wizard dialog box appears, click the Finish button.

9. If you see a dialog box indicating that you must restart your computer before the change can be successfully implemented, select the option to restart the computer.

Exam Essentials

Know how to update a device driver.   When an update is required, use Device Manager in the System Tools folder of the Computer Management utility to perform the update.

Know how to verify whether a device is compatible with Windows 2000 Server.   The Microsoft Hardware Compatibility List (HCL) lists all the devices that are compatible with Windows 2000 Server. This list is included on the Windows 2000 Server distribution CD as well as at the Microsoft Web site.

Know how to access the Windows Update Web site.   You can access Windows Update directly through your browser; from the Start menu; from Device Manager; or from the Add Printer Wizard.

Key Term and Concept

device driver   Software through which a specific piece of hardware communicates with the Windows 2000 operating system.

Sample Questions

1. You have found an updated driver at the manufacturer's Web site. Which utility will help you update the device driver?

A. Device Manager

B. Windows 2000 Diagnostics

C. System Information

D. Device Diagnostics

Answer: A. You can update device drivers through the Device Manager utility.

2. You want to update Windows. How can you access the Windows Update Web site?

A. From Internet Explorer

B. From an icon in the Start menu

C. From Print Manager

D. From Device Manager

Answer: A, B, C, and D. You can access the Windows Update Web site from all the sources listed.

▶ Troubleshoot problems with hardware.

As a general troubleshooting step, always make sure that you are using updated drivers. You can get updated drivers from the Windows Update Web site. Also, make sure that Microsoft has digitally signed your drivers. Although troubleshooting hardware problems can be very difficult, Microsoft will test you only on the tools you will use to check the devices. The exam does not test on troubleshooting techniques.

Critical Information

When you're having a problem with a hardware device, you can check its properties through the Device Manager utility. If the source of the problem isn't obvious from the device's properties, or if the device isn't listed in Device Manager, you can use the Windows 2000 Troubleshooter Wizard to help you figure out what's wrong.

Checking Device Properties

When Device Manager does not properly recognize a device, it reports the problem by displaying an exclamation point icon next to the device in the device tree. Double-click the device to open its Properties dialog box, and make sure that you have the most up-to-date driver for the controller. Other device Properties dialog boxes contain a Troubleshooter button, which you can click to run the Troubleshooter Wizard.

Running the Troubleshooter Wizard

If a device connected to your computer doesn't appear in Device Manager, you can get some hints on troubleshooting through the Troubleshooter Wizard. The Troubleshooter Wizard will walk you through various steps to help you identify and correct device-related problems and issues.

Necessary Procedures

The Troubleshooter Wizard is a key component in identifying problems with devices.

Using the Troubleshooter Wizard

If a device isn't working properly and isn't listed in Device Manager, you can get help from the Troubleshooter Wizard as follows:

1. From the Desktop, right-click My Computer and select Manage. In Computer Management, select System Tools, then Device Manager.

2. In Device Manager, double-click Computer, and then double-click Standard PC.

3. In the computer Properties dialog box, click the Troubleshooter button. The Windows 2000 Help window opens, with the Hardware Troubleshooter section displayed in the right pane. You can choose from a wide range of problems.

4. Select the problem device in the Device Manager window and the Troubleshooter Wizard window for the device. You may have to resize the windows to be able to see both, side-by-side. Here, you specify whether or not you have the device.

5. The Troubleshooter Wizard asks if the device is compatible with Windows 2000. If your device isn't on the HCL, the Wizard directs you to the card manufacturer for assistance.

6. Next the Troubleshooter Wizard identifies a possible problem and solution. It may suggest that your PCI card might be in a faulty slot. You are advised to move your PCI card to a different slot to see if this corrects the problem. (You may prefer to have this tested at a computer repair center.)

7. After you've followed the suggested procedure, the Wizard asks if this fixed your problem. In this example, the suggested correction works. (If your device still isn't working, the Troubleshooter Wizard will suggest other possible courses of action.)

Exam Essentials

Know how to use the Troubleshooter Wizard.   The Troubleshooter Wizard is launched from the Device Manager. You use the Wizard to help identify what is wrong with your computer.

Know how to check a device's properties.   Double-clicking on the device in Device Manager opens its properties dialog box. Here you can check the device's status, the date of its driver, and other properties.

Key Term and Concept

Troubleshooter Wizard   A troubleshooting utility that walks you through various steps to help identify and correct device-related problems.

Sample Questions

1. You suspect that a device is misbehaving. Which utility will give you access to the Troubleshooter Wizard to figure out what's wrong?

   A. Device Manager

   B. Windows 2000 Diagnostics

   C. System Information

   D. Device Diagnostics

   Answer: A. You access the Troubleshooter Wizard through the Device Manager utility.

2. You see a yellow exclamation point beside a device in Device Manager. What does this indicate?

   A. The device driver is out-of-date.

   B. The system did not recognize the device.

   C. The device is reporting hardware problems.

   D. It's time to see if Microsoft has released a new driver for this device in the Windows Update Web site.

   Answer: B. The yellow exclamation point indicates that the system did not recognize the device driver.

Chapter

4

System Performance, Reliability, and Availability

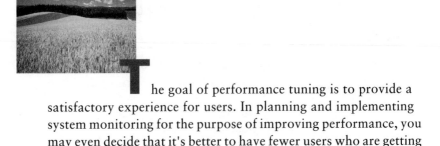

he goal of performance tuning is to provide a satisfactory experience for users. In planning and implementing system monitoring for the purpose of improving performance, you may even decide that it's better to have fewer users who are getting the level of performance that they need, rather than to serve more people at a less-than-satisfactory level.

Optimization is key to performance tuning. To define what optimization means for a particular server and identify how to achieve that optimization, you begin by looking at the server's role in the network. Also, it's important to keep in mind that a server's content and purpose changes over time, as does the hardware itself. A server is not something that you can just set up and then walk away from. Good performance tuning requires management, oversight, and review.

This chapter discusses the basics of monitoring and optimizing your system. Microsoft will of course test your knowledge of these important principles. The objectives here address the tools that you will use, namely System Monitor, Performance Logs and Alerts, and Task Manager. With these aids you can manage and optimize your system resources, processors, and hard drives.

Since every system performs imperfectly at least sometimes, this chapter also discusses ways to ensure that you can back up and restore System State and user data. It also explains how to use the Recovery Console and how to start the system in Safe mode. You'll be expected to be competent in these areas, able to restore your system should a disaster occur.

Monitor and optimize usage of system resources.

This section covers the important fundamental mechanics of monitoring and optimizing your system's resources. This includes assessing system performance by using Performance Logs and Alerts to collect information and by using the System Monitor to view the performance statistics. This objective also covers the most important subsystems to be monitored: memory, processors, and networks.

Monitoring and optimizing usage of system resources is the most critical objective in this chapter. It's the area on which the Microsoft exam will focus. The test tends to be very detail oriented on this topic; you'll be expected to know the specific performance counters and their thresholds. You'll also have to answer questions about which administrative tools are used and in what specific situations.

Critical Information

Before you can successfully optimize the performance of Windows 2000 Server, you must monitor critical subsystems. You need to determine how your system is currently performing and what (if anything) is causing system bottlenecks. Windows 2000 Server ships with two helpful snap-in tools for tracking and monitoring system performance: the *System Monitor* utility and the *Performance Logs and Alerts* utility. The Performance Logs and Alerts utility is useful for collecting information over time. System Monitor is useful for viewing data, either real-time data or the data collected in the Performance Logs and Alerts utility.

You access these monitoring tools by adding the System Monitor snap-in and the Performance Logs and Alerts snap-in to the MMC. They are both available under the Monitor heading. The System Monitor snap-in is added as an ActiveX control.

Assessing System Performance

The monitoring tools allow you to assess your server's current health and determine what it requires to improve its present condition. You'll use the System Monitor and Performance Logs and Alerts utilities to create baselines, identify bottlenecks, determine trends, and create thresholds for issuing alerts.

Creating Baselines

A *baseline* is a snapshot of your system's current performance. Suppose your computer's hardware has not changed over the last six months, but performance seems to have slowed. If you've been using the Performance Logs and Alerts utility and taking baseline logs, as well as noting the changes in your workload, you can more easily determine what resources are causing the system to slow down.

You should create baselines at the following times:

- When the system is first configured without any load

- At regular intervals of typical usage

- Whenever changes are made to the system's hardware or software configuration

Baselines are particularly useful for determining the effect of changes that you make to your computer. For example, if you add more memory, you should take baselines before and after you install the memory to determine the effect of the change. Along with hardware changes, system configuration modifications, too, can affect your machine's performance, so you should create baselines before and after you make any changes to your Windows 2000 Server configuration.

TIP For the most part, Windows 2000 Server is a self-tuning operating system. If you decide to tweak it, take baselines before and after each change. If you don't notice a performance gain after the tweak, consider returning the computer to its original configuration. Some tweaks cause more problems than they solve.

To create baselines, you use the Performance Logs and Alerts utility to create a baseline counters log file, as described in Necessary Procedures.

Identifying System Bottlenecks

A *bottleneck* is a system resource that is inefficient compared with the rest of the computer system as a whole. The bottleneck can cause the rest of the system to run slowly. To correct a bottleneck, you need to pinpoint its cause. Consider, for instance, a system with a Pentium 166 processor with 128MB of RAM. If the system's applications are memory intensive, and if lack of memory is the bottleneck, then upgrading your processor will not eliminate the bottleneck.

Using the System Monitor utility, you can measure the performance of various parts of your system, which allows you to identify system bottlenecks scientifically.

Determining Trends

Many of us tend to manage situations reactively rather than proactively. With reactive management, you focus on a problem when it occurs. With proactive management, you take steps to avoid the problem before it happens. In a perfect world, all management would be proactive.

System Monitor and Performance Logs and Alerts are excellent tools for proactive network management. If you are creating baselines on a regular basis, you can identify system trends and upgrade the hardware before performance degrades beyond repair.

Creating Alert Thresholds

The Performance Logs and Alerts utility provides another tool for proactive management: *alerts*. You can specify alert thresholds (the point when a counter reaches a critical value) and have the utility notify you when these thresholds are reached.

Using System Monitor

Through System Monitor, you view current data or data from a log file. When you view current activity, you are monitoring real-time activity. When you view data from a log file, you are importing a log file from a previous session.

After you've added the System Monitor snap-in to the MMC, open it by selecting Start ➤ Programs ➤ Administrative Tools ➤ Monitor. Figure 4.1 shows the main System Monitor window when it is first opened.

FIGURE 4.1: The System Monitor window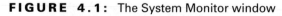

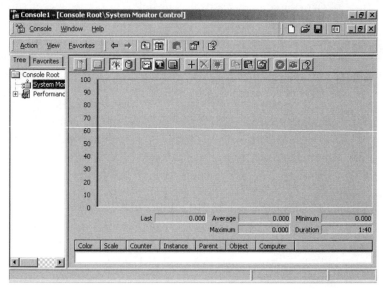

When you first start System Monitor, you'll notice that nothing is tracked by default. In order for System Monitor to be useful, you must configure it to track some type of system activity, which is done by adding counters. After you've added counters, they'll be listed at the bottom of the System Monitor window. The fields just above the counter list will contain data based on the counter that is highlighted in the list, as follows:

- The Last field displays the most current data.

- The Average field shows the average of the counter.

- The Minimum field shows the lowest value that has been recorded for the counter.

- The Maximum field shows the highest value that has been recorded for the counter.

- The Duration field tells you how long the counter has been tracking data.

Selecting the Appropriate View

By clicking the appropriate button in the System Monitor toolbar, you can see your data in three views.

Chart view is the default view for System Monitor. This view is useful for examining a small number of counters in a graphical format. The main advantage of chart view is that you can see how the data has been tracked during the defined time period. When you start to track a large number of counters, however, this view of the data is difficult to read.

Histogram view shows System Monitor data in bar graph form. This view is useful for examining large amounts of data, but it only shows performance for the current period. You do not see a record of performance over time, as you do with the chart view.

Report view gives you a logical report listing all the counters that are being tracked through System Monitor. The data displayed is for the current session. Watching these numbers in real-time is like watching someone on a pogo stick, because the numbers are constantly jumping up and down. The advantage of Report view is that it allows you to easily track large numbers of counters in real time.

Adding Counters

To use System Monitor, you must add *counters*. Counters have several characteristics: the computer being monitored, the performance object, the performance counter, and the performance instance. You can monitor counters on the local computer, or the counters from a specific computer on the network.

TIP You can monitor remote computers if you have Administrative permissions. This option is useful when you do not want the overhead of System Monitor running on the computer you are trying to monitor.

All Windows 2000 system resources, such as Cache, Memory, Paging File, Process, and Processor, are tracked as performance objects. The sum of all objects represents your total system. Some performance objects exist on all Windows 2000 computers; other objects appear only if specific processes or services are running.

Each performance object has an associated set of counters used to track specific information regarding the object. These counters are measurable. An *instance* is the mechanism that allows you to track how a specific object is performing if you have more than one item associated with a specific performance object.

NOTE In this book, we'll use the format *performance object > counter* to indicate the relationship between the object and what is counted. For example, Processor > % Processor Time denotes the Processor performance object and the Processor Time counter. Figure 4.2 shows you what you'll see in the Add Counters dialog box.

FIGURE 4.2: The Add Counters dialog box

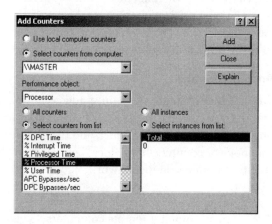

To highlight and select a counter in System Monitor, click it and then click the Highlight button on the System Monitor toolbar. Or just select the counter and press Ctrl+H. To remove a counter, highlight it and click the Delete button on the toolbar.

Managing System Monitor Properties

To configure the System Monitor properties, click the Properties button on the System Monitor toolbar. There are six tabs of options, as described in the following paragraphs.

GENERAL PROPERTIES

The General tab of the System Monitor Properties dialog box contains the following options:

- The view that will be displayed: graph, histogram, or report

- The display elements that will be used: legend, value bar, and/or toolbar

- The data that will be displayed: default (for reports or histograms, this is current data; for logs, this is average data), current, average, minimum, or maximum

- The appearance, either flat or 3-D

- The border, either none or fixed single

- How often the data is updated, in seconds

- Whether duplicate counter instances are allowed

SOURCE PROPERTIES

The Source tab allows you to specify the data source. This can be current activity, or data that has been collected in a log file. If you import data from a log file, you can specify the time range that you wish to view.

DATA PROPERTIES

In the Data tab, you specify the counters that you wish to track. Click the Add and Remove buttons to add and remove counters. You can also select a specific counter and define the color, scale, width, and size used to represent the counter in the graph.

GRAPH PROPERTIES

The Graph tab contains the following options for application to the chart or histogram view: a title; a vertical axis label; choice of a vertical grid, a horizontal grid, and/or vertical scale numbers; and the minimum and maximum numbers for the vertical scale.

COLOR AND FONT PROPERTIES

The Colors and Fonts tabs offer options for customizing the appearance of the System Monitor display.

Using Performance Logs and Alerts

Through the Performance Logs and Alerts utility, you can create counter logs and trace logs, and define alerts. The logs you create can then be viewed with the System Monitor. To open Performance Logs and Alerts, select Start ➢ Programs ➢ Administrative Tools ➢ Monitor and click Performance Logs and Alerts.

Counter logs record data about hardware usage and the activity of system services. You can configure logging to occur manually or on a predefined schedule. Trace logs measure data continually rather than through periodic samples. Trace logs are also used to track data that is collected by the operating system or programs. Alerts can be generated when a specific counter exceeds or falls below a specified value. The alert itself can be a message that's sent, a program that's run, or generation of a more detailed log file.

Managing Performance Tasks

The Performance tab of the Task Manager dialog box is accessed by pressing Ctrl+Alt+Del and selecting Task Manager. This data provides an overview of your computer's CPU and memory usage. It's information similar to what System Monitor tracks, but you don't need to configure it first as you do with System Monitor. You can view the following:

- CPU usage, real-time and history graph

- Memory usage, real-time and history graph

- Totals for handles, threads, and processes

- Physical memory statistics

- Commit change memory statistics

- Kernel memory statistics

Monitoring and Optimizing Memory

When the operating system needs a program or process, the first place it looks is in physical memory. If the program or process is not in physical memory, the OS looks in logical memory (the page file). If the program or process is not in logical memory, the OS must retrieve the program or process from the hard disk. Estimates say it can take up to 1,000 times longer to get information from the hard disk than from physical RAM.

Memory usage is the most likely cause of system bottlenecks. If you have no idea what is causing a bottleneck, system memory is usually a good place to start checking. To determine how memory is being used, there are two areas you need to examine:

- Physical memory, which is the physical RAM you have installed on your computer—and you can never have too much. It's actually a good idea to have more memory than you think you'll need just to be on the safe side. As you've probably noticed, each time you add or upgrade applications, you require more system memory.

- The *page file*, which is logical memory that exists on the hard drive. If you're using excessive paging (swapping between the page file and physical RAM), it's a clear sign that you don't have enough RAM and need to add more memory. Excessive paging can be determined by looking at the Memory > Pages/Sec counter in the Memory object.

Following are the three most important counters for monitoring memory:

- Memory > Available MBytes measures the amount of physical memory available to run processes on the computer. If this number is less than 4MB, you should consider adding more memory.

- Memory > Pages/Sec shows the number of times the requested information was not in memory and the request had to be retrieved from disk. This counter's value should be below 20; for optimal performance, 4 to 5.

- Paging File > %Usage indicates how much of the allocated page file is currently in use. If this number is consistently over 99%, you may need to add more memory.

These counters work together to show what is happening on your system. Use the Paging File > % Usage counter value in conjunction with the Memory > Available Bytes and Memory > Pages/Sec counters to determine how much paging is occurring on your computer.

NOTE Some documentation suggests that you can optimize memory by manipulating the page file. This generally applies to Windows 2000 Server running on a high-end server. In most cases, the best way to optimize memory is to add more physical memory.

Monitoring and Optimizing Processors

Windows 2000 Server supports multiple processors. If your computer is capable of supporting multiple processors, follow the manufacturer's instructions for installation. Then, in Windows 2000 Server, use the Upgrade Device Driver Wizard to update the processor's driver to take advantage of the additional processors.

Once you've installed the second processor, you can monitor both processors through the System Monitor utility. Task Manager allows you to verify that Windows 2000 Server is recognizing both processors and to configure the processors. You should continue to monitor this subsystem to make sure that processor utilization is at an efficient level.

NOTE To configure multiple processors, you can associate each processor with specific processes that are running on the computer. This is called *processor affinity*.

Following are the two most important counters for monitoring the system processor:

- Processor > %Processor Time measures the time that the processor spends responding to system requests. If this value is consistently above an average of 80%, you may have a processor bottleneck.

- Processor > Interrupts/Sec shows the average number of hardware interrupts the processor receives each second. If this value is more than 3,500 on a Pentium-class computer, it may be that a program or hardware is generating spurious interrupts.

If you suspect that you have a processor bottleneck, you can try the following solutions:

- Use applications that are less processor-intensive.

- Upgrade your processor.

- If your computer supports multiple processors, add a processor. Windows 2000 Server can support up to two, which will help if you use multithreaded applications.

WARNING Beware of running 3-D screen savers on your computer. They can use quite a bit of the processor's time.

Monitoring and Optimizing the Network Subsystem

Windows 2000 Server does not have a built-in mechanism for monitoring the entire network. However, you can monitor and optimize the traffic that is generated on the specific Windows 2000 computer. You can monitor the network interface (your NIC), and you can monitor the network protocols that have been installed on your computer.

The following two counters are useful for monitoring the network subsystem:

- Network Interface > Bytes Total/Sec measures the total number of bytes that are sent or received from the network interface and includes all network protocols.

- TCP > Segments/Sec measures the number of bytes sent or received from the network interface and includes only the TCP protocol.

NOTE Normally, you monitor and optimize the network subsystem from a network perspective rather than from a single computer. For example, you can use a network protocol analyzer to monitor all traffic on the network to determine if the network bandwidth is acceptable for your requirements or if the network bandwidth is saturated.

The following suggestions can help to optimize and minimize network traffic:

- Use only the network protocols you need.

- If you require multiple network protocols, place the most commonly used protocols higher in the binding order.

- Use NICs that take full advantage of your bus width.

- Use faster NICs.

Necessary Procedures

The following procedures will help you to understand how to monitor your system. The procedure for setting processor affinity has been provided to show you how to associate processes with a processor.

Adding Counters

Here are the steps to add counters for monitoring with the System Monitor utility:

1. Select Start ➤ Programs ➤ Administrative Tools ➤ Monitor. In System Monitor, click the Add button on the toolbar. This brings up the Add Counters dialog box.

TIP   To see information about a specific counter, select it in the Add Counters dialog box and click the Explain button in the upper-right corner.

---

2. Select the Use Local Computer Counters radio button to monitor the local computer. Alternatively, to select counters from a specific computer, select the Select Counters from Computer radio button and choose a computer from the drop-down list.

3. Select the performance object from the drop-down list.

4. Select the All Counters radio button to track all the associated counters, or you can select the Select Counters from List radio button and choose specific counters from the list box below.

TIP You can select multiple counters of the same performance object; Shift+click for contiguous items, or Ctrl+click for noncontiguous items.

---

5. Select the All Instances radio button to track all the associated instances, or click the Select Instances from List radio button and choose specific instances from the list box below.

6. Click the Add button to add the counters for the performance object.

7. Repeat steps 2 through 6 to specify any additional counters you want to track. When you're finished, click the Close button.

Creating a Counter Log

1. Select Start ➢ Programs ➢ Administrative ➢ Tools ➢ Monitor. Expand Performance Logs and Alerts, right-click Counter Logs, and select New Log Settings from the pop-up menu.

2. In the New Log Settings dialog box, type the name for the log file.

3. The counter log file's Properties dialog box appears. You can configure counter log properties as follows:

   - In the General tab, specify the counters you want to track in the log and the interval for sampling data. Click the Add button to add counters.

   - In the Log Files tab, you can configure the location, filename, type, and size of the log file.

   - In the Schedule tab, you can specify when the log file will start and stop, and what action should be taken, if any, when the log file is closed.

4. When you're finished configuring the counter log file properties, click the OK button. The log will be created and will record the activity for the counters you specified.

Creating a Trace Log

1. Select Start ➢ Programs ➢ Administrative ➢ Tools ➢ Monitor. Expand Performance Logs and Alerts, right-click Trace Logs, and select New Log Settings from the pop-up menu.

2. In the New Log Settings dialog box, type a name for the log file and click the OK button.

3. The trace log file's Properties dialog box appears. You can configure trace log properties as follows:

   - In the General tab, select the system events you want to track; for example, Process Creations/Deletions and Thread Creations/Deletions. You can also specify which system providers you want to track.

   - In the Log Files tab, you can configure the location, filename, type, and size of the log file.

   - In the Schedule tab, you can configure when the log file will start and stop, and what action should be taken, if any, when the log file is closed.

   - In the Advanced tab, you can configure the buffer settings for the log file. By default, the log service will save the trace file to memory and then transfer the data to the log file.

4. When you're finished configuring the trace file properties, click the OK button. The log will be created and will record the activity for the system events you specified.

Creating an Alert

1. Select Start ➢ Programs ➢ Administrative ➢ Tools ➢ Monitor. Expand Performance Logs and Alerts, right-click Alerts, and select New Alert Settings from the pop-up menu.

2. In the New Alert Settings dialog box, type in a name for the alert file and click the OK button.

3. The alert file's Properties dialog box appears. You can configure alert properties as follows:

   - In the General tab, select the counters you want to track. When you add a counter, you must specify that the alert be generated when the counter is under or over a certain value. You can also set the interval for sampling data.

   - In the Action tab, specify what action should be taken if an alert is triggered. You can log an entry in the application event log, send a network message, start another performance data log, and/or run a specific program.

   - In the Schedule tab, you can configure start and stop times for scans of the counters you have defined.

4. When you're finished configuring the alert properties, click the OK button.

Setting Processor Affinity

If you've installed two processors on your computer, you can set processor affinity through the following steps:

1. Press Ctrl+Alt+Delete to access the Windows Security dialog box. Click the Task Manager button.

2. In the Task Manager dialog box, click the Processes tab to see a list of all the processes that are currently running on your computer.

3. Right-click the process you want to associate with a specific processor, and select Processor Affinity from the pop-up menu.

4. The Processor Affinity dialog box appears. Choose the specific processor that the process will use, and click OK.

Exam Essentials

Know when to use Performance Logs and Alerts.   The Performance Logs and Alerts utility allows you to create counter logs and trace logs. You can also define alerts to notify you when set values are reached by the system.

Know what a baseline is and how to use it to monitor performance.
Baselines give you snapshots of system performance at a given time
and a given configuration. By comparing baselines, you can determine trends and then take proactive steps to eliminate problems
before they arise. Baseline comparisons also show you the effective-
ness of changes and modifications to the system.

Know what a bottleneck is and how it affects performance. A bottleneck is any system resource that is limiting performance of the system. Identifying the cause of the bottleneck tells you where system
improvements can be effective in bettering overall performance.

Know when to use alerts. Alerts help you to proactively manage
your systems, by predetermining threshold limits. When the limit is
reached, you can be notified.

Know when to use System Monitor. System Monitor lets you see
real-time data or import the data from a previous session in a log file.

Know the differences between the views in System Monitor. The
System Monitor has three views: Chart, Histogram, and Report View.

Know how to highlight a counter. Counters can be highlighted in
the System Monitor by pressing Ctrl+H.

Know the contents of a counter log. Counter logs record data
about hardware and the activity of system services. This data is either
manually logged or logged on a predefined schedule.

Know the contents of a trace log. A trace log continually measures
data and can be used to track data on the operating system or in programs.

Know the key memory counters. Memory counters are found in two
objects: Memory and Paging File. Key counters in Memory are Available
MBytes and Pages/Sec. The key counter in Paging File is %Usage.

TIP Microsoft likes to try to trick you on these counters by associating
them with the wrong object.

Know the threshold limits of the key memory counters.   Available MBytes should never be less than 4MB. Pages/Sec should be at least below 20, and optimally should be around 4 or 5. The %Usage should not exceed 99% on a continued basis.

Know the key processor counters.   The key counters for the processor object are %ProcessorTime and Interrupt/Sec.

Know the threshold limits of the key processor counters.   %ProcessorTime should not exceed 80% consistently. Spikes above this value are expected and normal. Continued operation above this limit indicates a bottleneck. Interrupts/sec should not exceed 3,500 on a Pentium-class system.

Know the key network counters.   The key counters for your network are Network Interface > BytesTotal/Sec, and TCP > Segments/Sec.

Key Terms and Concepts

alert   Notification when a threshold limit is reached on a counter.

baseline   A snapshot of how the system is performing. It can be used to show how the system is changing over time.

bottleneck   A system resource that limits the performance of the system.

counter   A measurable characteristic of an object.

instance   A mechanism that tracks a specific object when there is more than one item associated with a counter.

page file   The logical memory that resides on the hard drive.

Performance Logs and Alerts   A utility that creates log files. Also, it can create alerts using threshold limits for counters.

processor affinity   Established by associating a process with a specific processor in a multiple-processor environment.

System Monitor   A utility that allows you to view current data for the system, or data from a log file.

Sample Questions

1. Which view in the System Monitor is most appropriate to view the data collected over time in a log file?

   A. Chart view

   B. Histogram view

   C. Report view

   D. Alert view

   Answer: A. Chart view is most appropriate when viewing data over time. It allows you to track the data during a defined period of time.

2. You are the network administrator. You notice while monitoring that only 3MB remain available. What, if anything, needs to be done?

   A. Increase the page file size.

   B. Move the page file to a larger partition.

   C. Nothing; this is not a problem.

   D. Add RAM.

   Answer: D. Available MBytes is a counter that shows how much physical memory is available on the system. If this value is under 4MB, you should add more RAM.

►Manage processes.

- **Set priorities and start and stop processes.**

   There has never been a quick and easy way to monitor Windows NT. Sure, the Task List is available, but it only shows *applications* currently in memory. What about services? Of course, you can access the Services icon in Computer Management to see which ones are running—but how much RAM is each one consuming at any one time? You could try Performance Monitor, in the Monitor of Administrative Tool. It shows memory usage—but which of the hundreds of counters should you use?

Microsoft combines the best of all these tools into one handy feature in Windows 2000: *Task Manager,* available by right-clicking the Windows Taskbar and choosing Task Manager. From Task Manager, you can manage all processes that are running on the system.

Microsoft's exams tend to overlook this tool in favor of System Monitor and the Performance Logs and Alerts. However, you still need to know how to manage tasks. This is done using Task Manager.

Critical Information

For the most part, Windows 2000 is a "self-tuning" operating system—in most cases, it automatically adapts to perform optimally right "out of the box." For instance, when you deploy a Windows 2000 application, other services that are also present but not used are put into a state in which they occupy very few system resources (such as CPU and memory). It's important to periodically check to ensure that the system is behaving the way you want it to. Windows 2000 Server offers a couple of ways to monitor the behavior of processes: System Monitor and Task Manager. This objective covers both these tools, but the emphasis is on using Task Manager.

Managing with System Monitor

If you suspect that an application or process is consuming a large share of resources, you can monitor specific processes through the Process performance object. To collect this information, add the following counters to System Monitor (for a chart) and/or Performance Logs and Alerts (for a log):

- Process > %Processor Time, the instance of the application or process that you want to monitor. This counter allows you to see the amount of processor time that a specific process is using.

- Process > Page File Bytes, the instance of the application or process that you want to monitor. This counter allows you to see the number of bytes used in the page file for a specific process.

Managing with Task Manager

The Task Manager utility lists the applications and processes that are currently running on your computer, as well as CPU and memory usage information for those applications and processes. Task Manager has three tabs, for managing applications, processes, and performance tasks.

To access Task Manager, press Ctrl+Alt+Delete and click the Task Manager button. Alternatively, you can right-click an empty area in the Taskbar and select Task Manager from the pop-up menu.

Managing Application Tasks

The Applications tab of the Task Manager window lists all of the applications that are currently running on the computer. For each task, you see the name of the task and the current status (Running, Not Responding, or Stopped). You can manage application tasks as follows:

- To close an application, select it and click the End Task button at the bottom of the window. This option is especially useful for closing applications that have stopped responding.

- To make the application's window active, select it and click the Switch To button.

- To start an application, click the New Task button to bring up the Create New Task dialog box. Type in the name of the program you wish to start, or click the Browse button to find and select the program.

Managing Process Tasks

The Processes tab of the Task Manager window lists all processes that are currently running on the computer. This is a convenient way to get a quick look at how your system is performing. Unlike System Monitor, in Task Manager you don't have to configure the collection of this data; it's gathered automatically.

For each process, you'll see a unique process ID (PID) that changes each time a process is started; the amount of CPU utilization for the process; and the amount of time the processor spent running the process. You can organize the listing and control processes as follows:

- To organize the processes based on usage, click the column headings. For example, you can click the CPU column to start the listing with the processes that use the most CPU resources. If you click the CPU column a second time, the listing will be reversed.

- To manage a process, right-click it and choose an option from the pop-up menu. You can end the process, end the process tree, or set the priority of the process. If your computer has multiple processors installed, you can also set processor affinity.

- To customize the counters that are listed, select View ➤ Select Columns. This brings up the Select Columns dialog box, where you can select the information that you want to see listed on the Processes tab.

Stopping Processes

You may need to stop a process that isn't executing properly. To do this, select the process you want to stop in the Task Manager's Processes tab and click the End Process button. Task Manager displays a Warning dialog box. Click the Yes button to terminate the process.

NOTE By default, all DOS and Windows 16-bit applications run in a process called ntvdm.exe, which stands for NT Virtual DOS Machine. If you start DOS applications in separate memory spaces, you'll see a separate instance of each ntvdm session.

Some of the common processes that can be managed through Task Manager are listed in Table 4.1.

TABLE 4.1: Common Processes

Process	Description
System idle process	A process that runs when the processor is not executing any other threads
smss.exe	Session Manager subsystem
csrss.exe	Client/server runtime server service

TABLE 4.1: Common Processes *(continued)*

Process	Description
mmc.exe	Microsoft Management Console program (used to track resources used by MMC snap-ins, such as System Monitor)
explorer.exe	Windows 2000 Explorer interface
ntvdm.exe	MS-DOS and Windows 16-bit application support

Managing Process Priority

You can manage process priority through the Task Manager utility or through the start command-line utility.

- To change the priority of a process that is already running, use the Processes tab of Task Manager. Right-click the process you want to manage and select Set Priority from the pop-up menu. Choose from Realtime, High, Abovenormal, Normal, Belownormal, and Low priorities.

- To start applications and set their priority at the same time, use the start command. Table 4.2 lists the options that can be used with the start command.

TABLE 4.2: Options for the start Command-Line Utility

Option	Description
/low	Starts an application in the Idle priority class
/normal	Starts an application in the Normal priority class
/high	Starts an application is the High priority class
/realtime	Starts an application in the Realtime priority class
/min	Starts the application in a minimized window
/max	Starts the application in a maximized window

TABLE 4.2: Options for the start Command-Line

Option	Description
/separate	Starts a DOS or Windows 16-bit application in a separate memory space
/shared	Starts a DOS or Windows 16-bit application in a shared memory space

WARNING Running a process-intensive application in the Realtime priority class can have significant impact on Windows 2000 performance.

Necessary Procedures

There are no necessary procedures for this objective.

Exam Essentials

Know the key process counters.   The key counters for processes are %ProcessorTime and PageFileBytes. These counters are available in both System Monitor and Performance Logs and Alerts.

Know what information can be displayed in Task Manager.   The Task Manager can show you which applications or processes are running, as well as CPU and memory statistics.

Know how to determine application status.   The Applications tab of Task Manager lists all applications on the computer, with their status (Running, Not Responding, or Stopped).

Know how to create new tasks with Task Manager.   To start a new task, click the New Task button in Task Manager.

Know how to customize the counters in Task Manager.   You can customize the counters listed on the Processes tab by going to the View menu and selecting Select Columns.

Know how to stop a process. A process can be stopped in either the Applications or Processes tab of Task Manager.

Know how to change a process priority. A process priority can be controlled either through Task Manager or by using the `start` command with its options.

Know the `start` command switches. The `start` command switches important for the exam are `/low`, `/normal`, `/high`, and `/separate`.

Key Terms and Concepts

process A part of a running application that performs a single task.

process ID (PID) A unique identifier for each process running on a system.

`start` command A command that will launch a process and control how it is started (its priority).

Task Manager A utility that lets you examine application and process information, as well as CPU and memory usage information, on a computer.

Sample Questions

1. How do you access Task Manager?

A. Press Ctrl+Alt+Delete.

B. Press Ctrl+spacebar+Del.

C. Right-click on the Taskbar and select Task Manager from the pop-up menu.

D. Right-click on the Desktop and select Task Manager from the pop-up menu.

Answer: A and C. To get to the Task Manager, you can press Ctrl+Alt+Delete, or you can right-click the Taskbar and select Task Manager from the pop-up menu.

2. Every time you run a large report on the server, users complain that access to the files stored on that server slows way down. What can you do to improve user access to files on the server?

   A. Nothing; the users will have to wait for the reports to finish.

   B. On the Processes tab of Task Manager, change the priority to Low for the process running the report.

   C. On the Processes tab of Task Manager, change the priority to AboveAverage for the user processes.

   D. On the Processes tab of System Monitor, change the priority to Low for the process running the report.

   Answer: B. You can change the priority of any process on the Processes tab of Task Manager; options are Realtime, High, AboveNormal, Normal, BelowNormal, and Low.

Optimize disk performance.

This objective focuses on just the disk performance aspect of monitoring a system. You'll be expected to know the applicable counters and their threshold limits, just as for the monitoring tasks covered in other objectives. Additionally, the exam will test your understanding of the difference between a physical drive and a logical drive.

Critical Information

Monitoring disk access means monitoring the amount of time it takes your disk subsystem to retrieve data requested by the operating system. The two factors that determine how quickly your disk subsystem will respond to system requests are the average disk access time on your hard drive, and the speed of your disk controller.

You can monitor the PhysicalDisk object, which is the sum of all logical drives on a single physical drive, or the LogicalDisk object, which represents a specific logical disk. Following are the most important counters for monitoring the disk subsystem. These counters can be tracked for both the PhysicalDisk object and the LogicalDisk object.

- PhysicalDisk > %Disk Time shows the amount of time the physical disk is occupied with servicing read or write requests. If the disk is busy more than 90% of the time, you'll improve performance by adding another disk channel and splitting the disk I/O requests between the channels.

- PhysicalDisk > Current Disk Queue Length indicates the number of outstanding disk requests that are waiting to be processed. This value should be less than 2.

If you suspect that you have a disk subsystem bottleneck, the first thing you should check is your memory subsystem. A shortage of physical memory can cause excessive paging, which in turn affects the disk subsystem. If you don't have a memory problem, try the following solutions to improve disk performance:

- Use faster disks and controllers.

- Use disk striping to take advantage of multiple I/O channels.

- Balance heavily used files over multiple I/O channels.

- Add another disk controller for load balancing.

NOTE In Windows NT 4.0, you enabled all disk counters through the DISKPERF −Y command. Physical disk counters are automatically enabled in Windows 2000 Server, but you must enable DISKPERF in order to track logical disk counters.

Necessary Procedures

The one procedure necessary for this objective is for monitoring the disk subsystem.

Monitoring the Disk Subsystem

1. If System Monitor isn't already open, select Start ➢ Programs ➢ Administrative Tools ➢ Monitor.

2. In the System Monitor window, click the Add button on the toolbar.

NOTE Notice that there is a Performance object for PhysicalDisk, but not for LogicalDisk.

3. Select Start ➤ Programs ➤ Accessories ➤ Command Prompt.

4. At the command prompt, type **DISKPERF –Y** and press Enter. You'll see a message indicating that both logical and physical disk performance counters are set to start when the computer boots. Close the Command Prompt dialog box and restart your computer.

5. Select Start ➤ Programs ➤ Administrative Tools ➤ Monitor.

6. In the System Monitor window, click the Add button on the toolbar.

7. In the Add Counters dialog box:

- Select PhysicalDisk from the Performance Object drop-down list, select %Disk Time from the Counter list box, and click the Add button.

- Select PhysicalDisk from the Performance Object drop-down list, select Current Disk Queue Length from the Counter list box, and click the Add button.

- Select LogicalDisk from the Performance Object drop-down list, select %Idle Time from the Counter list box, and click the Add button.

8. Click the Close button. You should see these counters added to your chart.

9. To generate some activity, open and close some applications and copy some files between your domain controller and the member server.

10. Note the PhysicalDisk > %Disk Time counter. If this counter's average is below 90%, you are not generating excessive requests to this disk.

11. Note the PhysicalDisk > %Current Disk Queue Length counter. If this counter's average is below 2, you are not generating excessive requests to this disk.

TIP You can monitor your logical disk's amount of free disk space through the LogicalDisk > %Free Space counter. This counter can also be used as an alert. For example, you might set an alert to notify you when the LogicalDisk > %Free Space counter on drive C: is under 10%.

Exam Essentials

Know the difference between a physical disk and logical disk. "Physical disk" refers to the actual hard drive. "Logical disk" refers to the volumes and partitions on the hard drive.

Know the key counters for monitoring disk performance. The key disk counters are %DiskTime and CurrentDiskQueueLength.

Know the threshold limits of the key counters for disk performance. %DiskTime should not exceed 90% of the time. CurrentDiskQueueLength should not exceed 2. This is true for both physical and logical disks.

Know how to enable logical disk counters. Logical disk counters are enabled using the DISKPERF -Y command.

Key Terms and Concepts

DISKPERF   The command with which you enable the logical disk counters in Windows 2000 server.

LogicalDisk object   Represents a specific logical disk.

PhysicalDisk object   Represents a single physical drive.

Sample Questions

1. You want to enable the counters for the Physical Disk in Performance Logs and Alerts utility. How do you do this?

A. Do nothing; they are enabled by default.

B. Run DISKPERF -Y from the command prompt.

C. Select the Disk option in System Monitor.

D. Check the check box by PhysicalDisk in the Performance Logs and Alerts utility.

Answer: A. The counters are enabled by default for the physical disk. You must enable the counters for the logical disk, with the DISKPERF -Y command.

Manage and optimize availability of System State data and user data.

This objective focuses on ways to protect your system from damage caused by possible disasters. Nobody plans a disaster, but failure to plan *for* a disaster can lead to catastrophe, the worst result being the complete loss of all your data. Windows 2000 provides a number of tools that will help you manage and optimize availability of System State data and user data. These tools—if you use them— will help you manage in the event of a total disaster.

Study and learn about these critical tools: Windows Backup and its options, and Emergency Repair Disks (ERDs). Microsoft likes to test your knowledge thoroughly in this area, attempting to reinforce the facts that you need to protect your data.

Critical Information

Through the Windows Backup program, you manage the availability of System State data with regular backups of key system data. *System State data* is a collection of system-specific configuration information.

On any Windows 2000 computer, System State data consists of

- The Registry
- COM+ Class Registration database
- System boot files

On Windows 2000 servers, the System State data also includes

- Certificate Services database (if the server is configured as a Certificate server)

On Windows 2000 servers that are domain controllers, the System State data also includes

- Active Directory services database

- SYSVOL, which is a shared directory that stores the server copy of the domain's public files

---

NOTE If you need to restore System State data on a domain controller, restart your computer with the advanced startup option Directory Services Restore Mode. This allows the Active Directory service database and the SYSVOL directory to be restored. If the System State data is restored on a domain controller that is a part of a domain where data is replicated to other domain controllers, then you must perform an Authoritative Restore. With Authoritative Restore, you must use the Ntdsutil.exe command, and then restart the computer.

Using the Backup Utility

Use the *Windows 2000 Backup utility* to create and restore backups, and to create an *Emergency Repair Disk (ERD)*. Backups protect your data in the event of system failure, by storing the data on another medium such as another hard disk or a tape. If your original data is lost due to corruption, deletion, or media failure, you can restore the data using your backup. The ERD is a subset of a backup that you can use to restore configuration information quickly.

From the Backup window (Figure 4.3), you can start the Backup Wizard, start the Restore Wizard, or create an ERD.

FIGURE 4.3: The Backup window

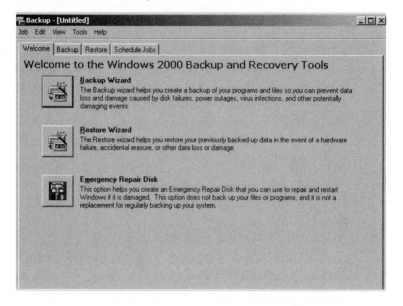

Creating and Using an ERD

You can use the ERD to repair and restart Windows 2000 Server in the event that your computer will not start or if the system files have been damaged. You should create an ERD when the computer is installed, and then update the ERD after making any changes to the configuration of your computer. Note that this process does not back up any system data.

You can repair the following items with the ERD:

- The basic system
- System files
- The partition boot sector
- The Startup environment
- The Registry (return the Registry to its original configuration)

Preparing an ERD

To create an ERD, click the Emergency Repair Disk button in the opening window of the Windows Backup utility. This brings up the Emergency Repair Disk dialog box, which asks you to insert a blank, formatted floppy disk into drive A:. At this point, you can also specify whether you want to back up the Registry to the ERD. If the Registry will fit onto your ERD, you should select this option. Click OK, and the system data will be copied to the ERD.

TIP   You should update your ERD after you make any major configuration changes to your computer.

Using the Backup Wizard

The *Backup Wizard* takes you through all the steps required for a successful system backup. Before you start the Wizard, you should be logged on as an Administrator or a member of the Backup Operators group. The procedure for using the Backup Wizard is described in the upcoming Necessary Procedures section.

Configuring Backup Options

You can configure specific backup configurations by setting the Backup program's options. The Options dialog box, shown in Figure 4.4, has five tabs with options for controlling the backup and restore processes: General, Restore, Backup Type, Backup Log, and Exclude Files.

FIGURE 4.4: The General tab of the Options dialog box

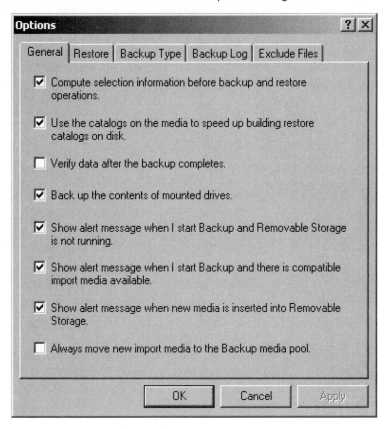

General Backup Options

The General tab contains the options listed in Table 4.3.

Restore Options

The Restore tab of the Options dialog box contains three options for restoring files when the file already exists on the computer:

- Do Not Replace the File on My Computer (Recommended)

- Replace the File on Disk Only If the File on the Disk Is Older

- Always Replace the File on My Computer

TABLE 4.3:   Backup Options, General Tab

Option	Description
Compute Selection Information before Backup and Restore Operations	Estimates the number of files and bytes that will be backed up or restored during the current operation; displays this information prior to the Backup or Restore operation
Use the Catalogs on the Media to Speed Up Building Restore Catalogs on Disk	Specifies that you want to use an on-media catalog to build an on-disk catalog that can be used to select folders and files to be restored during a Restore operation
Verify Data after the Backup Completes	Ensures that all data has been backed up properly
Back Up the Contents of Mounted Drives	Specifies that the data should be backed up on mounted drives; otherwise, only path information on mounted drives is backed up
Show Alert Message When I Start Backup and Removable Storage Is Not Running	Notifies you if Removable Storage is not running (when you are backing up to tape or other removable media)
Show Alert Message When I Start Backup and There Is Compatible Import Media Available	Notifies you when you start backup if new media have been added to the Removable Storage import pool
Show Alert Message When New Media Is Inserted into Removable Storage	Notifies you when new media are detected by Removable Storage
Always Move New Import Media to the Backup Media Pool	Specifies that if new media are detected by Removable Storage, that media should be directed to the backup media pool

Type of Backup

On the Backup Type tab, you can designate the default backup type that will be used (see Table 4.4). Select the default backup type based on the following:

- How much data you're backing up

- How quickly you want to be able to perform the backup

- The number of tapes you're willing to use if you perform a Restore operation

TABLE 4.4:   Backup Types

Option	Description
Normal	Backs up all files and sets the archive bit as marked for each file that is backed up. Requires only one tape for the Restore process.
Copy	Backs up all files but does not set the archive bit as marked for each file that is backed up. Requires only one tape for the Restore process.
Differential	Backs up only the files that have not been marked as archived; does not set the archive bit for each file that is backed up. Requires the last Normal backup and the last Differential tape for the Restore process.
Incremental	Backs up only the files that have not been marked as archived, and sets the archive bit for each file that is backed up. Requires the last Normal backup and all the Incremental tapes created since the last Normal backup, for use by the Restore process.
Daily	Backs up only the files that have been changed today; does not set the archive bit for each file that is backed up. Requires each Daily backup and the last Normal backup for the Restore process.

Backup Log Options

In the Backup Log tab, you can specify the amount of information that is logged during the backup process. Choose from the following options:

- Detailed, which logs all information, including the names of the folders and files that are backed up

- Summary, which logs only key backup operations, such as starting the backup

- None, which specifies that a log file will not be created

Excluding Files

The Exclude Files tab of the Options dialog box allows you to explicitly exclude specific files during the backup process.

Necessary Procedures

In order to manage System State data and user data, it's important that you understand the process of creating an Emergency Repair Disk, as well as how to perform system backups with the Windows Backup utility. The following procedures are for creating the ERD and for backing up your data and System State data.

Creating an Emergency Repair Disk (ERD)

1. Select Start ➢ Programs ➢ Accessories ➢ System Tools ➢ Backup.

2. Click the Emergency Repair Disk button. The Emergency Repair Disk dialog box appears.

3. Insert a blank, formatted floppy disk into drive A:.

4. Select the option Also Back Up the Registry to the Repair Directory.

5. Click OK. The system data will be copied to the ERD.

6. Click OK to close the confirmation dialog box that appears.

Using the Backup Wizard

1. Create a folder on drive D: called DATA. Create some small text files in this folder. The size of all of the files combined should not exceed 1MB.

2. Select Start ➢ Programs ➢ Accessories ➢ System Tools ➢ Backup.

3. In the opening Backup window, click the Backup Wizard button. When the Wizard welcome window appears, click the Next button to continue.

4. In the What to Back Up dialog box, select the radio button for Back Up Selected Files, Drives, or Network Data. Then click the Next button.

5. In the Items to Back Up dialog box, select My Computer, expand D:, and check the DATA folder. Click the Next button.

6. In the Where to Store the Backup dialog box, click the Browse button. In the Open dialog box, select 3 1/2 Floppy (A:). For the filename, enter the date (in the *mmddyy* format). Then click the Open button.

7. In the Where to Store the Backup dialog box, click the Next button.

8. Verify your selections in the Completing the Backup Wizard dialog box, and click the Finish button.

9. When the Backup Wizard is finished, click the Report button in the Backup Progress dialog box. This will display the backup log in a Notepad window. Examine the report and close the window.

10. Close all the Backup Wizard dialog boxes that remain open.

Backing Up System State Data

1. Select Start ➢ Programs ➢ Accessories ➢ System Tools ➢ Backup.

2. In the opening Backup window, click the Backup tab.

3. Under My Computer, click the System State check box and select the backup media or filename that will be used for the backup.

4. Click the Start Backup button.

5. Click Start Backup on the Backup Job Information Screen. When the Backup operation is complete, click the Report button in the Backup Progress dialog box. This displays the backup log in a Notepad window. Examine the report and close the window.

6. Close all Backup dialog boxes that remain open.

Exam Essentials

Know the tools available in the Backup utility. The Windows Backup utility gives you access to the Backup Wizard, Restore Wizard, and the button to create an Emergency Repair Disk.

Know how to create or update the Emergency Repair Disk (ERD). The ERD is created in the Windows 2000 Backup utility window, by clicking on the Emergency Repair Disk button.

Know how to specify the type of backup to be performed. In the Backup Type tab, you select the type of backup to be performed: Normal, Copy, Differential, Incremental, or Daily.

Know the options for restoring files from a backup. The options for restoring files are Do Not Replace, Replace the File If File on Disk Is Older, and Always Replace.

Know the backup log options. The backup log options are Detailed, Summary, and None.

Key Terms and Concepts

Backup Wizard A utility that walks through the steps required for a successful system backup.

Copy backup Backs up all files and does not set the archive bit as marked for each file that is backed up. Requires only one tape for the Restore process.

Daily backup Backs up only the files that have been changed today and does not set the archive bit for each file that is backed up. For the Restore process, requires each Daily backup and the last Normal backup.

Differential backup Backs up only the files that have not been marked as archived; does not set the archive bit for each file that is backed up. For the Restore process, requires the last Normal backup and the last Differential tape.

excluded files Files that have been specifically excluded from the backup.

Emergency Repair Disk (ERD)   A disk that stores system configuration information for the server.

Incremental backup   Backs up only the files that have not been marked as archived, and sets the archive bit for each file that is backed up. For the Restore process, requires the last Normal backup and all of the Incremental tapes that have been created since the last Normal backup.

Normal backup   Backs up all files, and sets the archive bit as marked for each file that is backed up. Requires only one tape for the Restore process.

System State data   System State data on a Windows 2000 Server consists of the Registry, the COM+ Class Registration database, the system files, and the Certificate Services database (if the server is configured as a Certificate server). On domain controllers, the Active Directory Services database and the SYSVOL directory are added.

Windows Backup utility   The utility with which you can create and restore system backups, and create an Emergency Repair Disk (ERD).

Sample Questions

1. You are designing a backup plan. It is decided that a speedy recovery is more important than an easy backup. Which type of backup operation will fit this situation?

A. Detailed

B. Differential

C. Incremental

D. Daily

Answer: B. Differential backup requires the last Normal backup and the last Differential tape for the Restore process.

2. System data comprises which of the following on a Windows 2000 Server configured as a Certificate Server? Select all that apply.

A. The Registry

B. Active Directory services database

C. System boot files

D. Certificate Services database

Answer: A, C, D. On any Windows 2000 computer, the System State data includes the Registry, the COM+ Class Registration database, and the system boot files. On Windows 2000 servers, the System State data also includes the Certificate Services database (if the server is configured as a Certificate server). And on Windows 2000 servers that are domain controllers, the System State data includes the Active Directory services database.

Recover System State data and user data.

- **Recover System State data by using Windows Backup.**
- **Troubleshoot system restoration by starting in safe mode.**
- **Recover System State data by using the Recovery Console.**

System recovery is the process of making your computer work again in the event of failure. In this objective, you will learn how to safeguard your computer and how to recover from a disaster. The benefit of having a disaster recovery plan is that when you expect the worst to happen and are prepared for it, you can easily recover from most system failures.

This objective focuses on how to protect you from the possibility of disasters. Nobody plans a disaster, but failure to plan for a disaster can lead to catastrophic results, the worst of which is the complete loss of all of your data. Windows 2000 has given you a number of tools that will help you avoid total disaster if they are used. Because of the critical importance of these tools, Microsoft likes to test your knowledge of these tools. They will try to reinforce the facts that you need to protect your data.

Of course, you can only recover what has been backed up; see the preceding objective for backing up System State and user data.

Critical Information

If a catastrophic event occurs that prevents the server from starting normally, Windows 2000 has several options to repair and/or recover the system. These include running in Safe mode, using the Event Viewer's tracking functions, restarting with the Emergency Repair Disk and/or various boot options, and using the Recovery Console. Coverage of this objective begins by examining Event Viewer, which gives you insight as to what is happening inside your computer. Then we'll look at the boot process and BOOT.INI, and see how to determine if the problems you are having are related to booting the machine. This section also includes information on how to create a Windows 2000 Boot Disk to get you into the operating system files, should the boot process fail.

The latter sections of this objective are concerned with restoring your system. You need to know how to recover using the Emergency Repair process with the Emergency Repair Disk. Windows 2000 has some additional tools, as well, including the Restore Wizard and some advanced startup options, that can act independently of the operating system to restore critical files. Safe mode and the Recovery Console can help, too.

Safeguarding Your Computer and Recovering from Disaster

One of the most unpleasant events you'll experience as a system professional is working with a computer that won't boot. An even worse experience is discovering that there is no recent backup for that computer.

The first step in preparing for disaster recovery is to expect that a disaster *will* occur at some point and take proactive steps beforehand to plan for recovery. Some of the preparations you can make are

- Performing regular system backups

- Using virus-scanning software

- Regularly performing administrative functions, such as monitoring the logs in the Event Viewer utility

When the dreaded day arrives and your system fails, you will have recovery options available. There are several system processes you can analyze, and Windows 2000 Server provides helpful utilities that will get you back up and running. These options are summarized in Table 4.5.

TABLE 4.5: Windows 2000 Server Recovery

Recovery Technique	When to Use
Use Event Viewer	If you're able to load the Windows 2000 OS in Normal or Safe mode, one of the first places to look for hints about the problem is Event Viewer. Event Viewer displays System, Security, and Application logs. On a domain controller, the Event Viewer will display Directory Services, DNS Server, and File Replication in addition to the other three logs.
Load in Safe mode	This is generally your starting point for system recovery. Safe mode loads the absolute minimum of services and drivers needed to boot Windows 2000. If you can load in Safe mode, you may be able to troubleshoot and determine the devices or services that keep Windows 2000 from loading normally.
Use the Last Known Good Configuration option during startup	You can use this option if you made changes to your computer and are now having difficulty running it. Last Known Good Configuration is an Advanced Options menu item that you can select during startup. It loads the configuration that was used the last time the computer booted successfully. (This option won't help if you have hardware errors.)
Boot with Windows 2000 Server Setup Boot Disk	You can try this option if you suspect that Windows 2000 is not loading due to missing or corrupt boot files. The Setup Boot Disks allow you to load all the Windows 2000 boot files. If you can boot from a boot disk, you can then restore the necessary files from the Emergency Repair Disk (ERD).

TABLE 4.5:   Windows 2000 Server Recovery   *(continued)*

Recovery Technique	When to Use
Boot with Emergency Repair Disk (ERD)	You can use the ERD when you need to correct configuration errors or to repair system files. You may be able to repair problems that prevent computer startup. The ERD stores portions of the Registry, the system files, a copy of your partition boot sector, and information that relates to the startup environment.
Plan ahead with Windows Backup	Use this utility regularly to safeguard your computer. Through the Backup utility, you can create an ERD, back up the system or parts of it, and restore data from existing backups.
Use the Recovery Console	Try this option if none of the other recovery options or utilities works. The Recovery Console starts Windows 2000 without the graphical interface and allows the administrator limited capabilities, such as adding or replacing files and starting and stopping services.

Getting Help from Event Viewer

The *Event Viewer* utility tracks information about your computer's hardware and software and helps you monitor security events. Tracked information is stored in three types of log files:

- The *System log* tracks events related to the overall Windows 2000 operating system.

- The *Security log* tracks Windows 2000 auditing events.

- *Application logs* track events related to applications that are running on your computer.

- The *Directory Services log* tracks events related to Directory Services running in the domain.

- *DNS Server* tracks events related to the running of DNS.

- *File Replication* tracks Dfs events.

In the log files, you'll see all the events that have been recorded. By default, you see the oldest events at the bottom of the screen and the newest events at the top of the screen. Watch out—this can be misleading in troubleshooting, because one error can precipitate other errors. Always resolve the oldest errors first.

Event Types

The Event Viewer logs display five types of event. Table 4.6 describes each event type and the icon representing it in Event Viewer.

TABLE 4.6: Event Viewer Log Events

Event Type	Icon	Description
Information	White dialog bubble with blue exclamation mark	Informs you that a specific action has occurred, such as a system shutting down or starting. Information events are logged for informative purposes.
Warning	Yellow triangle with black exclamation mark	Indicates that you should be concerned about the event. Warning events may not be critical in nature but may be indicative of future errors.
Error	Red circle with white X	Indicates that an error has occurred, such as a driver failing to load. Error events are cause for serious concern.
Success Audit	Yellow key	Indicates the occurrence of an event that has been audited for success. An example of a Success Audit event is a successful logon when system logons are being audited.
Failure Audit	Yellow lock	Indicates the occurrence of an event that has been audited for failure. An example of a Failure Audit event is a failed logon due to an invalid username and/or password when system logons are being audited.

Event Details

Clicking an event in an Event Viewer log brings up the Event Properties dialog box, which shows details about the event. Table 4.7 describes the information that appears in this dialog box.

TABLE 4.7: Event Properties

Property	Description
Date	The date the event was generated.
Time	The time the event was generated.
Type	The type of event generated: Information, Warning, Error, Success Audit, or Failure Audit.
User	The name of the user to which the event is attributed, if applicable (not all events are attributed to a user).
Computer	The name of the computer on which the event occurred.
Source	The software that generated the event (for instance, operating system components and drivers).
Category	The source that logged the event (this field will say None until this feature has been fully implemented in Windows 2000 Server).
Event ID	The event number specific to the type of event generated (for instance, a print error event has the event ID 45).
Description	A detailed description of the event.
Data	The binary data generated by the event (if any; some events do not generate binary data) in hexadecimal bytes or DWORD format. (Programmers can use this information to interpret the event.)

Managing Log Files

Over time, your Event Viewer log files will grow, and you'll need a way to manage them. One option is to clear a log file for a fresh start. You may want to save the existing log file before you clear it, to keep that log file available for reference or future analysis. The Clear Log button in the General tab of the log Properties dialog box clears all log events.

You can also set properties in Event Viewer logs. Each log has two sets of associated properties:

- General properties control items such as the log filename, the log's maximum size, and the action to take when the log file reaches its maximum size.

- Filter properties specify which events are displayed in the log.

Understanding the Windows 2000 Boot Process

Some of the problems that cause system failure are related to the Windows 2000 boot process. The boot process starts when you turn on your computer and ends when you log on to Windows 2000. To identify problems related to the boot process, you need to understand the steps involved in the process, as well as how the BOOT.INI file controls the process. Also, you should create a Windows 2000 Server boot disk that you can use to boot the operating system if your computer suffers a boot failure.

The Windows 2000 boot process consists of five major stages: the preboot sequence, the boot sequence, kernel load, kernel initialization, and logon. Many files are used during these stages of the boot process.

The Preboot Sequence

A normal boot process begins with the preboot sequence, in which your computer starts up and prepares for booting the operating system.

FILE ACCESSED IN THE PREBOOT SEQUENCE

During the preboot sequence, your computer accesses the NTLDR file. This file is used to control the Windows 2000 boot process until control is passed to the NTOSKRNL file for the boot sequence. The NTLDR file is located in the root of the system partition. It has the file attributes of System, Hidden, and Read-only.

STEPS IN THE PREBOOT SEQUENCE

1. When the computer is powered on, it runs a *Power On Self Test (POST)* routine. The POST detects the processor you are using, how much memory is present, what hardware is recognized, and whether the BIOS (Basic Input/Output System) is standard or has Plug-and-Play capabilities. The system also enumerates and configures hardware devices at this point.

2. The BIOS points to the boot device, and the *Master Boot Record (MBR)* is loaded.

3. The MBR points to the active partition, which is the partition that should be used to boot the operating system. This is normally the C: drive. Once the MBR locates the active partition, the boot sector is loaded into memory and executed.

4. As part of the Windows 2000 installation process, the NTLDR file is copied to the active partition. The boot sector points to the NTLDR file, and this file executes. The NTLDR file is used to initialize and start the Windows 2000 boot process.

POSSIBLE ERRORS DURING THE PREBOOT SEQUENCE

If you see errors during the preboot sequence, they are probably not related to Windows 2000 Server because the operating system has not yet been loaded. Following are some common causes for errors during the preboot stage:

Improperly configured hardware	If the POST cannot recognize your hard drive, the preboot stage will fail. This error is most likely to occur in a computer being configured for the first time. If everything has been working properly and you have not made any changes to your configuration, a hardware error is unlikely.
Corrupt MBR	Viruses that are specifically designed to infect the MBR can corrupt it. You can protect your system from this type of error by using virus-scanning software. Also, most virus-scanning programs can correct an infected MBR.

No partition is marked as active	This can happen if you used the FDISK utility and did not create a partition from all of the free space. If the partition is FAT16 or FAT32 and on a basic disk, you can boot the computer to DOS or Windows 9x with a boot disk, run FDISK, and mark a partition as active. If you created your partitions as a part of the Windows 2000 installation and have dynamic disks, an active partition is marked for you during installation.
Corrupt or missing NTLDR file	If the NTLDR file does not execute, it may have been corrupted or deleted (by a virus or malicious intent). You can restore this file through the ERD.
SYS program run from DOS or Windows 9x after Windows 2000 installation	The NTLDR file may not execute because the SYS program was run from DOS or Windows 9x after Windows 2000 was installed. If you have done this, the only solution is to reinstall Windows 2000.

The Boot Sequence

When the preboot sequence is completed, the boot sequence begins. The phases in this stage include initial boot loader, operating system selection, and hardware detection.

FILES ACCESSED IN THE BOOT SEQUENCE

Along with the NTLDR file, described in the preceding section, the following files are used during the boot sequence:

- BOOT.INI is used to build the operating system menu choices that are displayed during the boot process. This file is also used to specify the location of the boot partition. Located in the root of the system partition, BOOT.INI has the file attributes of System and Hidden.

- BOOTSECT.DOS is an optional file that is loaded if you choose to load an operating system other than Windows 2000. This file is only used in dual- or multi-boot computers. Located in the root of the system partition, BOOTSECT.DOS has the file attributes of System and Hidden.

- NTDETECT.COM is used to detect any hardware that is installed and add information about the hardware to the Registry. Located in the root of the system partition, NTDETECT.COM has the file attributes of System, Hidden, and Read-only.

- NTBOOTDD.SYS is an optional file that is used when you have a SCSI (Small Computer Standard Interface) adapter with the onboard BIOS disabled. (This option is not commonly implemented.) Located in the root of the system partition, NTBOOTDD.SYS has the file attributes of System and Hidden.

- NTOSKRNL.EXE is used to load the Windows 2000 operating system. This file is located in *%systemroot%*\System32 and has no file attributes.

STEPS IN THE BOOT SEQUENCE

1. For the initial boot loader phase, NTLDR switches the processor from real mode to 32-bit flat memory mode and starts the appropriate mini file system drivers. Mini file system drivers are used to support your computer's file systems and include FAT16, FAT32, and NTFS.

2. For the operating system selection phase, the computer reads the BOOT.INI file. If you have configured your computer to dual-boot or multi-boot and Windows 2000 recognizes that you have choices, a menu of operating systems that can be loaded is built. If you choose an OS other than Windows 2000, the BOOTSECT.DOS file is used to load the alternate OS, and the Windows 2000 boot process terminates. If you choose a Windows 2000 OS, the Windows 2000 boot process continues.

3. If you choose a Windows 2000 operating system, the NTDETECT.COM file is used to perform hardware detection. Any detected hardware is added to the Registry, in the HKEY_LOCAL_MACHINE key. Some of the hardware recognized by NTDETECT.COM includes communication and parallel ports, the keyboard, the floppy disk drive, the mouse, the SCSI adapter, and the video adapter.

4. Control is passed to NTOSKRNL.EXE to start the kernel load process.

POSSIBLE ERRORS DURING THE BOOT SEQUENCE

Some common causes for errors during the boot stage include the following:

Missing or corrupt boot files	If NTLDR, BOOT.INI, BOOTSECT.DOS, NTDETECT.COM, or NTOSKRNL.EXE is corrupt or missing (because of a virus or malicious intent), the boot sequence will fail. You'll see an error message indicating which file is missing or corrupt. You can restore these files through the ERD.
Improperly configured BOOT.INI file	If you've made any changes to your disk configuration and your computer won't restart, chances are the BOOT.INI file is configured incorrectly.
Unrecognizable or improperly configured hardware	If you have serious errors that cause NTDETECT.COM to fail, you should resolve the hardware problems. On a computer with a lot of hardware, remove all of it that's not required to boot the computer. Add each piece of hardware one at a time, and boot the computer. This process helps identify which piece of hardware is bad or conflicting for a resource, such as an IRQ, with another device.

The Kernel Load Sequence

In the kernel load sequence, the Hardware Abstraction Layer (HAL), computer control set, and low-level device drivers are loaded. The NTOSKRNL.EXE file is used during this stage. The kernel load sequence consists of the following steps:

1. The NTOSKRNL.EXE file is loaded and initialized.

2. The HAL is loaded. The HAL is what makes Windows 2000 Server portable to support platforms such as Intel and Alpha.

3. The control set to be used by the operating system is loaded. The control set is used to control system configuration information, such as a list of device drivers that should be loaded.

4. Low-level device drivers, such as disk drivers, are loaded.

If you have problems loading the Windows 2000 Server kernel, you'll most likely need to reinstall the operating system.

The Kernel Initialization Sequence

In the kernel initialization sequence, the HKEY_LOCAL_MACHINE\HARDWARE Registry and Clone Control set are created, device drivers are initialized, and high-order subsystems and services are loaded. Here are the steps of the kernel initialization sequence:

1. Once the kernel is successfully loaded, the Registry key HKEY_ LOCAL_MACHINE\HARDWARE is created. This Registry key is used to specify the configuration of hardware components when the computer is started.

2. The Clone Control set is created. This is an exact copy of the data used to configure the computer and does not include changes made by the startup process.

3. Device drivers that were loaded during the kernel load phase are initialized.

4. Higher-order subsystems and services are loaded.

If you have problems during the kernel initialization sequence, you might try to boot to the Last Known Good Configuration.

The Logon Sequence

In the logon sequence, the user logs on to Windows 2000 Server and any remaining services are loaded. This sequence consists of the following steps:

1. After the kernel initialization is complete, the Log On to Windows dialog box appears. At this point, you type in a valid Windows 2000 Server username and password.

2. The service controller executes and performs a final scan of HKEY_ LOCAL_MACHINE\SYSTEM\CurrentControlSet\Services to see if any remaining services need to be loaded.

If logon errors occur, they are usually due to an incorrect username or password, or the unavailability of a domain controller to authenticate the request (if the computer is a part of a domain). Errors can also occur if a service cannot be loaded. If a service fails to load, you will see a message in Event Viewer.

Editing the BOOT.INI File

The BOOT.INI file is located in the active partition and is used to build the boot loader menu and to specify the location of the Windows 2000 Server boot partition. This file also specifies the default operating system that should be loaded if no selection is made within the default time allotment. You can open and edit this file to add switches or options for controlling the loading of the OS. Figure 4.5 shows a fairly common example of a BOOT.INI file, opened in Notepad.

FIGURE 4.5: A sample BOOT.INI file

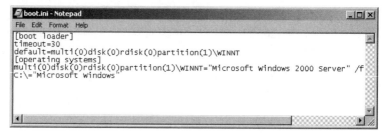

The following sections describe the BOOT.INI ARC (Advanced RISC Computing; RISC stands for Reduced Instruction Set Computing) naming conventions and how to edit the BOOT.INI file.

WARNING If you make changes to your disk configuration, you may see a dialog box stating that the number of the BOOT.INI file needs to be changed. This is the ARC number that points to the boot partition. If you try to restart your computer before you edit this file, you'll find that the system will not start.

ARC Naming Conventions

In the BOOT.INI file, the ARC path is used to specify the location of the boot partition within the disk channel. ARC names are constructed according to the conventions in Table 4.8.

TABLE 4.8:   ARC Naming Conventions

ARC Path Option	Description
multi (*w*) or scsi (*w*)	Identifies the type of disk controller being used by the system. The multi option is used by IDE controllers and SCSI adapters that use the SCSI BIOS. The scsi option is used by SCSI adapters that do not use the SCSI BIOS. The (*w*) value represents the number of the hardware adapter you are booting from.
disk (*x*)	Indicates the SCSI adapter you are booting from if you use the scsi option. If you use multi, the (*x*) setting is always 0.
rdisk (*y*)	Specifies the number of the physical disk to be used. In an IDE environment, it is the ordinal of the disk attached to the controller and will always be a 0 or a 1. On a SCSI system, this is the ordinal number of the SCSI drive.
partition (*z*)	Specifies the partition number that contains the operating system files. The first partition is always 1.

Here is a line from a sample BOOT.INI file:

```
multi(0)disk(0)rdisk(0)partition(1)\WINNT=
"Microsoft Windows 2000 Server"
```

This indicates that the boot partition is in the following location:

- multi(0) is an IDE controller or a SCSI controller with the BIOS enabled.

- disk(0) is 0 because the multi option was used.

- rdisk(0) specifies that first disk on the controller is being used.

- partition(1) specifies that the system partition is on the first partition.

- \WINNT indicates the folder that is used to store the system files.

- "Microsoft Windows 2000 Server" is what the user sees in the boot menu.

BOOT.INI Switches

When you edit your BOOT.INI file, you can add switches or options to control how the operating system is loaded. Table 4.9 defines the BOOT.INI switches.

TABLE 4.9: BOOT.INI Switches

Switch	Description
/basevideo	Boots the computer using a standard VGA video driver. This option is used when you change your video driver and then cannot use the new driver.
/fastdetect=comx	Keeps the computer from auto-detecting a serial mouse attached to a serial port.
/maxmem:n	Specifies the maximum amount of RAM that is recognized. This option is sometimes used in test environments where you want to analyze performance using various amounts of memory.
/noguiboot	Boots Windows 2000 without loading the GUI. With this option, a command prompt appears after the boot process ends.

Creating the Windows 2000 Server Boot Disk

Once you've created a *Windows 2000 Server boot disk,* you can use it to boot to the Windows 2000 Server operating system in the event of a boot failure. The procedure for creating this disk is included in the Necessary Procedures for this objective.

If the BOOT.INI file for the computer has been edited, you'll need to update the BOOT.INI file on the Windows 2000 Server boot disk.

WARNING   The BOOT.INI file on the Windows 2000 Server boot disk contains a specific configuration that points to the computer's boot partition. This might keep a boot disk made on one computer from working on another computer.

Using an ERD

The ERD is not a bootable disk and can be accessed only by using the Windows 2000 Server Setup CD or the Windows 2000 Server Setup diskettes that are created from the CD.

NOTE   In Windows NT, you create ERDs through the RDISK command. This command is not available in Windows 2000 Server.

Using the Restore Wizard

Having a complete backup won't help you when your system fails unless you can successfully restore that backup. To be sure that you can restore your data, you should test the restoration process before anything goes wrong. You can use the *Restore Wizard* for testing purposes, as well as when you actually need to restore your backup (see the Necessary Procedures section for this object).

Using Advanced Startup Options

The Windows 2000 Advanced Startup options can be used to troubleshoot errors that keep Windows 2000 Server from successfully booting. To access the Windows 2000 Advanced Startup options, press the F8 key when prompted during the beginning of the Windows 2000 Server boot process. This will bring up the Windows 2000 Advanced Options menu, which allows you to boot Windows 2000 with the following options:

- Safe Mode
- Safe Mode with Networking
- Safe Mode with Command Prompt
- Enable Boot Logging

- Enable VGA Mode

- Last Known Good Configuration

- Directory Services Restore Mode

- Debugging Mode

- Boot Normally

Starting in Safe Mode

When your computer won't start, one of the most basic troubleshooting techniques is to simplify the configuration as much as possible. This is especially important in a complex configuration when you don't know the cause of your problem. After you've simplified the configuration, you can determine whether the error is in the basic configuration or is a result of your more complex configuration. When the problem is in the basic configuration, you have a starting point for troubleshooting. When the problem is not in the basic configuration, you proceed to restore each configuration option that was removed, one at a time. This helps you to identify what's causing the error.

If Windows 2000 Server won't load, you can attempt to load the OS through *Safe mode*. Running in Safe mode, you're simplifying the Windows configuration as much as possible. Safe mode loads only the drivers and services needed to get the computer up and running, including basic files and drivers for the mouse (unless you have a serial mouse), monitor, keyboard, hard drive, standard video driver, and default system services. Safe mode is considered a diagnostic mode, so you don't have access to all the same features and devices in Windows 2000 Server as when you boot normally, including networking capabilities.

If you boot to Safe mode, check all your hardware and software settings in Control Panel and try to determine why Windows 2000 Server will not boot properly. After you take steps to fix the problem, attempt to boot to Windows 2000 Server normally.

Enabling Boot Logging

Boot logging creates a log file that tracks the loading of drivers and services. When you choose *Enable Boot Logging* from the Advanced Options menu, Windows 2000 Server loads normally, not in Safe mode. This allows you to log all the processes that take place during a normal boot sequence.

This log file can be used to troubleshoot the boot process. When logging is enabled, the log file is written to *%systemroot%*\ntbtlog.txt.

Other Advanced Options Menu Modes

The other selections on the Advanced Options menu work as follows:

- *Safe Mode with Networking* is the same as the Safe Mode option, but it adds networking features. You might use this mode if you need networking capabilities in order to download drivers or service packs from a network location.

- *Safe Mode with Command Prompt* starts the computer in Safe mode, but instead of loading the Windows 2000 graphical interface, it loads a command prompt. Experienced troubleshooters use this mode.

- *Enable VGA Mode* loads a standard VGA driver without starting the computer in Safe mode. You might use VGA mode if you changed your video driver, didn't test it, and tried to boot to Windows 2000 with a bad driver that wouldn't allow you to access video. The Enable VGA Mode option bails you out by loading a default driver, providing access to video so that you can properly install (and test!) the correct driver for your computer.

NOTE   When you boot to any form of Safe mode, you automatically use VGA Mode.

- *Last Known Good Configuration* boots Windows 2000 using the Registry information that was saved the last time the computer was successfully booted. You would use this option to restore configuration information if you have improperly configured the computer and can't successfully reboot. When you use the Last Known Good

Configuration option, you lose any system configuration changes that were made since the computer last successfully booted.

- *Directory Services Restore Mode* is used by Windows 2000 Server computers that are configured as domain controllers, to restore the Active Directory. This option is not available on Windows 2000 Server computers that are installed as member servers.

- *Debugging Mode* runs the Kernel Debugger, if that utility is installed. The Kernel Debugger is an advanced troubleshooting utility.

- *Boot Normally* boots to Windows 2000 in the default manner. This option is on the Advanced Options menu in case you got trigger happy and hit F8 during the boot process, but you really wanted to boot Windows 2000 normally.

NOTE   Windows 2000 handles startup options slightly differently from Windows NT 4.0. In Windows NT 4.0, the boot loader menu shows an option to load VGA mode, which appears each time you restart the computer. In Windows 2000, this function has been moved to the Advanced Options menu to present the user with a cleaner boot process. Also, in Windows NT 4.0, you have to press the spacebar as a part of the boot process to access the Last Known Good Configuration option.

Startup and Recovery Options

You use the Startup and Recovery options to specify the default operating system that is loaded and to specify which action should be taken in the event of system failure. You can access the Startup and Recovery options from your Desktop by right-clicking My Computer, selecting Properties, clicking the Advanced tab, and then clicking the Startup and Recovery button. Or you can select Start ➢ Settings ➢ Control Panel ➢ System ➢ Advanced ➢ Startup and Recovery. Table 4.10 lists the options that can be specified through the Startup and Recovery dialog box.

TABLE 4.10: Startup and Recovery Options

Option	Description
Default Operating System	Specifies the operating system that is loaded by default if no selection is made from the OS selection menu (if your computer dual-boots or multi-boots and an OS selection menu appears during bootup). By default, this option is set to Microsoft Windows 2000 Server.
Display List of Operating Systems for x Seconds	Specifies how long the OS selection menu is available before the default selection is loaded (if your computer dual-boots or multi-boots and an OS selection menu appears during bootup). The default setting is 30 seconds.
Write an Event to the System Log	Specifies that an entry is made in the System log any time a system failure occurs. By default, this option is enabled, which allows you to track system failures.
Send an Administrative Alert	Specifies that a pop-up alert message will be sent to the Administrator any time a system failure occurs. By default, this option is enabled, so the Administrator is notified of system failures.
Automatically Reboot	Specifies that the computer will automatically reboot in the event of a system failure. By default, this option is enabled, so the system restarts after a failure without intervention. You would disable this option if you wanted to see the blue screen for analysis.
Write Debugging Information	Specifies that debugging information (a memory dump) is written to a file. You can choose not to create a dump file or to create a small memory dump (64KB) file, a kernel memory dump file, or a complete memory dump file. Complete memory dump files require free disk space equivalent to your computer's memory, and a page file that is at least as large as your memory with an extra 2MB. The default setting is to write debugging information to a complete memory dump.
Overwrite Any Existing File	If you create dump files, you can choose to create a new dump file that overwrites the old one, or to keep all dump files each time a system failure occurs. Overwrite Any Existing File is selected by default.

Using the Recovery Console

If your computer won't start and you have tried to boot to Safe mode with no luck, there's one more option you can try. The *Recovery Console* is designed for administrators and advanced users. It allows you limited access to FAT16, FAT32, and NTFS volumes without starting the Windows 2000 Server graphical interface. Through the Recovery Console, you can perform the following tasks:

- Copy, replace, or rename operating system files and folders. This might be an option if you suspect your boot failure is the result of missing or corrupt files.

- Enable or disable the loading of services when the computer is restarted. If you suspect that a particular service is keeping the OS from booting, you could disable the service. If a particular service is required for successful booting, you want to make sure that service loading was enabled.

- Repair the file system boot sector or the MBR. You might use this option if it's possible a virus has damaged the system boot sector or the MBR.

- Create and format partitions on the drives. This is an option if your disk utilities will not delete or create Windows 2000 partitions. Normally, you use a disk-partitioning utility for these functions.

Starting the Recovery Console

If you have created the Windows 2000 Server Setup Disks, you can start the Recovery Console from them.

Alternatively, you can add the Recovery Console to the Windows 2000 startup options so it will be available in the event of a system failure. You'll need to configure this arrangement prior to the failure, as described in the Necessary Procedures section for this objective. This configuration takes about 7MB of disk space to hold the CMDCONS folder and files.

Using the Recovery Console

After you add the Recovery Console, you can access it by restarting your computer. In the OS selection menu, select the option for Microsoft Windows 2000 Recovery Console. The Recovery Console presents you with a command prompt and very limited access to system resources. This keeps unauthorized users from using the Recovery Console to access sensitive data. You can only access the following folders through the Recovery Console. (You'll get an "access denied" error message if you try to access any others.)

- Root

- *%systemroot%* and the subfolders of the Windows 2000 Server installation

- CMDCONS

- Removable media drives such as CD-ROM drives

In the Recovery Console, you cannot copy files from a local hard disk to a floppy disk. You can only copy files from a floppy disk or CD to a hard disk, or from one hard disk to another hard disk. This is for security purposes.

WARNING Use the Recovery Console with extreme caution. Improper use may cause even more damage than the problems you're trying to fix.

If your computer dual-boots with other Windows 2000 operating systems, you'll first have to specify which OS you will log on to. Next, you'll specify the Administrator password for the system you are logging on to.

When the Recovery Console starts, you can use the commands listed in Table 4.11.

TABLE 4.11:   Commands Available with the Recovery Console

Command	Description
ATTRIB	Sets file attributes. You can set Read-only (R), System (S), Hidden (H), or Compressed (C).
BATCH	Executes commands in a specified input file.

TABLE 4.11: Commands Available with the Recovery
Console *(continued)*

Command	Description
CHDIR (CD)	Navigates the directory structure. If executed without a directory name, the current directory is displayed. (CHDIR and CD work the same way.)
CLS	Clears any text currently displayed on the Console.
CHKDSK	Checks the disk and display a disk status report.
COPY	Copies a single file from one location to another. This COPY command does not support wildcards and does not copy files to removable media such as floppy disks.
DELETE (DEL)	Deletes a single file. Wildcards are not supported. (DELETE and DEL work the same way.)
DIR	Displays lists of files and subdirectories in the current directory.
DISABLE	Disables Windows 2000 system services and drivers.
DISKPART	Manages disk partitions. If executed without a command-line argument, a user interface is displayed.
ENABLE	Enables Windows 2000 system services and drivers.
EXIT	Quits the Recovery Console and restarts the computer.
EXPAND	Expands compressed files.
FIXBOOT	Writes a new boot sector onto the computer's system partition.
FIXMBR	Repairs the MBR of the computer's boot partition.
FORMAT	Prepares a disk for use with Windows 2000 by formatting the disk as FAT16, FAT32, or NTFS.
HELP	Displays help information for Recovery Console commands.
LISTSVC	Lists all available services and drivers on the computer, as well as the current status of each service and driver.

TABLE 4.11: Commands Available with the Recovery Console *(continued)*

Command	Description
LOGON	If the computer is configured for dual-booting or multi-booting, logs on to other installations as the local Administrator.
MAP	Displays the current drive letter mappings.
MKDIR (MD)	Creates new directories (MKDIR and MD work the same way).
MORE	Displays a text file on the console screen (same as TYPE).
RENAME (REN)	Renames a single file (RENAME and REN work the same way).
RMDIR (RD)	Deletes directories (RMDIR and RD work the same way).
SYSTEMROOT	Specifies that the current directory is the system root.
TYPE	Displays a text file on the Console screen (same as MORE).

Necessary Procedures

Following are the procedures necessary for recovering the System State data and user data after a system failure.

Using the Event Viewer Utility

1. Select Start ➢ Programs ➢ Administrative Tools ➢ Event Viewer.

2. Click System Log in the left pane of the Event Viewer window to display the System log events.

3. Double-click the first event in the right pane of the Event Viewer window to see its Event Properties dialog box. Click the Cancel button to close the dialog box.

4. Right-click System Log in the left pane of the Event Viewer window and select Properties.

5. Click the Filter tab. Clear all the check marks under Event Types except those in the Warning and Error check boxes; then click the OK button. You should see only Warning and Error events listed in the System log.

6. To remove the filter, return to the Filter tab of the log Properties dialog box, click the Restore Defaults button at the bottom of the dialog box, and click OK. All the event types will be listed again.

7. Right-click System Log and select Clear All Events.

8. When you're asked if you want to save the System log before clearing it, click the Yes button. Specify the path and filename for the log file, and click the Save button. All the events will be cleared from the System log.

Creating a Windows 2000 Boot Disk

1. Put a blank diskette in your floppy drive.

2. Select Start ➢ Programs ➢ Accessories ➢ Windows Explorer.

3. In Windows Explorer, expand My Computer, right-click 3^1/$_2$ Floppy (A:), and select Format. Accept all the default options and click the Start button.

4. A dialog box warns you that all the data will be lost. Click the OK button.

5. When you see the Format Complete dialog box, click OK, and then click the Close button to close the Format dialog box.

6. Select Start ➢ Programs ➢ Accessories ➢ Command Prompt.

7. In the Command Prompt dialog box, type **ATTRIB** and press Enter. You'll see all the files at the root of the C: drive. Note the file attributes of the NTLDR, NTDETECT.COM, and BOOT.INI files.

8. Type **ATTRIB NTLDR −S −H −R** and press Enter.

9. Type **COPY NTLDR A:** and press Enter.

10. Type **ATTRIB NTLDR +S +H +R** and press Enter.

11. Repeat steps 8 through 10 for the NTDETECT.COM and BOOT.INI files. These commands remove the file attributes, copy the file, and

replace the file attributes. If you have a SCSI adapter with the BIOS disabled, you'll also need to copy the NTBOOTDD.SYS file.

12. Verify that all the files are on the boot disk by typing **DIR A:**.

13. Type **Exit** to close the Command Prompt dialog box.

14. To test your Windows 2000 boot disk, select Start ➢ Shut Down ➢ Restart and click the OK button.

15. Label your Windows 2000 boot disk and put it in a safe place.

Restoring Your System with an Emergency Repair Disk

1. Restart using the Windows 2000 Server Setup Boot Disk. When prompted, insert Windows 2000 Server Setup Disk #2, #3, and #4, pressing Enter after you insert each one.

2. From the Welcome to Setup dialog box, press R to choose to repair a Windows 2000 installation.

3. From the Windows 2000 Repair Options dialog box, press R to repair the Windows 2000 installation using the Emergency Repair process.

4. Press F to choose Fast Repair.

5. Insert your ERD and press Enter. Then press Enter again in the next dialog box.

6. Press Enter to indicate that you want the Setup program to examine your computer's drives.

7. Insert the Windows 2000 Server CD into your CD-ROM drive and press Enter. The Emergency Repair process will examine the files on your drive.

8. When prompted, remove any floppies from your floppy drives, and the Windows 2000 Server CD from the CD-ROM drive. You computer will restart automatically.

Using the Restore Wizard

1. Select Start ➢ Programs ➢ Accessories ➢ System Tools ➢ Backup.

2. In the opening Backup window, click the Restore Wizard button. When the Welcome dialog box appears, click Next to continue.

3. In the What to Restore dialog box, click the filename of the backup session. Check the box for drive D:, and then click the Next button.

4. In the Completing the Restore Wizard dialog box, verify that everything is configured properly. Then click the Finish button.

5. When the Restore Wizard is finished, click the Report button in the Restore Progress dialog box. Examine the report, and close the Notepad window when you are finished.

6. Close all Restore and Backup dialog boxes that remain open.

Booting Your Computer to Safe Mode

1. If your computer is currently running, select Start ➤ Shutdown ➤ Restart.

2. During the boot process, press F8 to access the Windows 2000 Advanced Options menu.

3. Highlight Safe Mode and press Enter. Then log on as Administrator.

4. When you see the Desktop dialog box letting you know that Windows 2000 is running in Safe mode, click the OK button.

5. Select My Network Places ➤ Entire Network. You should see an error message stating that you are unable to browse the network (because you are in Safe mode). Click OK to close the message box.

6. Select Start ➤ Settings ➤ Control Panel ➤ System ➤ Hardware ➤ Device Manager. Look in Device Manager to see if any devices are not working properly.

NOTE   For this exercise, you shouldn't have any nonworking devices. If you use this procedure as a result of actual problems, select the device that is not working properly and update or reinstall the drivers. Chapter 3 gives procedures for updating a device driver.

Using Boot Logging

1. Start your computer. (If your computer is currently running, select Start ➤ Shutdown ➤ Restart.)

2. During the boot process, press F8 to access the Windows 2000 Advanced Options menu.

3. Highlight Enable Boot Logging and press Enter. Then log on as Administrator.

4. Select Start ➢ Programs ➢ Accessories ➢ Windows Explorer.

5. In Windows Explorer, expand My Computer, then C:. Open the WINNT folder and double-click `ntbtlog.txt`.

6. Examine the contents of your boot log file.

7. Shut down your computer and restart in Normal mode.

NOTE   The boot log file is cumulative. Each time you boot to any Advanced Options menu mode (except Last Known Good Configuration), you are writing to this file. This allows you to make changes, reboot, and see if you have fixed any problems. If you want to start from scratch, you should manually delete the boot log file and reboot to an Advanced Options menu selection that supports logging.

Using Startup and Recovery Options

1. From your Desktop, right-click My Computer and choose Properties. Click the Advanced tab, and then click the Startup and Recovery button.

2. Change the Display List of Operating Systems option from 30 seconds to 10 seconds.

3. In the Write Debugging Information section, choose (None) from the drop-down list.

4. Click the OK button to close the Startup and Recovery dialog box.

5. You'll be reminded that the changes won't take effect until the server is rebooted; click OK to close this message box.

Adding the Recovery Console to the Windows 2000 Setup

1. Insert the Windows 2000 Server CD in your CD-ROM drive. Hold down the Shift key as the CD is read to prevent auto-play.

2. Select Start ➢ Programs ➢ Accessories ➢ Command Prompt.

3. Change the drive letter to your CD-ROM drive.

4. From the CD drive prompt (x:\>), type **CD I386** and press Enter.

5. From x:\I386>, type **WINNT32 /CMDCONS**.

6. In the Windows 2000 Setup dialog box, click the Yes button to confirm that you want to install the Recovery Console.

7. After the installation files are copied to your computer, a dialog box tells you that the Recovery Console has been successfully installed. Click the OK button.

8. Shut down and restart your computer. In the startup selection screen, select the option for Microsoft Windows 2000 Recovery Console.

9. At the command prompt, type **EXIT** to close the Recovery Console and return to the Windows Desktop.

Using the Recovery Console

1. Restart the computer. In the operating system selection menu, select the Microsoft Windows 2000 Recovery Console option.

2. Select the Windows 2000 installation you want to manage and press Enter. (If the computer has been configured as specified in this book, this will be option 1.)

3. Enter the Administrator password and press Enter. You see the C:\WINNT> prompt.

4. Type **DIR** and press Enter to see a current listing of available files and folders. In the listing, you can press Enter to scroll down line by line, or the spacebar to scroll continuously.

5. Type **CD ..** and press Enter to move to the root of the C: drive. You see the C:\> prompt.

6. Type **DIR BOOT.INI** and press Enter to see the file attributes of the BOOT.INI file.

7. Type **MORE BOOT.INI** and press Enter to see the contents of the BOOT.INI file.

8. Type **LISTSVC** and press Enter to see a list of all the services and drivers.

9. Type **EXIT** to exit the Recovery Console and restart your computer.

Exam Essentials

Know what information is stored in each of the Event Viewer logs.
The System log tracks events related to the Windows 2000 operating system. The Security log tracks events related to auditing. The Application log tracks events related to the applications running on your computer. On a domain controller there are additional logs that track events related to Directory Services, DNS Server, and File Replication (Dfs).

Understand the Windows 2000 boot process. The Windows 2000 boot process consists of five stages: the preboot sequence, the boot sequence, kernel load, kernel initialization, and logon.

Know the possible errors that can occur in the boot sequence. The most common errors that occur in the boot sequence are missing or corrupt boot files, improper configuration of the BOOT.INI file, and unrecognized or improperly configured hardware.

Understand the ARC naming convention. The ARC naming convention is used to identify three things for the boot process: the controller, the device, and the partition where the Windows 2000 operating system files are located.

Know when to use the MULTI or SCSI option in ARC paths. The SCSI option is used when the controller is a SCSI device that does not have or is not using the SCSI BIOS. All other controllers are MULTI.

Know the BOOT.INI switches. Especially, you will need to know about /basevideo, which boots the computer using standard VGA mode, and /fastdetect=comx, which disables the mouse auto-detect on serial ports and allows you to add UPS devices to the serial ports.

Understand the Advanced Startup options. The Windows 2000 Advanced Startup options are used to troubleshoot errors that keep Windows 2000 Server from successfully booting.

Know what happens when the computer starts up in Safe mode.
Safe mode simplifies the Windows 2000 configuration to include only the drivers and services required to get the computer up and running.

Many features that are available during normal operations are not available while the computer is in Safe mode.

Know what functions are available in the Recovery Console. The Recovery Console allows you limited access to your files without starting the GUI. You can copy or replace OS files and folders, enable or disable loading of services, repair the file system boot sector or the MBR, and create and format partitions.

Key Terms and Concepts

Application logs   Event Viewer logs that track events related to applications running on your computer.

Boot Normally   An Advanced Startup option that boots to Windows 2000 in the default manner.

BOOT.INI   A file used to build the operating system menu choices that are displayed during the boot process. It is also used to specify the location of the boot partition. Located in the root of the system partition, BOOT.INI has the file attributes of System and Hidden.

BOOTSECT.DOS   An optional file that is loaded if you choose to load an OS other than Windows 2000. It is only used in dual- or multi-booting computers. Located in the root of the system partition, BOOTSECT.DOS has the file attributes of System and Hidden.

Debugging Mode   An option that runs the Kernel Debugger, if that utility is installed. The Kernel Debugger is an advanced trouble-shooting utility.

Directory Services Restore Mode   An option used by Windows 2000 Server computers that are configured as domain controllers, to restore the Active Directory. This option is not available on Windows 2000 Server computers that are installed as member servers.

Enable Boot Logging   An Advanced Startup option that uses a log file that tracks the loading of drivers and services.

Enable VGA Mode   An Advanced Startup option that loads a standard VGA driver without starting the computer in Safe mode. You might use this mode if you changed your video driver, did not test it, and tried to boot to Windows 2000 with a bad driver that would not allow you to access video. Enable VGA Mode bails you out by loading a default driver, providing access to video so that you can properly install (and test!) the correct driver for your computer.

Event Viewer   A utility to track information about your computer's hardware and software, as well as to monitor security events.

Last Known Good Configuration   An Advanced Startup option that boots Windows 2000 using the Registry information that was saved the last time the computer was successfully booted. You would use this option to restore configuration information if you have improperly configured the computer and have not successfully rebooted the computer. When you use the Last Known Good Configuration option, you lose any system configuration changes that were made since the computer last successfully booted.

`NTBOOTDD.SYS`   An optional file that is used when you have a SCSI (Small Computer Standard Interface) adapter with the onboard BIOS disabled. (This option is not commonly implemented.) Located in the root of the system partition, `NTBOOTDD.SYS` has the file attributes of System and Hidden.

`NTDETECT.COM`   A file used to detect any hardware that is installed and to add information about the hardware to the Registry. Located in the root of the system partition, `NTDETECT.COM` has the file attributes of System, Hidden, and Read-only.

`NTLDR`   A file used to control the Windows 2000 boot process until control is passed to the `NTOSKRNL` file for the boot sequence.

`NTOSKRNL.EXE`   A file used to load the Windows 2000 operating system. This file is located in the system partition in the folder `%systemroot%\System32` and has no file attributes.

POST (Power On Self Test)   A routine that detects the computer's processor, how much memory is present, what hardware is recognized, and whether the BIOS (Basic Input/Output System) is standard or has Plug-and-Play capabilities.

Recovery Console   A startup option that allows limited access to FAT16, FAT32, and NTFS volumes without starting the Windows 2000 Server graphical interface.

Restore Wizard   A Wizard that walks through the steps of restoring from a backup, as well as testing the restoration process.

Safe Mode with Command Prompt   An Advanced Startup option that starts the computer in Safe mode but loads a command prompt instead of the GUI. Experienced troubleshooters use this mode.

Safe Mode with Networking   An Advanced Startup option that is the same as Safe mode but adds networking features. Useful if you need networking capabilities in order to download drivers or service packs from a network location.

Safe Mode   An Advanced Startup option that loads only the drivers and services needed to get the computer up and running.

Security log   An Event Viewer log that tracks events related to Windows 2000 auditing.

System log   An Event Viewer log that tracks events related to the Windows 2000 operating system.

Windows 2000 Server Boot Disk   A disk used to boot to Windows 2000 Server operating system in the event of a boot failure.

Sample Questions

1. You have recently made changes to some device drivers. Now when you try to restart your computer, it fails to initialize. You suspect that the new drivers are the cause. The original driver files are located on another server. Which mode should you use to reboot the system in order to fix the problems?

   A. Debugging Mode

   B. Save Mode

   C. Safe Mode with Command Prompt

   D. Safe Mode with Networking

   Answer: D. Safe Mode with Networking is an option that allows entering the Safe mode with networking capabilities, so that you can access resources over the network.

2. You suspect that the reason you can't boot is due to corrupt system files. How can you repair the damage?

A. Boot from the ERD.

B. Start the computer in Safe mode.

C. Use the Recovery Console.

D. Start the computer with the Last Known Good Configuration option.

Answer: C. The Recovery Console is designed to give you limited access to volumes without starting the GUI, so you can replace operating system files. You cannot boot from the ERD. Safe mode allows you to fix problems with device drivers, services, or configuration problems. The Last Known Good Configuration option allows you to try to recover from configuration errors.

3. You have a SCSI controller that has its BIOS disabled. There are three hard drives connected to the controller. The Boot partition is located on the third device, on the second partition. What is the correct ARC path?

A. `multi(1)disk(0)rdisk(3)partition(2)`

B. `scsi(1)disk(3)rdisk(0)partition(2)`

C. `multi(0)disk(0)rdisk(2)partition(2)`

D. `scsi(0)disk(2)rdisk(0)partition(2)`

Answer: D. The correct ARC path is `scsi(0)disk(2)rdisk(0)partition(2)`. You use `scsi` because you have an SCSI controller with its BIOS disabled. The number is 2 because it's the third device. (Remember that the numbering system starts at 0.) The correct device parameter is `disk`, the one associated with SCSI. The partition number is 2 because ordinal numbers are used for the `partition` value.

Chapter

5

Managing, Configuring, and Troubleshooting Storage Use

MICROSOFT EXAM OBJECTIVES COVERED IN THIS CHAPTER:

▶ Monitor, configure, and troubleshoot disks and volumes. *(pages 248 – 277)*

▶ Configure data compression. *(pages 277 – 281)*

▶ Monitor and configure disk quotas. *(pages 281 – 290)*

▶ Recover from disk failures. *(pages 290 – 293)*

Most networks are installed to offer safe, reliable sharing and storage of information. Networked organizations store most, if not all, of their important information on file servers, so security and safety are critical issues. Today's network operating systems, including Windows 2000, offer many services to protect network data files. They also provide file storage options that can increase the speed, fault tolerance, and convenience of data storage.

Network administrators who handle day-to-day network operations and who know the requirements of data management and storage systems need to become familiar with new Microsoft Windows 2000 Server features related to storage management. When you're planning your Windows 2000 deployment, it's recommended that you incorporate these features into your strategy for storage management. Making wise use of disk management, data compression, and disk quotas can help you improve your storage management arrangement.

Microsoft has improved the tools and functionality of data management in Windows 2000, and the exam will focus on these topics. Make sure that you're comfortable using these tools because they'll be the primary focus of the questions relating to these objectives. Considerations for selecting a data storage system, designating fault tolerance, and ways to improve your disaster recovery capabilities are also discussed in this chapter.

Monitor, configure, and troubleshoot disks and volumes.

Improving your storage systems and their management is not only an important consideration when deploying Microsoft Windows 2000

Server; it's a critical part of managing any enterprise network infrastructure. Considering the enormous amount of data that must be protected in a network environment, it's essential that you are aware of the latest technologies so you can select the hardware and software that best meet your network's needs.

Microsoft Windows 2000 provides several features for managing disk resources to enhance performance and protect data.

Critical Information

When you install Windows 2000 Server, you choose the setup for initial configuration of your disks. Windows 2000 Server's utilities and features help you change your configuration and perform the necessary disk-management tasks.

For your file system configuration, you can choose FAT, FAT32, or NTFS. You can also convert a FAT16 or FAT32 partition to NTFS.

Another factor in disk management is choosing the configuration for your physical drives. Windows 2000 Server supports basic storage and dynamic storage. When you install Windows 2000, or if you upgrade from Windows NT, the drives are configured as basic storage. Dynamic storage is new to Windows 2000 Server and allows you to create simple, spanned, striped, mirrored, and RAID-5 volumes (RAID stands for Redundant Array of Inexpensive Disks).

Once you decide how your disks should be configured, you implement the configurations through the Disk Management utility. This utility allows you to view and manage your physical disks and volumes.

Configuring File Systems

File systems are used to store and locate the files you save on your hard drive. Windows 2000 Server supports the *FAT16, FAT32,* and *NTFS* file systems. Choose FAT16 or FAT32 if you want to dual-boot your computer, because these two file systems are backward compatible with other operating systems. Choose NTFS when you want to take advantage of features such as local security, file compression, and file encryption. Table 5.1 summarizes the capabilities of each file system.

TABLE 5.1: File System Capabilities

Feature	FAT16	FAT32	NTFS
Operating system support	Most	Windows 95 OSR2, Windows 98, and Windows 2000	Windows NT and Windows 2000
Long filename support	Yes	Yes	Yes
Efficient use of disk space	No	Yes	Yes
Compression support	No	No	Yes
Quota support	No	No	Yes
Encryption support	No	No	Yes
Local security support	No	No	Yes
Network security support	Yes	Yes	Yes
Maximum volume size	2GB	32GB	2TB

NOTE Windows 2000 Server also supports *CDFS (Compact Disk File System)*. However, CDFS cannot be managed. It is only used to mount and read CDs.

Windows 2000 provides the CONVERT command-line utility for converting a FAT16 or FAT32 partition to NTFS. The syntax for the CONVERT command is

```
CONVERT [drive:] /fs:ntfs
```

Configuring Disk Storage

Windows 2000 Server supports two types of disk storage: *basic storage* and *dynamic storage*. Basic storage is backward compatible with other operating systems and can be configured to support up to four partitions. Dynamic storage is a new system in which storage is configured as volumes.

NOTE   You can convert a basic disk to a dynamic disk in Windows 2000 Server; however, you cannot convert a dynamic disk to a basic disk.

Basic Storage

At the highest level of disk organization, you have a physical hard drive. You cannot use space on the physical drive until you have logically partitioned the physical drive. A *partition* is a logical definition of hard drive space. When you configure *basic storage,* you work with primary and extended partitions.

The first partition created on a hard drive is called a *primary partition;* it uses all the space that is allocated to it. Each physical drive can have up to four partitions, configured as four primary partitions or as three primary partitions and one extended partition.

With *extended partitions,* you can allocate the space in whatever arrangement you like.

NOTE   Laptops support basic disks only.

Dynamic Storage

Dynamic storage is a new Windows 2000 feature that consists of a *dynamic disk* divided into dynamic *volumes*. Dynamic volumes cannot contain partitions or logical drives and are not accessible through DOS.

Windows 2000 Server dynamic storage supports five types of dynamic volumes: simple volumes, spanned volumes, striped volumes, mirrored volumes, and RAID-5 volumes. These are similar to the disk configurations used with Windows NT 4. When you install Windows 2000 or if you've upgraded from NT 4, you are using basic storage and you can't add volume sets. Fortunately, you can upgrade from basic storage to dynamic storage, as explained later in the "Necessary Procedures" section of this chapter.

To set up dynamic storage, you create or upgrade a disk to a dynamic disk. Then you create dynamic volumes within the dynamic disk. All this is accomplished with the Windows 2000 Disk Management utility, covered later in this chapter.

Simple Volumes

A *simple volume* contains space from a single dynamic drive. The space from the single drive can be contiguous or noncontiguous. Simple volumes are used when you have enough disk space on a single drive to hold your entire volume.

Spanned Volumes

Spanned volumes consist of disk space on two or more dynamic drives; up to 32 dynamic drives can be used in a spanned volume configuration. Spanned volume sets are used to dynamically increase the size of a dynamic volume. When you create spanned volumes, the data is written sequentially, filling space on one physical drive before writing continues to the space on the next physical drive in the spanned volume set. You don't have to allocate the same amount of space to the volume sets on each physical drive.

Because data is written sequentially, you don't see any performance enhancement with spanned volumes, as you do with striped volumes (discussed next). The main disadvantage of spanned volumes is that if any drive in the spanned volume set fails, you lose access to all the data in the spanned set.

Striped Volumes

Striped volumes store data in equal stripes between two or more (up to 32) dynamic drives. Because the data is written sequentially in the stripes, you can take advantage of multiple I/O performance and increase the speed at which data reads and writes take place.

The main disadvantage of striped volumes is that if any drive in the striped volume set ("stripe set") fails, you lose access to all the data in the stripe set.

Mirrored Volumes

Mirrored volumes are copies of two simple volumes stored on two separate physical partitions. In a mirrored volume set, you have a *primary drive* and a *secondary drive*. The data written to the primary drive is mirrored to the secondary drive.

Mirrored volumes provide fault tolerance—if one drive in the mirrored volume fails, the other drive still works without any interruption in service or loss of data.

Another advantage of mirrored volumes is enhanced disk-read performance, because the drive head closest to the sector being read is accessed for the operation. On the other hand, disk-write performance degrades somewhat because one disk controller has to write to two separate drives. To increase your system's fault tolerance and improve write performance as well, you can use a variation of mirroring called *duplexing*. In duplexing, you add another disk controller. (Windows 2000 Server does not distinguish between mirroring and duplexing, essentially viewing both configurations as mirrored volumes.)

TIP   The system and boot partitions can exist on a mirrored volume set.

The main disadvantage of mirrored volumes is high overhead. All of your data is written to two locations.

RAID-5 Volumes

RAID-5 volumes are similar to striped volumes in that they stripe the data over multiple disk channels. In addition, RAID-5 volumes place a parity stripe across the volume. (*Parity* is a mathematical calculation performed on the data; the calculation provides information that can be used to rebuild data on failed drives.) If a single drive within the volume set fails, the parity information stored on the other drives can be used to rebuild the data on the failed drive. RAID-5 volumes require at least three physical drives (up to a maximum of 32), with each volume using an equal amount of free space on all the drives.

WARNING   Unlike mirrored volumes, RAID-5 volumes cannot be used to mount the system and boot partitions.

RAID-5 volumes are fault tolerant and provide good performance because the configuration uses multiple disk I/O channels. The other advantage of RAID-5 volumes is that they require less disk space for fault tolerance than is needed for mirrored volumes. (A mirrored volume set uses half of the volume set to store the mirror.) In contrast, a RAID-5 volume set requires only the storage space of one drive in the set to use for storing the parity information.

The primary disadvantage of using a RAID-5 volume is that once a drive fails, system performance suffers until you rebuild the RAID-5 volume. This is because the parity information must be recalculated through memory to reconstruct the missing drive.

WARNING   If more than one drive fails, the RAID-5 volume becomes inaccessible. At that point, you must restore your data from your backup media.

NOTE   The RAID-5 technology offered through Windows 2000 Server is *software RAID*. Most hardware server vendors offer *hardware RAID,* the features of which are far superior to software RAID. Software RAID, however, has the advantage of not requiring any special hardware.

Using the Disk Management Utility

The *Disk Management utility* is a graphical tool for managing disks and volumes within the Windows 2000 Server environment.

To have full permissions to use the Disk Management utility, you should be logged on with Administrative privileges. To access the utility, open the Control Panel and select Administrative Tools, then Computer Management. Expand the Storage folder to see the Disk Management utility.

NOTE   You can also access the Disk Management utility by right-clicking My Computer, selecting Manage, expanding Computer Management, expanding Storage, and finally expanding Disk Management. Another alternative is to add Disk Management as a Microsoft Management Console (MMC) snap-in.

The Disk Management window shows the following information:

- The volumes that are recognized by the computer
- The type of partition (basic or dynamic)
- The type of file system used by each partition
- The status of the partition and whether the partition contains the system or boot partition
- The capacity (amount of space) allocated to the partition
- The amount of free space remaining on the partition
- The amount of overhead associated with the partition

Managing Basic Tasks

With the Disk Management utility, you can perform a variety of basic tasks, as described in the following sections.

Viewing Disk Properties

To view the properties of a disk, right-click the drive in the lower half of the Disk Management main window and choose Properties from the pop-up menu. This brings up the Disk Properties dialog box, which displays the following disk properties:

- Disk number
- Type of disk (basic, dynamic, CD-ROM, removable, DVD, or unknown)
- Status (online or offline)
- Capacity
- Amount of unallocated space
- Hardware device type
- Hardware vendor that produced the drive
- Adapter name
- Logical volumes that have been defined on the physical drive

Viewing Volume and Local Disk Properties

On a dynamic disk, you manage volume properties. On a basic disk, you manage local disk properties. Volumes and local disks perform the same function, and the options discussed in the following sections apply to both. If you're using basic storage, you'll view the local disk properties rather than the volume properties.

To view the properties of a volume, right-click the volume in the upper half of the Disk Management main window and choose Properties. This brings up the volume's Properties dialog box.

In the dialog box, the volume properties are organized on tabs named General, Tools, Hardware, Sharing, Security, Quota, and Web

Sharing. (The Security and Quota tabs appear only for NTFS volumes, not for FAT volumes).

GENERAL

The information on the General tab represents the fundamental configuration of the volume. You can see the volume's label, type, file system, used and free space, and capacity. The label is shown in an editable text box, and you can change it if desired. The space allocated to the volume is shown graphically as well as in text.

NOTE   The label for a volume or local disk is for informational purposes only.

The Disk Cleanup button starts the Disk Cleanup utility, which allows you to delete unnecessary files and free disk space. This utility is described in more detail later in this chapter.

TOOLS

The Tools tab of the volume Properties dialog box provides access to three tools:

- The Check Now button runs the Check Disk utility. You might use this to check the volume for errors if you were experiencing problems accessing it, or if the volume was open during a system restart that didn't go through a proper shutdown sequence. (The Check Disk utility is covered later in this chapter in the "Recover from disk failures" objective.)

- The Backup Now button runs the Backup Wizard, which steps you through the process of backing up the files on the volume.

- The Defragment Now button runs the Disk Defragmenter utility. This program defragments files on the volume by storing the files contiguously on the hard drive.

HARDWARE

The Hardware tab lists the hardware associated with the disk drives that are recognized by the Windows 2000 operating system. The bottom half of the page shows the properties of the device that's highlighted in the top half of the page.

For more details about a hardware item, highlight it and click the Properties button in the lower-right corner of the dialog box. This brings up the properties for the item. If the device is working correctly, your device status will report that. If you find that the device isn't running smoothly, you can click the Troubleshooter button to bring up a Wizard to help you search out the problem.

SHARING

The Sharing tab allows you to specify whether or not the volume is shared. By default, all volumes are shared. The share name is the drive letter followed by a $ (dollar sign). The $ indicates that the share is hidden. From this page of the volume's Properties dialog box, you can also set the user limit, permissions, and caching for the share.

SECURITY

You'll see the Security tab in the volume's Properties dialog box only if it's an NTFS volume. The Security tab contains settings for the NTFS permissions.

WARNING   Notice that the default permissions give the Everyone group Full Control permissions at the root of the volume. This could cause major security problems if any user decides to manipulate or delete the data within the volume.

QUOTA

Like the Security tab, the Quota tab appears only if the volume is NTFS. Through the settings on this tab, you can limit the amount of space users can access within the volume.

WEB SHARING

By default, Internet Information Server (IIS) is installed and started on a Windows 2000 Server computer. If this service is running, you'll see a tab for Web Sharing in the Properties dialog box. The Web Sharing tab is used to configure folder sharing for IIS.

Adding a New Disk

To increase the amount of disk storage you have, you can add a new disk. This is a fairly common task that you will likely need to perform as your applications and files grow larger. The procedure for adding a disk depends on whether your computer supports hot swapping of drives. *Hot swapping* is the ability to add new hard disks while the computer is turned on. Most computers do not support this capability.

- **Your Computer Doesn't Support Hot Swap:** If your computer doesn't support hot swapping, you need to shut down the computer before you add a new disk. Then add the drive according to the manufacturer's directions. When you're finished, restart the computer. The new drive should be listed in the Disk Management utility. Start the Disk Management utility, and you'll be prompted to write a signature to the disk so that it will be recognized by Windows 2000 Server. By default, the new drive will be configured as a dynamic disk.

- **Your Computer Supports Hot Swap:** If your computer does support hot swapping, you don't need to turn off your computer before adding a new disk. Just add the disk according to the manufacturer's directions. Then open the Disk Management utility and select Action ➢ Rescan Disks. The new drive should appear in the Disk Management utility.

Creating Partitions and Volumes

If you have unallocated (free) space on a basic disk and you want to create a logical drive, you create a partition. If you have unallocated space on a dynamic disk and you want to create a logical drive, you create a volume. The steps for these tasks are explained in the "Necessary Procedures" section for this objective.

Upgrading a Basic Disk to a Dynamic Disk

To take advantage of the features offered by Windows 2000 dynamic disks, you must upgrade your basic disks to dynamic disks, as explained in the "Necessary Procedures" section for this objective.

WARNING   Upgrading basic disks to dynamic disks is a one-way process. If you decide to revert back to a basic disk, you'll have to first delete all volumes associated with the drive. This operation is potentially dangerous. Before you do this upgrade (or make any major change to your drives or volumes), create a new backup of the drive or volume and verify that you can successfully restore the backup.

Changing the Drive Letter and Path

When you want to reassign drive letters, right-click the affected volume in the Disk Management window and choose the Change Drive Letter and Path option. In the dialog box that appears, click the Edit button to access the Edit Drive Letter or Path dialog box. Use the drop-down list next to the Assign a Drive Letter option to select a drive letter. Finally, confirm the change when prompted.

Deleting Partitions and Volumes

You may need to delete a partition or volume when you're reorganizing your disk, or when you want to make sure that data won't be accessed. Proceed with caution here—once you delete a partition or volume, it's gone forever.

To delete a partition or volume, right-click it in the Disk Management window and choose Delete Volume (or Delete Partition). You'll see a warning that all the data on the partition or volume will be lost. If you're sure, click Yes to confirm that you want to delete the volume or partition.

Managing Basic Storage

The Disk Management utility offers limited support for managing basic storage. You can create, delete, and format partitions on basic drives. You can also delete volume sets and stripe sets that were created under Windows NT. For most other disk management tasks, you'll have to upgrade your drive to dynamic disks.

Managing Dynamic Storage

A dynamic disk can contain simple, spanned, stripped, mirrored, or RAID-5 volumes. Through the Disk Management utility, you can create volumes of each type. You can also create an extended volume, which is the process of adding disk space to a single simple volume. The following sections describe all these disk-management tasks.

Creating Extended Volumes

When you create an extended volume, you are taking a single simple volume and adding more disk space to it, from the free space that exists on the same physical hard drive. When a volume is extended, it is still seen as a single drive letter. In order to extend a volume, the simple volume must be formatted as NTFS. You cannot extend a system or boot partition. Nor can you extend volumes that were originally created as basic disk partitions and then converted to a dynamic disk.

WARNING   Once a volume is extended, no portion of the volume can be deleted without losing data on the entire set.

Creating Spanned Volumes

When you create a spanned volume, you are forming a new volume from scratch that includes space from two or more physical drives, up to a maximum of 32 drives. Spanned volumes can be formatted as FAT, FAT32, or NTFS. In order to create a spanned volume, you must have at least two drives installed on your computer and each drive must contain unallocated space.

WARNING Once a spanned volume is created, no portion of the volume can be deleted without losing the data on the entire set.

Creating Striped Volumes

When you create a striped volume, you are forming a new volume that combines free space on 2–32 drives into a single logical partition. Data in the striped volume is written across all the affected drives in 64KB stripes. (Data in spanned and extended volumes is written sequentially.) In order to create a striped volume, you must have at least two drives installed on your computer and each drive must contain unallocated space. The free space on all drives must be equal in size.

WARNING Once a striped volume is created, no portion of the volume can be deleted without losing the data on the entire set.

Creating Mirrored Volumes

When you create a mirrored volume, you are setting up two physical drives that contain volumes that mirror each other. You create the mirrored volumes from areas of free space on the two drives. You must have at least two drives installed on your computer, and each drive must contain unallocated space. The space on each drive used for the mirror set must be equal in size.

Creating RAID-5 Volumes

When you choose the RAID-5 volume, you are creating a new volume that combines free space on from 3 to 32 physical drives. The volume will contain stripes of data, and parity information for increased performance and fault tolerance. You must choose at least three disks that will be part of the RAID-5 volume. The free space on all the drives must be equal in size.

Using the Disk Defragmenter Utility

Data is normally stored sequentially on the disk as space is available. Fragmentation naturally occurs as users create, delete, and modify files. The access of noncontiguous data is transparent to the user. However, when data is stored in this manner, the operating system must search through the disk drive to find all the pieces of a file. This slows down data access, which is apparent to the user.

Disk defragmentation rearranges existing files so that they are stored contiguously, which optimizes access to those files. In Windows 2000 Server, you use the *Disk Defragmenter utility* to defragment your disk.

To access the Disk Defragmenter utility, select Start ➢ Programs ➢ Accessories ➢ System Tools ➢ Disk Defragmenter. The main Disk Defragmenter window lists each volume, the file system used, capacity, free space in bytes, and the percent of free space.

Along with defragmenting, this utility can analyze your disk and report on the current file arrangement.

Defragmenting Disks

To defragment a disk, open the Disk Defragmenter utility, select the drive to be defragmented, and click the Defragment button (to the right of the Analyze button at the bottom of the window). Defragmenting causes all files to be stored more efficiently in contiguous space. When defragmentation is complete, you can view a report of the process.

Analyzing Disks

To analyze a disk, open the Disk Defragmenter utility, select the drive to be analyzed, and click the Analyze button at the bottom-left of the window. The Disk Defragmenter utility checks for fragmented files, contiguous files, system files, and free space. The results of the disk analysis are shown in the Analysis display bar, color-coded as follows:

Fragmented files	Red
Contiguous files	Blue

| System files | Green |
| Free space | White |

The disk analysis also produces a report, which is displayed when you click the View Report button. The report contains the following:

- Whether or not the volume needs defragmenting
- Volume information, including general volume statistics, volume fragmentation, file fragmentation, page file fragmentation, directory fragmentation, and master file table (MTF) fragmentation
- A list of the most fragmented files

Using the Disk Cleanup Utility

The *Disk Cleanup utility* identifies areas of disk space that can be retrieved by deleting certain files. Disk Cleanup works by identifying temporary files, Internet cache files, and unnecessary program files.

This utility calculates the amount of disk space you can free. After the analysis is complete, the Disk Cleanup dialog box lists the files suggested for deletion and shows how much space will be gained by deleting those files. You can select and deselect files in the list. After you've chosen the files to be deleted and clicked the OK button, you'll be asked to confirm the deletions. If you click Yes, the Disk Cleanup utility will delete the files and automatically close the Disk Cleanup dialog box.

Troubleshooting Disk Devices and Volumes

If you're having trouble with your disk devices or volumes, an important source of aid is the Windows 2000 *Check Disk utility*. This program detects bad sectors, attempts to fix errors in the file system, and scans for and attempts to recover bad sectors. The Check Disk utility is discussed under the "Recover from disk failures" objective later in the chapter.

Necessary Procedures

Before you can start saving files to any volume, the hard drive must be configured. This configuration includes partitioning the space and determining the type of volume that will best meet your needs. The following procedures show how to create the various types of volumes, as well as how to monitor the volumes after they've been created.

Creating a Partition

To create a partition from unallocated space on a basic disk, use the Create Partition Wizard.

1. Right-click an area of free space and choose the Create Partition option from the pop-up menu.

2. The Welcome to the Create Partition Wizard dialog box appears. Click the Next button to continue.

3. Next you'll see the Select Partition Type dialog box, where you'll choose the type of partition you want to create: primary, extended, or logical drive. (Only the options supported by your computer's hardware configuration will be available.) Click the radio button for the partition type, and click the Next button.

4. In the Specify Partition Size dialog box, specify the maximum partition size, up to the amount of free disk space that is recognized. Click the Next button.

5. Next up is the Assign Drive Letter or Path dialog box. You can specify a drive letter, mount the partition as an empty folder, or choose not to assign a drive letter or drive path. Make your selections; then click the Next button.

TIP   If you choose to mount the volume as an empty folder, you can have an unlimited number of volumes, negating the drive-letter limitation.

WARNING If you choose not to assign a drive letter or path, users will not be able to access the partition.

---

6. The Format Partition dialog box appears next, in which you choose whether or not you will format the partition. If you format the volume, you can format it as FAT, FAT32, or NTFS. You can also select the allocation unit size, enter a volume label (for information purposes), specify a quick format, or choose to enable file and folder compression. Note that the quick format operation is risky because it will not scan the disk for bad sectors (as is done in a normal format operation). After you've made your choices, click the Next button.

7. In the Completing the Create Partition Wizard dialog box, you verify the selections you've made for the partitioning operation. If you need to change any of them, click the Back button to reach the appropriate dialog box. When you're satisfied with your settings, click the Finish button.

Upgrading a Basic Disk to a Dynamic Disk

To take advantage of the features offered by Windows 2000 dynamic disks, you must upgrade your basic disks to dynamic disks.

WARNING Upgrading basic disks to dynamic disks is a one-way process. If you decide to revert back to a basic disk, you'll have to first delete all volumes associated with the drive. Also, this operation is potentially dangerous. Before you do this upgrade (or make any major change to your drives or volumes), create a new backup of the drive or volume and verify that you can successfully restore the backup.

---

1. In the Disk Management utility, right-click the drive you want to convert and select the Upgrade to Dynamic Disk option.

2. In the Upgrade to Dynamic Disk dialog box, select the disk that you want to upgrade and click the OK button.

3. The Disks to Upgrade dialog box appears. Click the Upgrade button.

4. A confirmation dialog box warns you that if you complete this upgrade you will no longer be able to boot previous versions of Windows from this disk. Click the Yes button to continue.

5. Another confirmation dialog box warns you that any file systems mounted on the disk will be dismounted. Click the Yes button to continue.

6. Finally, an information dialog box tells you that a reboot is required to complete the upgrade. Click the OK button. Your computer will restart, and the disk upgrade is complete.

Creating Extended Volumes

1. In the Disk Management utility, right-click the volume you want to extend and choose the Extend Volume option.

2. The Extend Volume Wizard starts. Click the Next button.

3. The Select Disks dialog box appears. Select the disk that you want to use for the extended volume and click the Next button.

4. In the Completing the Extend Volume Wizard dialog box, click the Finish button.

Creating Spanned Volumes

1. In the Disk Management utility, right-click an area of unallocated space on one of the drives that will be part of the spanned volume. Select Create Volume from the pop-up menu.

2. When the Create Volume Wizard starts, click the Next button.

3. In the Select Volume Type dialog box, select the Spanned Volume radio button and click the Next button.

NOTE Only the options that are supported by your computer's hardware will be available in the Select Volume Type dialog box.

---

4. The Select Disks dialog box appears next. By default, the disk that you originally selected to create the spanned volume is selected. You have to select at least one other dynamic disk by highlighting it and clicking the Add button. The disks that you select appear in the Selected Dynamic Disks list box. When you have added all the disks that will make up the spanned volume, click the Next button.

5. Next up is the Assign Drive Letter or Path dialog box. You can specify a drive letter, mount the volume at an empty folder that supports drive paths, or choose not to assign a drive letter or drive path. Then click the Next button.

6. The Format Partition dialog box appears next. Choose whether or not you will format the partition, and if so, what file system will be used. After you've made your choices, click the Next button.

7. The Completing the Create Volume Wizard dialog box appears last, offering you the opportunity to verify your selections. If you need to make changes, click the Back button to get to the appropriate dialog box. When the configuration is correct, click the Finish button. In the Disk Management window, you'll see that the spanned volume consists of two or more drives that share a single drive letter.

Creating Striped Volumes

1. In the Disk Management utility, right-click an area of unallocated space on one of the drives that will be a part of the striped volume set. Select Create Volume from the pop-up menu.

2. When the Create Volume Wizard starts, click the Next button.

3. The Select Volume Type dialog box appears. Select the Striped Volume radio button and click the Next button.

4. Next up is the Select Disks dialog box. By default, the disk you originally chose for creating the striped volume is selected. You have to select at least one other dynamic disk by highlighting it and clicking the Add button. The disks that you select appear in the Selected Dynamic Disks list box. When you have added all the disks that will make up the striped volume, click the Next button.

5. The Assign Drive Letter or Path dialog box appears next. You can specify a drive letter, mount the volume at an empty folder that supports drive paths, or choose not to assign a drive letter or drive path. Then click the Next button.

6. The Format Partition dialog box appears. You can choose whether or not you will format the partition, and if so, what file system will be used. After you've made your choices, click the Next button.

7. You'll end up at the Completing the Create Volume Wizard dialog box, which lets you verify your selections. If you need to make changes, click the Back button to get to the appropriate dialog box. When the configuration is correct, click the Finish button. In the Disk Management window, you'll see that the striped volume consists of two or more drives that share a single drive letter.

Creating Mirrored Volumes

1. In the Disk Management utility, right-click an area of unallocated space on one of the drives that will be a part of the mirrored volume set. Select Create Volume from the pop-up menu.

2. When the Create Volume Wizard starts, click the Next button.

3. The Select Volume Type dialog box appears. Select the Mirrored Volume radio button and click the Next button.

4. Next up is the Select Disks dialog box. By default, the disk that you originally selected to create the mirrored volume is selected. Select one other dynamic disk by highlighting it and clicking the Add button. Then click the Next button.

5. The Assign Drive Letter or Path dialog box appears next. You can specify a drive letter, mount the volume at an empty folder that supports drive paths, or choose not to assign a drive letter or drive path. Then click the Next button.

6. In the Format Partition dialog box, choose whether or not you will format the partition, and if so, what file system will be used. After you've made your choices, click the Next button.

7. The Completing the Create Volume Wizard dialog box appears last. If you need to make changes, click the Back button to get the appropriate window. If the configuration is correct, click the Finish button. In the Disk Management window, you'll see that the mirrored volume consists of two drives that share a single drive letter.

Creating RAID-5 Volumes

1. In the Disk Management utility, right-click an area of unallocated space on one of the drives that will be a part of the RAID-5 volume set. Select Create Volume from the pop-up menu.

2. When the Create Volume Wizard starts, click the Next button.

3. The Select Volume Type dialog box appears. Select the RAID-5 Volume radio button and click the Next button.

4. Next up is the Select Disks dialog box. By default, the disk that you originally selected to create the RAID-5 volume is selected. Select at least two other dynamic disks by highlighting each disk and clicking the Add button. The disks that you select appear in the Selected Dynamic Disks list box. When you've finished adding the disks that will make up the RAID-5 volume, click the Next button.

5. The Assign Drive Letter or Path dialog box appears next. You can specify a drive letter, mount the volume at an empty folder that supports drive paths, or choose not to assign a drive letter or drive path. Then click the Next button.

6. In the Format Partition dialog box, choose whether or not you will format the partition, and if so, what file system will be used. After you've made your choices, click the Next button.

7. Last up is the Completing the Create Volume Wizard dialog box. If you need to make changes, click the Back button. If the configuration is correct, click the Finish button. In the Disk Management window, you'll see that the RAID-5 volume consists of three or more drives that share a single drive letter.

Analyzing and Defragmenting Disks

1. Select Start ➢ Programs ➢ Accessories ➢ System Tools ➢ Disk Defragmenter.

2. Highlight the C: drive and click the Analyze button.

3. When analysis is complete, click the View Report button to see the analysis report.

4. Click the Defragment button.

5. When defragmentation is complete, click the Close button.

Using the Disk Cleanup Utility

1. Select Start ➢ Programs ➢ Accessories ➢ System Tools ➢ Disk Cleanup.

2. Highlight the C: drive and click the OK button.

3. In the Disk Cleanup dialog box, leave all the boxes checked and click the OK button.

4. When you are asked to confirm that you want to delete the files, click the Yes button.

Using the Check Disk Utility

1. Select Start ➢ Settings ➢ Control Panel ➢ Administrative Tools. Expand Computer Management, then Storage, then Disk Management.

2. Right-click the D: drive and choose Properties.

3. Click the Tools tab, then click the Check Now button.

4. In the Check Disk dialog box, check both of the disk options check boxes. Then click the Start button.

Exam Essentials

Know the difference between basic and dynamic storage. Basic storage is backward compatible with other operating systems and can be configured to support up to four primary partitions. Dynamic storage is a new system that is configured as volumes. Dynamic volumes cannot contain partitions or logical drives and are not accessible through DOS.

Know how to manage basic tasks, basic storage, and dynamic storage. The Disk Management Utility is the graphical tool for managing disks and volumes within the Windows 2000 Server environment.

Know when to select FAT16, FAT32, or NTFS as the file system for a partition. Choose FAT16 or FAT32 if you want to dual-boot your computer, because these file systems are backward compatible with other operating systems. Choose NTFS if you want to take advantage of features such as local security, file compression, and file encryption.

Know what kind of volumes are supported by dynamic storage. Dynamic storage supports five types of dynamic volume: simple, spanned, striped, mirrored, and RAID-5 volumes.

Know what kinds of volumes are fault tolerant. Windows NT 2000 supports two fault-tolerant volume types: mirrored volumes and RAID-5 volumes.

Know how to launch the Backup Wizard. In a volume's Properties dialog box, the Tools tab provides access to the Backup Wizard. This Wizard steps you through the process of backing up the files on a volume.

Know how to launch the Disk Defragmenter utility. In a volume's Properties dialog box, the Tools tab provides access to the Disk Defragmenter utility. This utility defragments files on the volume by storing files contiguously on the hard disk.

Know how to add a new device when the computer supports hot swapping. If the computer supports hot swapping of drives, add the new hard drive to the system. Then open the Disk Management utility and select Action ➤ Rescan Disks.

Know how to use the Disk Cleanup utility. When you run the Disk Cleanup utility, it calculates the amount of disk space you can free up. The utility does this by identifying temporary files, Internet cache files, and unnecessary program files that can be deleted. After the analysis is complete, the utility lists the files suggested for deletion and shows how much space will be gained by deleting those files.

Know how to use the Check Disk utility to troubleshoot disk and volume problems. The Windows 2000 Check Disk utility detects bad sectors, attempts to fix errors in the file system, and scans for and attempts to recover bad sectors. You will run this utility when you're having trouble with your disk devices or volumes.

Key Terms and Concepts

basic storage Consists of primary and extended partitions.

CDFS (Compact Disk File System) A file system used to mount and read CDs.

Check Disk utility A System Tools utility that detects bad sectors and attempts to fix file-system errors.

CONVERT A command-line utility that converts FAT and FAT32 partitions to NTFS.

Disk Cleanup utility A System Tools utility that identifies files that can be deleted to free up space on the hard drive.

Disk Defragmenter utility A System Tools utility that rearranges files on the hard drive so they can be stored in contiguous space.

Disk Management utility A graphical utility used for managing disks and volumes.

duplexing Having a mirrored volume that has separate controllers for each physical disk.

dynamic disk A dynamic disk is a physical disk that has been upgraded by and is managed with the Disk Management utility. Dynamic disks do not use partitions or logical drives. They can contain only dynamic volumes created by Disk Management.

dynamic storage New in Windows 2000, this storage is provided by a dynamic disk divided into dynamic volumes.

extended partition Any partition created from free space on a hard disk can be subdivided into logical drives. Only one of the partitions allowed per physical disk can be an extended partition, and you don't need a primary partition in order to create an extended partition.

extended volume A volume created from free space on a dynamic disk; it can be subdivided into logical drives.

FAT16 (File Allocation Table) A widely supported file system that is compatible with DOS and other older operating systems.

FAT32 An upgraded version of FAT16 that can recognize larger volumes and is more efficient than FAT16. Can be used with Windows 95 OSR2, Windows 98, and Windows 2000.

hot swapping Adding or removing hard disks from a system that is powered on.

mirrored volume A fault-tolerant volume consisting of two separate physical partitions that have identical data written to them. If one fails, the other is available without interruption of service or loss of data.

NTFS   A file system that is compatible with Windows NT and Windows 2000; provides support for large volumes, data compression, encryption, quota support, and security.

parity   Information that provides data redundancy. The data redundancy method used in Windows 2000 for striping with parity is a function of the Boolean operation called exclusive OR, also called XOR. Regeneration uses the parity information with the data on the good disks to re-create the data on the failed disk.

primary drive   In a mirrored set, data is written to the primary drive.

primary partition   A portion of a physical disk that can be marked for use by an operating system. A primary partition cannot be subpartitioned.

RAID (Redundant Array of Inexpensive Disks)   A system that can support multiple physical disks. It is often associated with fault-tolerant volumes.

RAID-5 volume   A fault-tolerant volume that consists of from 3 to 32 separate physical partitions; a data stripe is placed across the multiple disks. Parity information is stored on one of the drives, which can be used to rebuild the data if one drive fails.

secondary drive   In a mirrored set, the data written to the primary drive is duplicated to the secondary (mirrored) drive. This drive provides the data redundancy.

simple volume   A volume that consists of space from a single dynamic drive.

spanned volume   A volume that consists of disk space on two or more dynamic drives.

striped volume   A volume that consists of equal disk space on 2–32 dynamic drives; data is stored in equal stripes.

Sample Questions

1. Which of the following disk configurations is/are supported as dynamic storage on a Windows 2000 Server computer? Choose all that apply.

   A. Primary partition

   B. Extended partition

   C. Mirrored volume

   D. RAID-5 volume

   Answer: C, D. Primary partitions and extended partitions are supported disk configurations for Windows 2000 Server, but they are basic storage, not dynamic storage.

2. Which of the following dynamic disk configurations provide(s) fault tolerance on a Windows 2000 Server computer? Choose all that apply.

   A. RAID-0 volumes

   B. Mirrored volumes

   C. RAID-3 volumes

   D. RAID-5 volumes

   Answer: B, D. RAID 0 is actually disk striping and is not fault tolerant; RAID-3 is not a supported dynamic disk configuration in Windows 2000 Server. Windows 2000 Server supports mirrored volumes and RAID-5 volumes, which provide fault tolerance.

3. You are installing Windows 2000 Server on a computer with an 8GB drive and three 80GB drives. You want to make sure that you use the maximum amount of disk space with fault tolerance. What configuration should you use?

   A. Install Windows 2000 Server on the 8GB drive. Create a spanned volume set with the three remaining drives.

B. Install Windows 2000 Server on the 8GB drive. Create a striped volume set with the three remaining drives.

C. Install Windows 2000 Server on the 8GB drive. Create a RAID-3 volume set with the three remaining drives.

D. Install Windows 2000 Server on the 8GB drive. Create a RAID-5 volume set with the three remaining drives.

Answer: D. You would create a striped volume set and a spanned volume set if you wanted to maximize the amount of storage and increase performance, but you'd have no fault tolerance. Only a RAID-5 volume set would maximize space while providing fault tolerance. Windows 2000 Server does not support RAID-3.

Configure data compression.

Data compression is the process of storing data in a form that takes less space than what is required for uncompressed data. If you have ever "zipped" or "packed" a file, you have used data compression. Data compression is a file attribute that can be set through Windows Explorer. It can be applied to any NTFS folder or file.

Microsoft will test this subject only lightly, if at all. This feature's ease of use, as well as its support in other versions of Microsoft operating systems, make extensive coverage unnecessary. You do need to be familiar with the terminology.

Critical Information

You implement compression through the Windows Explorer utility or through My Computer. In both cases, compression is an advanced attribute in the properties of a folder or file. Access the attributes by right-clicking the folder or file and selecting Properties.

Files as well as folders in the NTFS file system can be compressed or uncompressed. Files and folders are managed independently, which means that a compressed folder could contain uncompressed files, and an uncompressed folder could contain compressed files.

Data compression is only available on NTFS partitions. If you copy or move a compressed folder or file to a FAT partition (or a floppy disk), Windows 2000 will automatically decompress the folder or file. Similarly, compressed NTFS files copied or moved to a FAT partition or floppy disk are automatically decompressed.

NOTE   Access to compressed files by DOS or Windows applications is transparent. For example, if you access a compressed file through Microsoft Word, the file will be decompressed automatically when it is opened, and then automatically compressed again when it is closed. You cannot have a folder or file compressed and encrypted at the same time.

Using the Compact Program

The Compact program is the command-line version of the compression attribute for files and folders in My Computer or Windows Explorer. Using the `compact` command, you can display and alter the compression of folders and files on NTFS volumes. It also displays the compression state of folders.

There are two reasons why you might want to use Compact instead of My Computer:

- You can use Compact in a batch script.

- If the system fails during compression or decompression, the file or folder is nevertheless marked as Compressed or Uncompressed. If the operation was not completed successfully, Compact forces the operation to complete in the background.

NOTE   Unlike My Computer, the Compact program does not prompt you to compress or expand files and subfolders when you set the compression state of a folder. Rather, the program automatically compresses or expands any files that are not already in the compression state that you set for the folder.

For more information about the Compact program, you can type **compact /?** at the command prompt.

Necessary Procedures

You can set the compression state of NTFS folders, and compress or decompress files, by using My Computer. When using My Computer, you can set the compression state of an NTFS folder without changing the compression state of existing files in that folder. If you have Read or Write permission, you can change the compression state locally or across a network. For the compress and decompress operations, you can select individual folders or files.

Compressing Folders or Files

Here are the steps to compress a folder or file:

1. Open Windows Explorer by selecting Start ➢ Programs ➢ Accessories ➢ Windows Explorer, or open My Computer by double-clicking the Desktop icon.

2. Navigate to the folder or file you wish to compress, and select it.

3. Right-click the folder or file to be compressed, and select Properties from the pop-up menu.

4. In the General tab of the Properties dialog box, click the Advanced button.

5. In the Advanced Attributes dialog box, check the Compress Contents to Save Disk Space check box. Then click the OK button.

6. If you are compressing a folder and it contains any files, the Confirm Attribute Changes dialog box appears. Specify whether you want to compress only this folder (Apply Changes to This Folder Only) or to also compress the subfolder and files within the folder (Apply Changes to This Folder, Subfolder, and Files). Then click the OK button.

To uncompress folders and files, repeat the foregoing steps, but uncheck the Compress Contents to Save Disk Space option in the Advanced Attributes dialog box.

TIP You can specify that compressed and uncompressed files be displayed in different colors. To do so, in Windows Explorer select Tools ➤ Folder Options ➤ View. Under Files and Folders, check the option to Display Compressed Files and Folders with an Alternate Color.

Exam Essentials

Know how to configure data compression.   Data compression is configured through file and folder attributes. This attribute can be accessed through either My Computer or Windows Explorer.

Know what happens to the file's compression attribute when a file is moved or copied.   Whenever a file is moved or copied, the data compression attribute changes to reflect the compression attribute of the target directory. The only exception is when the file is moved within the same partition; in this case, the file retains its original compression attribute.

Know when to use My Computer and when to use the compact command to compress a file or folder.   Normally, you would use My Computer or Windows Explorer to configure compression. The attributes portion of the file's or folder's Properties in these tools will give the maximum flexibility in designating which files or folders need compression. Use the compact command, on the other hand, when you want to enable compression as part of a batch file, or if you are having difficulties in using My Computer or Windows Explorer.

Key Term and Concept

data compression   The process of storing data in a form that takes less space.

Sample Questions

1. You want to compress your folder in a partition. Which of the following tools should you use?

   A. convert

   B. Windows Explorer

   C. Disk Administrator

   D. Disk Management

   Answer: B. In Windows Explorer, right-click the folder that you want to compress and select Properties. In the General tab, click the Advanced button. In the Advanced Attributes dialog box, turn on the Compress Contents to Save Disk Space option.

2. You move a compressed file from an uncompressed folder on the C: drive to an uncompressed folder on the D: drive. What compression attribute does the file now have?

   A. Nothing. A compressed file cannot exist within an uncompressed folder.

   B. It inherits the uncompressed attribute from the target directory.

   C. It inherits the uncompressed attribute from the original directory.

   D. It remains compressed.

   Answer: B. When a file is moved to different partition, the data compression attribute changes to reflect the compression attribute of the target directory.

▶ Monitor and configure disk quotas.

Suppose you have a server with an 18GB drive that is used mainly for users' home folders, and you start getting "out of disk space" error messages for that server. On closer inspection, you find that a single user has taken up 10GB of space by storing some multi-media files downloaded from the Internet. This type of problem can be avoided through the use of disk quotas.

This new feature of Windows 2000 gives network administrators control of how a user can utilize user space on the servers, and Microsoft will test your ability to use this feature. The exam questions will cover the tasks of planning for storing user data on the server, controlling individual users, and monitoring the quotas.

Critical Information

Disk quotas are used to specify how much disk space a user is allowed to consume on specific NTFS volumes. You can specify disk quotas for all users, or you can limit disk space on a per-user basis.

Before you administer disk quotas, you should be aware of the following:

- Disk quotas can be specified only for NTFS volumes.

- Disk quotas apply only at the volume level, even if the affected NTFS partitions reside on the same physical hard drive.

- Disk usage is calculated based on file and folder ownership. When a user creates, copies, or takes ownership of a file, that user is the owner of the file.

- When a user installs an application, the free space that the application will see is based on the disk quota availability, not the actual amount of free space on the volume.

- Disk quota space used is based on actual file size. There is no mechanism in NTFS to support or recognize file compression when used with disk quotas.

NOTE Disk quotas are not applicable to the Administrator account or to members of the Administrators group.

Configuring Disk Quotas

You configure disk quotas through the NTFS volume's Properties dialog box. You can access the volume Properties dialog box through either the Disk Management utility or from Windows Explorer, by right-clicking the drive letter and selecting Properties from the pop-up menu. In the volume's Properties dialog box, click the Quota tab, shown in Figure 5.1.

Notice the big traffic light icon in the Quota tab; it gives you a quick indicator of the disk quotas, as follows:

- Red light: Disk quotas are disabled.

- Yellow light: Windows 2000 Server is rebuilding disk quota information.

- Green light: The disk quota system is enabled and active.

When you first open the Quota tab, you'll see that disk quotas are disabled by default. The options that can be configured in this tab are described in Table 5.2.

FIGURE 5.1: The Computer Management window

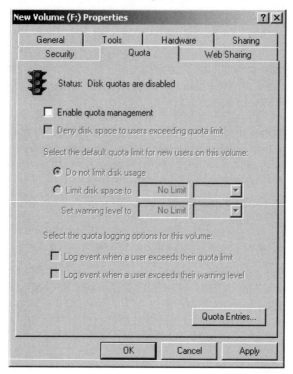

TABLE 5.2: Disk Quota Configuration Options

Disk Quota Option	Description
Enable Quota Management	Specifies whether quota management is enabled for the volume.
Deny Disk Space to Users Exceeding the Quota Limit	If enabled, specifies that users who exceed their disk quota won't be able to override it. Those users will receive "out of disk space" error messages.

TABLE 5.2:   Disk Quota Configuration Options *(continued)*

Disk Quota Option	Description
Select the Default Quota Limit for New Users on This Volume	Allows you to define quota limits for new users. Options include not limiting disk space, limiting disk space, and specifying warning levels.
Select the Quota Logging Options for This Volume	Specifies whether log events that relate to quotas will be recorded. You can enable log events for users exceeding quota limits and/or for users exceeding warning limits.

Setting Default Quotas for a Volume

When you set default quota limits for new users on a volume, the quotas apply only to users who have not yet created files on that volume. This means users who already own files or folders on the volume will be exempt from the quota policy.

To set the default quota limit for new users, access the Quota tab of the volume's Properties dialog box. Check the Enable Quota Management box. Click the Limit Disk Space To radio button and enter a number in the first box next to the option. In the drop-down list in the second box, specify whether disk space is limited by KB (kilobytes), MB (megabytes), GB (gigabytes), TB (terabytes), PB (petabytes), or EB (exabytes). If you choose to limit disk space, you can also set a warning level, so that users will be warned if they come close to reaching their limit.

TIP   If you want to apply disk quotas for all users, apply the quota when the volume is first created. That way, no users will have already created files on the volume and thus be exempt from the quota.

Setting an Individual's Quota

You can also set quotas for individual users. There are several reasons for setting quotas this way:

- You can allow unlimited disk space for a user who routinely updates your applications, while restricting other users.

- You can set warnings at lower levels for a user who routinely exceeds disk space.

- You can apply the quota to users who already had files on the volume before the quota was implemented and thus have been granted unlimited disk space.

To set an individual quota, go to the Quota tab of the volume's Properties and click the Quota Entries button in the bottom-right corner. This brings up the Quota Entries for New Volume window shown in Figure 5.2.

FIGURE 5.2: The Computer Management window

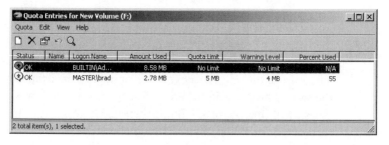

To modify a user's quota, double-click that user. You can then specify whether or not the user's disk space will be limited, the quota limit, and the warning level.

TIP You can also modify the quotas of several users at once. Ctrl+click to highlight several users and select Quota ➢ Properties.

Monitoring Disk Quotas

If you implement disk quotas, you will want to monitor disk quotas on a regular basis. Monitoring allows you to check the disk usage by all the users who own files on the volume with the quotas applied.

NOTE It is especially important to monitor quotas if you have specified that disk space should be denied to users who exceed their quota limit. Otherwise, some users may not be able to get their work done.

You monitor disk quotas through the Quota Entries window, shown in Figure 5.2, which appears when you click the Quota Entries button in the Quota tab of the volume's Properties dialog box. The dialog box shows the following information:

- One of the following icons representing the status of the user's disk quota:

Icon	Indication
A green arrow in a dialog bubble	The status is OK.
An exclamation point in a yellow triangle	The warning threshold has been exceeded.
An exclamation point in a red circle	The user threshold has been exceeded.

- The name and logon name of the user who has stored files on the volume

- The amount of disk space the user has consumed on the volume

- The user's quota limit

- The user's warning level

- The percent of disk space this user has consumed in relation to their disk quota

Necessary Procedures

Disk quotas are a new feature in NTFS that provide more precise control of network-based storage. Quotas are implemented on a per-volume basis and enable both hard and soft storage limits to be implemented on a per-user basis. The following procedure shows you how to implement user quotas for a local disk through Windows Explorer.

Setting User Quotas

User quotas for a volume are set as a property of the volume, through Windows Explorer.

1. Select Start ➤ Programs ➤ Accessories ➤ Windows Explorer.

2. In Windows Explorer, expand My Computer. Right-click Local Disk (D:) and select Properties.

3. In the Local Disk Properties dialog box, open the Quota tab.

4. Check the Enable Quota Management check box.

5. Click the radio button for Limit Disk Space To and use the adjacent boxes to specify the amount for the limit. In the Set Warning Level To line just below, specify a value less than the limit.

6. Click the Apply button and then the OK button.

7. If you currently have data stored on the volume, you'll see a Disk Quota message box specifying that the volume will need to be rescanned. Click the OK button.

To establish quota limits for the individual users on a volume, click the Quota Entries button in the volume's Properties dialog box.

Exam Essentials

Know how to monitor disk quotas.   Monitoring established quotas allows you to check the disk usage by all users who own files on the volume with the quotas applied.

Know when the volume's default quotas apply to users.   Default disk quotas apply to users who have not stored files on the disk where the quotas are established. Existing users are exempt from the disk quotas.

Know when to apply disk quotas for individual users.   You'll want to set individual disk quotas when some users have different requirements for disk access; when you want to establish warning levels for specific users; or when you want to apply quotas to users who have existing files on the volume.

Key Term and Concept

disk quotas   Settings that specify how much disk space a user is allowed on specific NTFS volumes.

Sample Questions

1. You want to impose individual disk quotas on certain users who continually abuse the storage on your server. Where can you configure these individual disk quotas?

   A. On any folder in a FAT partition

   B. On a FAT partition or volume

   C. On any folder in an NTFS partition

   D. On an NTFS partition or volume

   Answer: D. Disk quotas are set at the partition or volume level on partitions or volumes that have been formatted with NTFS. Quotas cannot be applied at any other level.

2. You have Windows 2000 Server running and are having a problem with users storing large files on the server. You want to impose disk quotas, but you realize that the volume storing users' files is a FAT32 volume, and in order to use quotas you must have an NTFS partition. What command or utility can be used to change the partition to NTFS without losing any data?

A. ntfsconv

B. convert

C. Disk Administrator

D. Disk Manager

Answer: B. You can't upgrade a partition to NTFS through any of the GUI utilities. You must use the convert command-line utility.

Recover from disk failures.

Windows 2000 Server offers many tools to maintain and troubleshoot your system. If you're having trouble with your disk devices or volumes, you can use the Windows 2000 Check Disk utility as a helpful tool after a failure. This utility detects bad sectors, attempts to fix file system errors, and scans for and attempts to recover bad sectors.

As a Windows 2000 certified professional candidate, you'll be tested on your knowledge of how to recover from disk or volume failures. This includes your ability to understand and use the Windows 2000 Check Disk utility to diagnose these failures.

Critical Information

File system errors can be caused from a corrupt file system or from hardware errors. If you have software errors, the Check Disk utility may be able to help you find them. If you have excessive hardware errors, you should replace your disk drive. There is no way to fix hardware errors through software. The Check Disk utility scans for and repairs physical problems such as bad blocks, as well as logical structure errors such as lost clusters, cross-linked files, and directory errors, on volumes on the hard disk.

Once file errors are discovered, the Check Disk utility can automatically fix the file errors or attempt to recover data from the bad sectors. This is accomplished by choosing the options to Automatically Fix File System Errors, and Scan for and Attempt Recovery of Bad Sectors, when Check Disk is started.

To access the Check Disk utility, open Control Panel and select Administrative Tools, then Computer Management. Expand the Storage folder to see the Disk Management utility. In the Disk Management utility, right-click the partition or volume you want to check and choose Properties. Open the Tools tab of the volume Properties dialog box, and click the Check Now button. This brings up the Check Disk dialog box containing options to Automatically Fix File System Errors, and Scan for and Attempt Recovery of Bad Sectors. Check the options you want and click the Start button.

NOTE   If the system cannot gain exclusive access to a partition, the Check Disk operation will be executed the next time the system is restarted. You cannot gain exclusive access to partitions or volumes that contain the system or boot partition.

WARNING   Back up key data files before performing any disk repair operations. Do not run any disk tools that are not specifically designed for Windows 2000. Earlier versions of disk repair tools may not work properly. To prevent possible data loss, use a disk tool such as Check Disk that is specifically designed for Windows 2000.

Necessary Procedures

You start the Check Disk utility from the Disk Management tool. Follow these steps to set Check Disk options:

1. Select Start ➢ Settings ➢ Control Panel ➢ Administrative Tools. Expand Computer Management, then Storage, then Disk Management.

2. Right-click the volume that you want to check, and choose Properties.

3. In the Properties dialog box, click the Tools tab, then click the Check Now button.

4. In the Check Disk dialog box, enable the options that you want to use for your Check Disk operation. Then click the Start button.

Exam Essentials

Know when to use the Check Disk utility. The Check Disk utility is used when you suspect that physical problems such as bad blocks exist on the hard disk; and when you think there may be logical structure errors such as lost clusters, cross-linked files, and directory errors on the volumes of the hard disk.

Key Term and Concept

Check Disk utility A utility in Control Panel ➢ Administrative Tools that scans for and repairs physical problems or logical errors on hard disk volumes.

Sample Questions

1. Which of the following problems can Check Disk help you correct? Choose all that apply.

   A. Lost clusters

   B. Cross-linked files

   C. Directory errors

   D. Logical structure errors

   Answer: A, B, C, D. The Check Disk utility scans for and repairs physical problems such as bad blocks, as well as logical structure errors such as lost clusters, cross-linked files, and directory errors, on volumes on the hard disk.

2. You have detected file system errors on the system partition. When will the error be fixed by Check Disk?

   A. Never. Files on the system partition cannot be fixed with the Check Disk utility.

   B. Immediately.

   C. Files will be fixed the next time the system is restarted.

   D. Files will be fixed during the emergency repair process.

   Answer: C. The Check Disk utility can only fix the file problems when it has exclusive access to the files. This occurs the next time the system is restarted.

Chapter

6

Configuring and Troubleshooting Windows 2000 Network Connections

---

MICROSOFT EXAM OBJECTIVES COVERED IN THIS CHAPTER:

Microsoft Windows 2000's Network and Dial-up Connections feature provides connectivity between your computer and another computer, a network, or the Internet. You can configure settings to reach local or remote network resources or functions.

Five types of connections can be created in the Network and Dial-up Connections folder. A permanent local area connection is automatically created for each network adapter that Plug and Play detects. You can also create connections dynamically, including dial-up, virtual private network (VPN), direct, and incoming connections. Each connection in the Network and Dial-up Connections folder contains a set of settings that create the link between your computer and another computer or network. These connections (except for the local area connections) are maintained in the Network and Dial-up Connections folder. Performing a task such as modifying a network protocol is as easy as right-clicking on a connection's icon.

Additionally, this chapter covers the primary network protocols TCP/IP, NWLINK, and NetBEUI, and the principal network services DHCP, DNS and WINS. The Terminal Services objectives have been added to this chapter because this feature allows thin-client technologies to be used on your network. You will find that Terminal Services gives you the potential to expand your network across the WAN without the usual slowdown in performance.

This section of the exam always carries a lot of weight. Skill in managing networking, after all, is the goal of the MCSE. This chapter includes the information and procedures necessary to help you understand and utilize the powerful networking tools in Windows 2000 Server.

Install, configure, and troubleshoot shared access.

With the Shared Access feature of Network and Dial-Up Connections, you can use Windows 2000 to connect your home network or small office network to the Internet. By enabling shared access on the computer that uses the dial-up connection, you are providing several services for all the computers on your small network: network address translation, addressing, and name.

Shared access is a valuable function for small networks, but the Microsoft certification exam will cover this topic at the definition level only. You need not have a thorough understanding of the mechanics of Shared Access. This section lightly covers the topic in general, along with the necessary procedure for implementing shared access on a network connection.

Critical Information

Shared access is intended for use in a small office or home office in which the network configuration and the Internet connection are managed by the Windows 2000-based computer on which the shared connection resides. It is assumed that this computer is the only Internet connection on the small network, is the only gateway to the Internet, and sets up all internal network addresses.

If your home office users need to gain access to a corporate network that is connected to the Internet by a tunnel server from a shared access network, they need to create a virtual private network (VPN) connection. This connection tunnels from the computer on the shared access network to the corporate tunnel server on the Internet. The VPN connection is authenticated and secure. Creating the tunneled connection allocates proper IP addresses, DNS server addresses, and WINS (Windows Internet Name Service) server addresses for the corporate network. VPNs are discussed at length throughout this chapter.

NOTE To enable shared access, you must have administrative rights.

In a network with shared access, you may need to configure programs and services to work properly across the Internet. Services that you provide must be configured so they can be accessed by Internet users.

WARNING Do not use shared access in a network with other Windows 2000 Server domain controllers, DNS servers, gateways, DHCP servers, or computers configured for static IP addresses. When you enable shared access, the network adapter connected to the home or small office network is given a new, static IP address configuration. TCP/IP connections existing on the shared access computer are lost, and must be reestablished if they'll be needed.

Necessary Procedures

The following procedure tells you how to enable shared access on a network connection:

1. From the Start menu, select Settings and then Network and Dial-Up Connections.

2. Right-click the connection you want to share, and then click Properties.

3. On the Sharing tab, select the check box to Enable Shared Access for this Connection.

4. If you want the connection to dial automatically when another computer on the network attempts to use external resources, select the check box to Enable On-demand Dialing.

Exam Essentials

Know the benefits of using shared access. By enabling shared access on a computer that has access to the Internet, you can provide network access translation, addressing, and name resolution services for all the computers on the network.

Know how to enable shared access. Shared access is enabled using the Network and Dial-Up Connections icon in Control Panel.

Key Term and Concept

shared access Internet access for all the computers on a small network through a single connection point.

Sample Question

1. You are the network administrator for a small network and want to provide Internet access for all the computers on the network. What is the simplest method of providing the access?

A. Implement a Proxy Server.

B. Install a modem on each computer and configure each computer for Internet access.

C. Use the Shared Access feature of Network and Dial-Up Connections.

D. Install a DNS server.

Answer: C. The Shared Access feature of the Network and Dial-Up Connections on a Windows 2000 computer can give the rest of the network Internet access.

Install, configure, and troubleshoot a virtual private network (VPN).

Microsoft Windows 2000 includes extensive support for virtual private networking technology, which takes advantage of the connectivity of the Internet to connect remote clients and remote offices. As a network professional, you should understand the important uses of virtual private networking for your organization, and the underlying technologies that make VPNs work. In conjunction with this knowledge, you should already be familiar with TCP/IP, IP routing, and the Windows 2000 Remote Access Service (RAS).

The exam will test, in particular, your knowledge of what elements make up VPN connections, the different types of connections, and how to troubleshoot problems related to VPN connections. The Necessary Procedures include the steps to set up a VPN.

Critical Information

Virtual private networks (VPNs) enable VPN clients to access VPN servers through a private network or through the Internet.

A virtual private network (VPN) is the extension of a private network that encompasses links across shared or public networks like the Internet. The VPN allows you to send data between two computers across a shared or public internetwork in a manner that emulates the properties of a point-to-point private link. Configuring and creating the VPN is known as *virtual private networking*.

To emulate a point-to-point link, data is encapsulated (wrapped) with a header that provides routing information allowing it to traverse the shared or public internetwork to reach its endpoint. To emulate a private link, the data being sent is encrypted for confidentiality. Packets that are intercepted on the shared or public network are indecipherable without the encryption keys. The link in which the private data is encapsulated and encrypted is known as a *VPN connection*.

A VPN server is installed and configured through the Routing and Remote Access utility, in a process similar to that for installing an RAS server.

Elements of a VPN Connection

The *VPN server* is a computer that accepts VPN connections from VPN clients. A VPN server can provide a remote access VPN connection or a router-to-router VPN connection. For more information, see "VPN Connection Types" later in this section.

The *VPN client* is a computer that initiates a VPN connection to a VPN server. A VPN client can be an individual computer that obtains a remote access VPN connection, or a router that obtains a router-to-router VPN connection. Microsoft Windows NT 4.0, Windows 2000, Microsoft Windows 95, and Microsoft Windows 98–based computers can create remote access VPN connections to a Windows 2000–based VPN server. Microsoft Windows 2000 Server and Microsoft Windows NT Server 4.0–based computers running the Routing and Remote Access service (RRAS) can create router-to-router VPN connections to a Windows 2000–based VPN server. VPN clients can also be any non-Microsoft Point-to-Point Tunneling Protocol (PPTP) client or any Layer Two Tunneling Protocol (L2TP) client using IPSec.

The *tunnel* is the portion of the connection in which your data is encapsulated.

The *VPN connection* is the portion of the connection in which your data is encrypted. For secure VPN connections, the data is encrypted and encapsulated along the same portion of the connection.

NOTE   It is possible to create a tunnel and send the data through the tunnel without encryption. This is not a VPN connection, however, because the private data is sent across a shared or public network in an unencrypted and easily readable form.

Tunneling protocols are communication standards used to manage tunnels and encapsulate private data. (Data that is tunneled must also be encrypted on a VPN connection.) Windows 2000 includes the PPTP and L2TP tunneling protocols.

Tunneled data is data that is usually sent across a private point-to-point link.

The *transit internetwork* is the shared or public internetwork crossed by the encapsulated data. For Windows 2000, the transit internetwork is always an IP internetwork. The transit internetwork can be the Internet or a private IP-based intranet.

VPN Connection Types

Creating the VPN is very similar to establishing a point-to-point connection using dial-up networking and demand-dial routing procedures. There are two types of VPN connections.

- **Remote Access VPN Connection:** A remote access VPN connection is made by a remote access client, or a single user computer, that connects to a private network. The VPN server provides access to the resources of the VPN server or to the entire network to which the VPN server is attached. The packets sent across the VPN connection originate at the remote access client. The remote access client (the VPN client) authenticates itself to the remote access server (the VPN server) and, for mutual authentication, the server authenticates itself to the client.

- **Router-to-Router VPN Connection:** A router-to-router VPN connection is made by a router and connects two portions of a private network. The VPN server provides a routed connection to the network to which the VPN server is attached. On a router-to-router VPN connection, the packets sent from either router across the VPN connection typically do not originate at the routers. The calling router (the VPN client) authenticates itself to the answering router (the VPN server); for mutual authentication, the answering router authenticates itself to the calling router.

Troubleshooting VPNs

Several tools are available to help you gather information about the source of VPN problems.

Unreachability Reason

When a demand-dial interface fails to make a connection, the interface is left in an unreachable state. In the Routing and Remote Access snap-in, right-click the failed connection demand-dial interface, and then select Unreachability Reason to obtain more information about why the interface was unable to connect. Demand-dial interfaces most often fail because there are no more ports available for the demand-dial interface; the RRAS is paused; the demand-dial interface is disabled; or dial-out hours are preventing the connection.

Event Logging

On the Event Logging tab in the properties of a VPN server, there are four levels of logging. Select the option to log the maximum amount of information, and then try the connection again. When the connection fails, check the system event log for events logged during the connection process. After you're done viewing remote access events, return to the Event Logging tab and select the option to log errors and warnings; this choice conserves system resources.

Tracing

The tracing feature of RRAS writes (to a file) the sequence of programming functions called during a process. In the Routing and Remote Access snap-in Properties, you enable PPP tracing by selecting Enable Point-to-Point Protocol (PPP) Logging from the Event Logging tab. When you want to gather programming calls and actual PPP packets, enable the tracing feature for remote access and VPN components and then try the connection again. After you have viewed the traced information, reset the tracing settings back to their default values to conserve system resources.

Tracing information can be complex and very detailed. Most of the time this information is useful only to Microsoft support professionals or to network administrators who are very experienced with the RRAS. Tracing information can be saved as files and sent to Microsoft Support for analysis.

Network Monitor

Use Network Monitor, a packet capture and analysis tool, to view the traffic sent between a VPN server and VPN client during the VPN connection process and during data transfer. To install Network Monitor, run the Add/Remove Windows Components Wizard, select Management and Monitoring Tools, and click Details. Once Network Monitor is installed, it is available in Administrative Tools.

NOTE You cannot interpret the encrypted portions of VPN traffic with Network Monitor.

Necessary Procedures

Here are the steps to install a Virtual Private Network (VPN):

1. Select Start ➢ Programs ➢ Administrative Tools ➢ Routing and Remote Access.

2. When the Routing and Remote Access (RRAS) utility starts, right-click your server and select Configure and Enable Routing and Remote Access from the pop-up menu.

3. When the Routing and Remote Access Server Wizard starts, click the Next button to continue.

4. In the Common Configurations dialog box, select the Virtual Private Network (VPN) Server option and click the Next button.

5. The Remote Client Protocols dialog box appears next. You can select the No, I Need to Add Protocols option and specify other protocols. Or you can accept the default selection (Yes, All of the Required Protocols Are on This List). Click Next to proceed.

6. In the Internet Connection dialog box, select the Internet connection that will be used by the VPN server. Click the Next button.

7. Next up is the IP Address Assignment dialog box. You can specify that IP addresses will be automatically assigned or that IP

addresses will be assigned from a specified range of addresses. In this example, IP addresses will be assigned automatically. Click the Next button.

8. The Managing Multiple Remote Access Servers dialog box appears. This dialog box allows you to specify whether you will install a RADIUS server that will be used to manage remote access servers centrally. In this example, a RADIUS server is not installed. Click the Next button.

9. In the final dialog box, Completing the Routing and Remote Access Server Setup Wizard, click the Finish button.

Exam Essentials

Know how VPNs work.   A VPN is the extension of a private network that encompasses links across shared networks or the Internet. The link is emulated by encapsulating the data with a header providing routing information along its path on the Internet.

Know the tunneling protocols.   Tunneling on a Windows 2000 computer is done by using either the PPTP or the L2TP tunneling protocol.

Know where to look for VPN information.   Trace records and event logging are two ways to gather information about the VPN. In addition, by right-clicking on the interface in Routing and Remote Access snap-in, you can select Unreachability Reason to obtain more information on why the connection failed.

Key Terms and Concepts

tunnel   The portion of the connection in which your data is encapsulated

tunneling protocols   Communication standards used to manage tunnels and encapsulate data. Windows 2000 uses PPTP and L2TP.

virtual private network (VPN)   An extension of a private network that encompasses links across shared or public networks like the Internet.

VPN client   A computer that initiates a VPN connection to a VPN server.

VPN connection   The portion of the connection that is encapsulated and encrypted.

VPN server   A computer that accepts VPN connections from VPN clients.

Sample Questions

1. You are the administrator of a network that has many users who need to connect to the network from remote locations. You are trying to avoid additional costs. All of these employees have Internet access. What can you do to give the employees access to the network?

   A. Grant dial-up access to the users.

   B. Implement a VPN.

   C. Implement a Proxy Server.

   D. Nothing can be done to allow these users access.

   Answer: B. A VPN will allow access to the network without additional costs. The users will then access the network via the Internet.

2. You are the network administrator. You have implemented a VPN. Your users are complaining about problems while connecting. Where can you view information that will help you troubleshoot the problem? Select all that apply.

   A. Access the Unreachability Reason.

   B. Look at the Event Logging tab of the VPN's Properties.

   C. Enable tracing.

   D. Use Network Monitor to capture the packets sent between the VPN Server and VPN client.

   Answer: A, B, C, and D. All of these options will give you information about the VPN connection.

Install, configure, and troubleshoot network protocols.

Windows 2000 has provided several network protocols to facilitate communication with many different network operating systems. Your success as a network professional will be greatly enhanced by a good understanding of the capabilities and features that these network protocols have to offer.

Knowing their features will allow you to select the particular network protocol that is most appropriate for a given situation. TCP/IP, of course, offers connectivity to many different network operating systems and is quickly becoming the networking standard. In addition, there are many other protocols with their own characteristics that may make them suitable for a given situation. The popularity and ease of use of Novell's NetWare in many networks makes NWLink another protocol that you need to be familiar with.

Connectivity is covered very heavily on Microsoft's certification exams. Your knowledge of connectivity begins with understanding how the protocols are used and configured to meet the various circumstances you'll encounter as a network professional. This section covers these fundamentals, and gives procedures for installing and configuring the primary protocols used in networking.

Critical Information

Network protocols function at the Network and Transport layers of the OSI model. These protocols are responsible for transporting data across an internetwork. You can mix and match among the following network protocols supported by Windows 2000 Server:

- TCP/IP, the most commonly used protocol, installed on Windows 2000 Server computers by default

- NWLink IPX/SPX/NetBIOS, used to connect to Novell NetWare networks

- NetBEUI, a nonroutable protocol useful for small networks

- AppleTalk, used to support Apple Macintosh computers; a fully functional, routable protocol

- DLC (Data Link Control), used primarily for printers and connections to IBM environments

Using TCP/IP

TCP/IP (Transmission Control Protocol/Internet Protocol) is nearly ubiquitous among the networking community. Originally developed in the 1970s for the Department of Defense (DoD) as a way of connecting dissimilar networks, TCP/IP has become an industry standard.

On a clean installation of Windows 2000 Server, TCP/IP is installed by default. This protocol has the following benefits:

- It is the most commonly used protocol and is supported by almost all network operating systems. It is the required protocol for Internet access.

- TCP/IP is scalable for use in small and large networks. In large networks, TCP/IP provides routing services.

- TCP/IP is designed to be fault tolerant and is able to dynamically reroute packets if network links become unavailable (assuming alternate paths exist).

- Companion protocols such as Dynamic Host Configuration Protocol (DHCP) and Domain Name System (DNS) offer advanced functionality.

Configuring TCP/IP

As explained in the following paragraphs, TCP/IP requires an IP address and a subnet mask. You can also configure many other optional parameters, such as the default gateway, DNS server, and Windows Internet Name Service (WINS) settings. Depending on your network setup, TCP/IP configuration is done either manually or dynamically.

IP ADDRESS

The *IP address,* which uniquely identifies your computer on the network, is a 32-bit address of four fields separated by periods. Part of the IP address is used to identify your network address, and part is used to identify the host (or local) computer's address.

If you use the Internet, you should register your IP addresses with one of the Internet registration sites. There are three main classes of IP addresses. Depending on the class you use, various parts of the address show the network portion of the address and the host address.

TIP   You can find more information about Internet registration at InterNIC's Web site, www.internic.net.

Table 6.1 shows the three classes of network addresses and the number of networks and hosts that are available for each network class.

TABLE 6.1:   IP Class Assignments

Network Class	Address Range of First Field	Number of Networks Available	Number of Host Nodes Supported
A	1–126	126	16,777,214
B	128–191	16,384	65,534
C	192–223	2,097,152	254

SUBNET MASK

The *subnet mask* is used to specify which part of the IP address is the network address and which part is the host address. By default, the following subnet masks are applied:

Class A   255.0.0.0

Class B   255.255.0.0

Class C   255.255.255.0

By using 255, you are selecting the octet or octets (or in some cases, a piece of an octet) used to identify the network address.

DEFAULT GATEWAY

You configure a *default gateway* if the network contains routers. A router is a device that connects two or more network segments together. Routers function at the Network layer of the OSI model.

You can configure a Windows 2000 server to act as a router by installing two or more network cards (NICs) in the server, attaching each NIC to a different network segment, and then configuring each NIC for the segment to which it will attach. You can also use third-party routers, which typically offer more features than Windows 2000 servers configured as routers.

You configure the computers on each segment to point to the IP address of the NIC router that is attached to their network segment.

DNS SERVERS

DNS servers are used to resolve host names to IP addresses. This makes it easier for people to access domain hosts. For example, the IP address for the White House is 198.137.240.91. Easier to remember is the host name of the White House: `www.whitehouse.gov`. When you access the Internet and type in `www.whitehouse.gov`, DNS servers resolve the host name to the proper IP address.

If you don't have access to a properly configured DNS server, you can configure a *HOSTS file* for your computer. A HOSTS file contains the mappings of IP addresses to the domain hosts that you need to access. DNS servers are discussed in greater detail in the later section "Using DNS."

WINS SERVERS

WINS servers, also discussed more in a later section, resolve *Network Basic Input/Output System (NetBIOS)* names to IP addresses. Windows 2000 uses NetBIOS names in addition to host names to identify network computers. This is mainly for backward compatibility with Windows NT 4.0, which used this addressing scheme extensively. When you attempt to access a computer using the NetBIOS name, the computer must be able to resolve the NetBIOS name to an IP address. This address resolution can be accomplished through a broadcast (if the computer you are trying to reach is on the same network segment); through a WINS server; or through an *LMHOSTS file*, which is a static mapping of IP addresses to NetBIOS computer names.

Manual IP Configuration

You can manually configure IP if you know your IP address and subnet mask. If you're using optional components such as a default gateway or a DNS server, you also need to know the IP addresses of the computers that host these services.

Advanced Configuration

Clicking the Advanced button in the Internet Protocol (TCP/IP) dialog box opens the Advanced TCP/IP Settings dialog box. From here, you can configure advanced DNS and WINS settings.

ADVANCED DNS SETTINGS

You can configure additional DNS servers that can be used for name resolution and other advanced DNS settings. The settings for these servers are in the DNS tab of the Advanced TCP/IP Settings dialog box, as described in Table 6.2.

TABLE 6.2: Advanced DNS TCP/IP Settings

Setting/Option	Description
DNS Server Addresses, in Order of Use	The DNS servers that are used to resolve DNS queries. Use the arrow buttons on the right side of the list box to move the servers up or down in the list.
Append Primary and Connection Specific DNS Suffixes	Method by which unqualified domain names are resolved by DNS.
Append Parent Suffixes of the Primary DNS Suffix	Specifies whether name resolution includes the parent suffix for the primary domain DNS suffix, up to the second level of the domain name.

TABLE 6.2: Advanced DNS TCP/IP Settings *(continued)*

Setting/Option	Description
Append These DNS Suffixes (in order)	The DNS suffixes that will be used to attempt unqualified name resolution.
DNS Suffix for This Connection	The DNS suffix for the connection. If this value is configured by a DHCP server and you specify a DNS suffix, it will override the value set by DHCP.
Register This Connection's Address in DNS	Specifies that the computer will try to register its address dynamically using the computer name that was specified through the Network Identification tab of the System Properties dialog box (accessed through the System icon in Control Panel).
Use This Connection's DNS Suffix in DNS Registration	Specifies that when the computer registers automatically with the DNS server, the computer should use the combination of the computer name and the DNS suffix.

ADVANCED WINS SETTINGS

You can configure advanced WINS options through the WINS tab in the Advanced TCP/IP Settings dialog box. The options in this dialog box are described in Table 6.3.

Dynamic IP Configuration

Dynamic IP configuration assumes that you have a DHCP (Dynamic Host Configuration Protocol) server on your network (see "Using DHCP" later in this chapter). DHCP servers are configured to provide DHCP clients with all their IP configuration information

TABLE 6.3:   Advanced WINS TCP/IP Settings Options

Option	Description
WINS Addresses, in Order of Use	The WINS servers that are used to resolve WINS queries. Use the arrow buttons on the right side of the list box to move the servers up or down in the list.
Enable LMHOSTS Lookup	Specifies whether an LMHOSTS file can be used for name resolution. If you configure this option, you can use the Import LMHOSTS button to import an LMHOSTS file to the computer.
Enable NetBIOS over TCP/IP	Allows you to use statically config-ured IP addresses so that the com-puter is able to communicate with pre–Windows 2000 computers.
Disable NetBIOS over TCP/IP	Allows you to disable NetBIOS over TCP/IP. Do this only if your network includes only Windows 2000 clients or only DNS-enabled clients.
Use NetBIOS Settings from the DHCP Server	Specifies that the computer should obtain its NetBIOS and WINS set-tings from the DHCP server.

automatically. When TCP/IP is installed on a Windows 2000 Server computer, the computer is by default configured for dynamic IP con-figuration.

Testing IP Configuration

After you've configured IP, you can test the IP configuration by using the IPCONFIG and PING commands.

The IPCONFIG command displays your IP configuration. Table 6.4 lists some of the command switches that can be used with IPCONFIG.

TABLE 6.4: IPCONFIG Switches

Switch	Description
/all	Shows verbose information about your IP configuration, including your computer's physical address, the DNS server you are using, and whether you are using DHCP
/release	Releases an address that has been assigned through DHCP
/renew	Renews an address through DHCP

The PING command is used to send an Internet Control Message Protocol (ICMP) echo request and echo reply to verify if the remote computer is available. PING is useful for verifying connectivity between two hosts. If you're having trouble connecting to a host on another network, you'd use PING to verify that a valid communication path exists. You'd ping the following addresses:

- The loopback address, 127.0.0.1

- The local computer's IP address (you can verify this with IPCONFIG)

- The local router's (default gateway's) IP address

- The remote computer's IP address

If PING fails to get a reply from any of these addresses, you have a starting point for troubleshooting the connection error.

NWLink IPX/SPX/NetBIOS

NWLink IPX/SPX/NetBIOS Compatible Transport is Microsoft's implementation of the Novell Internetwork Packet Exchange/ Sequenced Packet Exchange (IPX/SPX) protocol stack. The Windows 2000 implementation of the IPX/SPX protocol stack adds NetBIOS support. NWLink is easy to install and configure.

The main function of NWLink is to act as a transport protocol to route packets through internetworks. By itself, NWLink does not allow you to access NetWare File and Print Services. However, it does provide a method of transporting the data across the network. If you want to access NetWare File and Print Services, you need to install both NWLink and Client Services for NetWare (CSNW) on your Windows 2000 client, or you need to install Gateway Services for NetWare (GSNW) on your Windows 2000 Server computer. CSNW and GSNW are software packages that work at the upper layers of the OSI model to allow access to NetWare File and Print Services.

Configuring NWLink IPX/SPX

The only options that you need to configure for NWLink are the internal network number and the frame type. Normally, you leave both settings at their default values.

Usually, the *internal network number* identifies NetWare file servers. It's also used if you're running File and Print Services for NetWare or using IPX routing.

The *frame type* specifies how the data is packaged for transmission over the network. If the computers using NWLink use different frame types, they cannot communicate with each other. By default, the frame type is set to Auto Detect, which will attempt to automatically choose a compatible frame type for your network.

NetBEUI

NetBEUI, for NetBIOS Extended User Interface, was developed in the mid-1980s to connect workgroups that were running the OS/2 and LAN Manager operating systems. The NetBEUI protocol offers the following advantages:

- It is easy to install.

- There are no configuration requirements.

- It has self-tuning capabilities.

- It has less overhead than TCP/IP and IPX/SPX and thus offers better performance.

- It uses less memory than TCP/IP and IPX/SPX.

The main disadvantage of the NetBEUI protocol is that it is not routable, so you cannot use it in networks that have more than one network segment. Also, NetBEUI is not as commonly accepted as the TCP/IP protocol.

Managing Network Bindings

Bindings enable communication between your network adapter and the network protocols that are installed. If you have multiple network protocols installed on your computer, you can improve performance by binding the most common protocols higher in the binding order.

To configure network bindings, access the Network and Dial-up Connections window and then select Advanced ➢ Advanced Settings from the menu bar. The Adapters and Binding tab of the Advanced Settings dialog box appears. For each local area connection, if there are multiple protocols listed, you can use the arrow buttons on the right side of the dialog box to reposition the protocols in the binding order.

Necessary Procedures

The procedures offered here tell you how to install and configure, where possible, the most commonly used network protocols. Since TCP/IP is installed by default, we'll cover the steps for manually configuring it.

Setting Manual IP Configuration

If you want to manually configure IP, take the following steps:

1. From the Desktop, right-click My Network Places and choose Properties.

2. Right-click Local Area Connection and choose Properties.

3. In the Local Area Connection Properties dialog box, highlight Internet Protocol (TCP/IP) and click the Properties button.

4. The Internet Protocol (TCP/IP) Properties dialog box appears. Select the Use the Following IP Address radio button.

5. In the appropriate text boxes, specify the IP address, subnet mask, and default gateway (optional) that you want to use.

6. Optionally, select the radio button for Use the Following DNS Server Addresses and specify a preferred and alternate DNS server in the corresponding text boxes.

7. Click the OK button to save your settings and close the dialog box.

Setting Dynamic IP Configuration

If your computer is configured for manual IP configuration and you want to use dynamic IP configuration, take the following steps:

1. From the Desktop, right-click My Network Places and choose Properties.

2. Right-click Local Area Connection and choose Properties.

3. In the Local Area Connection Properties dialog box, highlight Internet Protocol (TCP/IP) and click the Properties button.

4. The Internet Protocol (TCP/IP) Properties dialog box appears. Choose the Obtain an IP Address Automatically radio button. Then click the OK button.

Installing and Configuring NWLink IPX/SPX/ NetBIOS

1. From the Desktop, right-click My Network Places and choose Properties.

2. Right-click Local Area Connection and choose Properties.

3. In the Local Area Connection Properties dialog box, click the Install button.

4. In the Select Network Component Type dialog box, highlight Protocol and click the Add button.

5. The Select Network Protocol dialog box appears next. Select NWLink IPX/SPX/NetBIOS Compatible Transport Protocol from the list. Then click the OK button.

6. When you close the dialog box, the NWLink IPX/SPX/NetBIOS Compatible Transport Protocol Properties dialog box automatically appears. In this dialog box you can configure your internal network number and frame type.

Installing NetBEUI

1. From the Desktop, right-click My Network Places and select Properties.

2. Right-click Local Area Connection and select Properties.

3. In the Local Area Connection Properties dialog box, click the Install button.

4. In the Select Network Component Type dialog box, highlight Protocol and click the Add button.

5. In the Select Network Protocol dialog box, choose NetBEUI Protocol from the list and click the OK button.

Exam Essentials

Know the role of TCP/IP.   This nearly universal protocol is supported by almost all network operating systems. It is scalable to allow for growth and provides fault tolerance to the network.

Know how to configure TCP/IP.   TCP/IP requires that you configure the IP address and a subnet mask. In a subnetted environment, you also have to provide the IP address of the default gateway. There are several other options that are configured if applicable, including DNS and WINS settings.

Know the address ranges for each TCP/IP network class.   The network class determines the number of hosts available for each network. Class A networks range from 1 to 126; Class B networks range from 128 to 191; and Class C networks range from 192 to 223.

Know the default subnet masks for each TCP/IP network class.
The subnet mask is used to distinguish between the network ID and the host ID in the IP address. The subnet mask for Class A is 255.0.0.0, for Class B is 255.255.0.0, and for Class C is 255.255.255.0.

Know how to make a Windows 2000 Server operate as a TCP/IP router.   A Windows 2000 Server can work as a router if you install two or more NICs; attach each NIC to a different network segment; configure each NIC with unique IP information for the segment; and enable IP routing.

Know how to display TCP/IP information.   To view the TCP/IP configuration information, you can use the IPCONFIG command. This will display the IP configuration for each network adapter in the computer.

Know how to test your TCP/IP configuration.   Your IP configuration can be tested using the PING command. You begin testing by pinging your loopback address of 127.0.0.1. Next, ping your local computer's IP address. Then ping the IP address of the default gateway. Finally, ping the IP address of a remote computer. The point where this process fails indicates where the problem lies.

Know what NWLink is.   NWLink is Microsoft's implementation of Novell's Internetwork Packet eXchange/Sequenced Packet eXchange (IPX/SPX) protocol stack. This is an easily implemented and configured network protocol.

Know how to troubleshoot NWLink.   NetWare server versions use various frame types. These frame types are unable to intercommunicate, however. Windows 2000 Server is capable of using more than one frame type. You may have to manually set the frame types you want the Windows 2000 Server to use.

Know what NetBEUI is.   NetBEUI is a small, self-tuning network protocol. There are no configuration options to set. It also has very little overhead. Its main disadvantage is that it's not routable.

Understand how bindings affect the network.   Bindings govern the order in which protocols are used. You want the protocol that is most frequently used listed first. Failure to do so results in slower network responses.

Key Terms and Concepts

bindings   Arrangements that enable communications between your network adapter and the network protocol.

default gateway   The router that connects you to remote network segments.

frame type   Identifies the method of data packaging for transmission over an IPX/SPX network.

HOSTS **file**   Contains mappings of IP address and host names; can be used to resolve host names to IP addresses.

internal network number   Used to identify NetWare servers.

IP address   Uniquely identifies computers and other devices on the network. It is a 32-bit address, divided into four octets separated by periods.

IPCONFIG   A command-line utility used to display current TCP/IP configuration information.

NetBEUI   A small, nonroutable network protocol used on networks with less than 200 computers.

NetBIOS (Network Basic Input/Output System) names   A convention that is used for naming computers using Microsoft software.

NWLink IPX/SPX/NetBIOS Compatible Transport   Microsoft's implementation of Novell's IPX/SPX protocol stack. The Windows 2000 implementation of the protocol stack adds NetBIOS support.

PING   A utility that is used to verify connectivity between two hosts.

subnet mask   Specifies which part of the IP address is the network address and which part is the host address.

TCP/IP (Transmission Control Protocol/Internet Protocol)   A protocol stack used to connect dissimilar networks. It has become the network standard for many network operating systems.

Sample Questions

1. You are administrator of a network using the TCP/IP protocol for the majority of its clients and servers. You are also running several NetWare servers. On a client, you notice that the binding lists NWLink first, followed by TCP/IP. What, if anything, can be done to improve network performance on this machine?

    A. Remove the NWLink protocol.

    B. Change the bindings order on the client to list TCP/IP first.

    C. Change the binding order on the servers to list NWLink first.

    D. Nothing. The network is running optimally already.

Answer: B. By changing the network binding order on the client, you can help it talk to the TCP/IP severs that represent the majority of the servers on the network.

2. You are the network administrator. You are trying to verify that a computer is properly configured to use TCP/IP. What steps, in what order, would you take using the PING command?

   A. Ping the remote computer, then the remote default gateway, then the local IP address, and then the loopback address.

   B. Ping the remote computer, then the local default gateway, then the local IP address, and then the loopback address.

   C. Ping the loopback address, then the local IP address, then the remote default gateway address, and then a remote address.

   D. Ping the loopback address, then the local IP address, then the local default gateway address, and then a remote address.

   Answer: D. To test connectivity between two computers, you can use the PING command. The sequence to test the configuration is as follows: First ping the loopback address, then the local IP address, then the local default gateway address, and finally a remote address.

Install and configure network services.

The complexity of the TCP/IP protocol suite can make managing and using it very difficult. These tasks are simplified by many services and protocols offered by TCP/IP. Microsoft has incorporated several of these services to help you implement the TCP/IP protocol stack. DHCP is the easiest way of configuring many network computers. With automatic IP configuration, many of the headaches of the past are gone. Dynamic DNS gives us the capability of using host names instead of having to remember the associated IP addresses, which would be impossible with automatic IP address configuration. WINS gives you backward compatibility with Windows NT networks that use the NetBIOS naming convention.

The examination process overall requires that you have a thorough understanding of how the network services work individually and together. For this particular Windows 2000 Server exam, however, you should have a solid foundation of familiarity with the services and their uses. A broader application of network service management is tested in other Microsoft exams.

Critical Information

The services that contribute most to network interoperability are DHCP, DNS, and WINS, all of which are covered in this section. In Windows 2000 networks, only Windows 2000 Server computers can act as DHCP, WINS, and DNS servers. A single computer can have all three services loaded on it.

The following operating systems are supported as clients of DHCP, DNS, and WINS:

- Windows 2000 Professional or Server

- Windows NT 3.51 or later Workstation or Server

- Windows 95 or Windows 98

- Windows for Workgroups 3.11 (with TCP/IP-32)

- Microsoft Network Client 3.0 for Microsoft MS-DOS with the real-mode TCP/IP driver

- Microsoft LAN Manager 2.2c (OS/2 version not supported)

DHCP

Keeping track of which host has which address can be a monumental task. Companies have used databases, spreadsheets, and even sticky labels to manage hosts and their IP addresses.

Unfortunately, the methods used to manage IP addresses manually are only as good as their last update. If an administrator forgets to record that an address is already assigned, that same address could be assigned twice. This is equivalent to the phone company's assigning the same phone number to two customers. Typing errors occur, as well, which can result in duplicate or incorrect addresses. Sometimes, users unwittingly contribute to the problem by copying configuration information from a coworker's computer or by trying to guess an IP address when the system administrator is not available.

Microsoft's implementation of TCP/IP goes a long way to minimizing the problems of duplicate IP addresses by sending out an *Address Resolution Protocol (ARP)* broadcast when a computer initializes the TCP/IP protocol stack. If another computer replies to the ARP broadcast, that means the requested IP address is already in use, and TCP/IP will not be initialized on the new computer. Both computers receive a warning message that an IP address has been duplicated.

When computers are moved from one subnet to another without having the IP address reconfigured, this can result in another common problem. If a computer's IP address isn't modified to reflect the new network and subnet address, TCP/IP will initialize but the computer won't be able to communicate with other computers on the network. That computer thinks local traffic is remote, and remote traffic is local. Each device that will use TCP/IP on your network must have a valid, unique IP address.

NOTE   To alleviate the problem of tracking and assigning valid IP addresses, the Internet Engineering Task Force (IETF) has worked with industry leaders to develop the Dynamic Host Configuration Protocol, DHCP. Like all development on the Internet, this protocol has been discussed in a series of Requests for Comments (RFCs), which are available at numerous Internet sites, including the IETF site at `http://www.ietf.org/rfc.html`. The RFCs that pertain to DHCP are 1533, 1534, 1541, and 1542.

In order to act as a DHCP server, the Windows 2000 Server computer must have

- The DHCP networking service installed

- A static IP address configured

- A valid range of IP addresses that can be assigned to DHCP clients

All the Microsoft operating systems listed earlier are supported as DHCP clients, as well as non-Microsoft systems such as Unix and Macintosh.

DHCP Implementation

DHCP is implemented as a client/server service and works as follows:

1. When the client computer starts up, it sends a broadcast DHCP-DISCOVER message, requesting a DHCP server. The request includes the hardware address of the client computer.

2. Any DHCP server receiving the broadcast that has available IP addresses will send a DHCPOFFER message to the client, offering an IP address for a set period of time (called a *lease*), a subnet mask, and a server identifier (the IP address of the DHCP server). The address offered by the server is marked as unavailable and will not be offered to any other clients during the DHCP negotiation period.

3. The client selects one of the offers and broadcasts a DHCPRE-QUEST message, indicating its selection. This allows any DHCP offers that were not accepted to be returned to the pool of available IP addresses.

4. The selected DHCP server sends back a DHCPACK message as acknowledgment, indicating the IP address, subnet mask, and the duration of the lease that the client computer will use. The server may also send additional configuration information, such as the address of the default gateway or the DNS server address.

TIP   A mnemonic device for remembering the four steps in the DHCP lease-generation process is *ROSA:* IP lease *R*equest, IP lease *O*ffer, IP lease *S*election, IP lease *A*cknowledgment.

WINS

Prior to Windows 2000, Windows clients such as Windows 9*x* and Windows NT 4.0 used NetBIOS names to communicate with other computers on the network. WINS servers are used to resolve Net-BIOS computer names to IP addresses.

When a client attempts to communicate with another computer using a NetBIOS name in a WINS environment, the following steps are used to resolve the NetBIOS name to an IP address:

1. The client checks its local NetBIOS name cache to see if it contains a NetBIOS-to-IP address mapping.

2. If the request is not resolved, the client sends a name query to the primary WINS server.

3. If the primary WINS server is not available after three attempts, the client sends a name query to the secondary WINS server.

4. If no WINS server can resolve the name, a network broadcast is initiated to locate the remote computer.

Once a WINS server is installed and the WINS clients are configured, WINS name registration will occur automatically. When the WINS client starts, it automatically sends its IP address and NetBIOS name to the designated WINS server. It queries the WINS server to verify that the NetBIOS name used by the client is not already in use. This verification process also occurs if the IP address information changes (for example, when the computer moves to another subnet or when DHCP assigns new configuration information). Name registration is temporary, so the WINS client must renew its name registration periodically.

In order to act as a WINS server, the Windows 2000 Server computer must have

- The WINS service installed
- A static IP address, subnet mask, and default gateway (if routing is used) configured

After WINS is installed, you'll see the WINS program item in the Administrative Tools group. You can view WINS database entries and configure the WINS server through this utility.

DNS

DNS is a hierarchical structure to logically organize domain names. The top of the hierarchy is represented by a period. Examples of top-level domains include .com, .edu, .gov, and extensions representing geographical locations. Companies, organizations, and individuals register second-level domains. DNS is used with the Internet and with private networks to resolve host (computer) names to IP addresses. The host name need not be the same as the Windows 2000 computer name, but that is the default setting.

In order to access a host, you use a fully qualified domain name (FQDN). DNS then uses the FQDN to resolve the host name to a specific IP address.

To act as a DNS server, the Windows 2000 Server computer must be configured with the TCP/IP protocol using a static IP address. DNS can only be installed on Windows 2000 Server computers.

Name Resolution

The following process is used when DNS clients query DNS servers for name resolution:

1. The DNS client queries the DNS server that it is configured to use for name resolution.

2. If the DNS server can resolve the query, it returns a response to the DNS client. This is called *an iterative query*.

3. If the DNS server cannot resolve the query, the DNS server contacts other DNS servers on behalf of the DNS client to attempt to resolve the query. This is called a *recursive query*.

When you query a DNS server, you can make two types of queries:

- *Forward lookup* queries are requests to map an FQDN address to an IP address.

- *Reverse lookup* queries are requests to map an IP address to an FQDN.

NOTE Windows 2000 supports dynamic DNS. If you use DHCP to assign IP addresses, the name-to-IP mapping will be automatically registered with DNS servers when the DHCP configuration information is registered with the DHCP configuration.

Necessary Procedures

Following are the steps for installing the network services, as well as for configuration of DHCP and DNS (WINS configuration is not included in the exam).

Installing Network Services

You install the DHCP, WINS, and DNS services through the Add/Remove Programs icon in Control Panel. Here are the steps to install a network service on a Windows 2000 Server computer:

1. Confirm that the server is configured with a static IP address by checking the TCP/IP properties.

2. Select Start ➤ Settings ➤ Control Panel. Double-click the Add/Remove Programs icon.

3. In the Add/Remove Programs window, click the Add/Remove Windows Components option.

4. When the Windows Components Wizard starts, select Networking Services and click the Details button.

5. Next you'll see the Networking Services dialog box. Check the check box for the service you want to install: Dynamic Host Configuration Protocol (DHCP), Windows Internet Name Service (WINS), or Domain Name System (DNS). Then click the OK button.

6. You return to the Windows Components dialog box. Click the Next button.

7. When you see the Completing the Windows Components Wizard dialog box, click the Finish button.

8. You return to the Add/Remove Programs window. Click the Close button. Close Control Panel.

Configuring a DHCP Server

After the DHCP service is installed, you'll see the DHCP program item in Administrative Tools. To configure your DHCP server, take the following steps:

TIP   You can also add the DHCP snap-in to the MMC.

---

1. Select Start ➤ Programs ➤ Administrative Tools ➤ DHCP.

2. The DHCP window appears. Right-click your server and select New Scope from the pop-up menu.

3. The New Scope Wizard starts. Click the Next button to proceed.

4. The Wizard first displays the Scope Name dialog box. Type in a name and comment that will be used to identify the scope. Click the Next button.

5. The IP Address Range dialog box appears. Type the starting and ending IP addresses in the corresponding text boxes to define the address range for the DHCP scope. Specify the subnet mask that will be used by the DHCP scope, either by selecting a length or by entering an IP address, and click the Next button.

6. The Add Exclusions dialog box appears. Here, you can identify any addresses to exclude within the specified DHCP scope. Exclusions are used to reserve IP addresses that are already in use or are reserved. To exclude a single address, type the address in the Start IP Address text box and click the Add button. To exclude a range of contiguous IP addresses, type the starting and ending IP addresses in the respective text boxes and click the Add button. Use the Remove button to remove excluded addresses. When you've configured any address exclusions, click the Next button.

7. Next up is the Lease Duration dialog box. Specify how long the client will be able to use the IP address before it's returned to the DHCP scope. By default, a DHCP client will attempt to renew its IP address when one-half the lease period has expired. The default lease period is eight days. You might want to shorten the lease period if you have a limited number of IP addresses in your scope compared to the number of clients who require IP addresses. After you configure your scope, click the Next button.

8. The Configure DHCP Options dialog box appears, offering you a choice of the most common IP configuration options. If none of these fits, select No, I Will Configure These Options Later; you'll be able to assign default gateways, DNS servers, and WINS servers at another time (but before clients use any of the IP addresses in the DHCP scope). In this example, the Yes, I Want to Configure These Options Now option is selected to configure additional DHCP settings. Click the Next button to continue.

9. Next you'll see the Router (Default Gateway) dialog box. Specify the IP address of the default gateway that will be used by your DHCP clients and click the Add button. Click the Next button to continue.

10. The Domain Name and DNS Servers dialog box appears, in which you configure the parent domain that your DHCP clients will use for DNS name resolution. You can also configure the server name and IP addresses of DNS servers that will be used for DNS name resolution. After you specify this information, click the Next button.

11. The WINS Servers dialog box appears. This dialog box allows you to configure the primary and secondary WINS servers that are used to resolve NetBIOS computer names to IP addresses. Specify the WINS server information and click the Next button.

12. The Activate Scope dialog box appears. Here you specify whether or not you will activate the DHCP scope. DHCP clients can only use the services of active DHCP scopes. You can choose to activate this scope now or later. Then click the Finish button.

13. When the Completing the New Scope Wizard dialog box comes up, click the Finish button.

14. If the DHCP server is a part of the Active Directory, you must also authorize the DHCP server. To do this, right-click the DHCP server in the main DHCP window and choose Authorize from the pop-up menu.

Configuring a DNS Server

After DNS is installed, you'll see the DNS program item in the Administrative Tools group. Here are the steps to configure a DNS server:

TIP You can also add the DNS snap-in to the MMC.

---

1. Select Start ➤ Programs ➤ Administrative Tools ➤ DNS.

2. The DNS window appears. Right-click your DNS server and select Configure the Server from the pop-up menu.

3. The Configure DNS Server Wizard starts. Click the Next button.

4. Next up is the Root Server dialog box. Indicate whether this is the first DNS server on your network, or that your network already has a DNS server. If you choose the This Is the First DNS Server on This Network option, this computer becomes the root server. If you are configuring DNS on a server in a network using the Active Directory, a DNS server will already be running. Click the Next button.

5. The Forward Lookup Zone dialog box appears. Forward lookup zones are database files that contain the DNS domain-name-to-IP-address mappings. Specify whether or not this file is created. Click the Next button.

6. You'll next see the Zone Type dialog box, where you specify the type of zone that is created. There are three types of zones; make your selection and then click the Next button.

- Active Directory-integrated, which is used with the Active Directory to store and replicate zone files. Zone database files are replicated when Active Directory replication occurs. This option is not available on a server that is not a part of the Active Directory.

- Standard primary, which is a master copy of a new zone and stores the zone database file as a text file.

- Standard secondary, which is a copy (replica) of an existing zone file. This option is used for redundancy and load balancing.

7. If you chose to create a standard primary zone in step 6, the Zone Name dialog box appears. Enter a name for the zone and click the Next button.

8. The Zone File dialog box appears. Here you can create a new file for the zone or use an existing file that may have been copied from another computer. After you make your selection, click the Next button.

9. Next, the Reverse Lookup Zone dialog box appears. A reverse lookup zone file is used to translate IP addresses to DNS names. Choose whether or not this file is created. In this example, the No, Do Not Create a Reverse Lookup Zone option is selected. Click the Next button.

10. The Completing the Configure the DNS Server Wizard dialog box appears. If all of the information is correct, click the Finish button.

Exam Essentials

Know the role of DHCP.   A DHCP server can automatically assign DHCP clients IP addresses. It can provide a unique IP address, subnet mask, default gateway, WINS server information, and DNS server information.

Know the DHCP server requirements.   A DHCP server requires a static IP address, the DHCP service, and a valid range of IP addresses that can be assigned to DHCP clients.

Know how a DHCP client gets an IP address.   The four steps in the DHCP address lease process are IP lease request, IP lease offer, IP lease selection, and IP lease acknowledgment.

Know the role of WINS.   WINS is used to resolve NetBIOS names to IP addresses. In Windows 2000, it's primarily used for backward compatibility with other Microsoft operating systems.

Know the requirements of a WINS server. A WINS server requires a static IP address and the WINS service installed.

Know what DNS server does. DNS is used to provide host-name-to-IP-address resolution. DNS must have a physical presence on the Internet.

Understand what a reverse lookup does. A reverse lookup is used to resolve an IP address to a host name.

Key Terms and Concepts

ARP (Address Resolution Protocol) A broadcast-based protocol used to resolve a NetBIOS name to an IP address.

DHCP (Dynamic Host Configuration Protocol) A protocol used to assign IP addresses to DHCP clients automatically.

DHCP server A server that is running the DHCP protocol.

DNS (Domain Name System) server A server used to resolve host names to IP addresses. In Windows 2000, it is a dynamic service.

forward lookup A query to a DNS server in which the domain name of a host computer is searched to find its IP address.

iterative query A query made to a DNS server in which the name server is expected to provide the best information, based on what the server knows from local zone files or from caching.

recursive query A query made to a DNS server, in which the requester asks the server to assume the full workload and responsibility for providing a complete answer to the query. The DNS server then uses separate iterative queries to other DNS servers, beginning with a root DNS server, on behalf of the requester to assist in completing an answer for the recursive query. When it receives a successful response from the other DNS servers, it then sends a response to the client.

reverse lookup A query to a DNS server in which the IP address is used to determine the DNS name for the computer.

WINS (Windows Internet Name Service) server   A server used to resolve NetBIOS names to IP addresses. In Windows 2000, it provides backward compatibility with other Microsoft operating systems.

Sample Questions

1. You are the administrator of a large network on which you've had problems manually configuring TCP/IP on all of the client computers. Which TCP/IP service can help you?

   A. DHCP

   B. DNS

   C. LMHOSTS

   D. WINS

   Answer: A. DHCP is used to assign IP addresses to client computers automatically.

2. You are the administrator of a large network and are using DHCP to assign the IP address to client computers. Now you're having difficulties when trying to connect to the computers using their computer names. Which TCP/IP service can help?

   A. DHCP

   B. DNS

   C. LMHOSTS

   D. WINS

   Answer: B. Although WINS can provide NetBIOS name resolution, dynamic DNS is designed to work with DHCP clients to register their name-to-IP-address mappings automatically. This is the preferred method in Windows 2000.

Configure, monitor, and troubleshoot remote access.

- **Configure inbound connections.**
- **Create a remote access policy.**
- **Configure a remote access profile.**

Remote access gives your users substantial flexibility in how they connect to the network. Without remote access, you needed to be physically connected to a network in order to access its data and services. Now, through a dial-up connection, users can connect to network resources from other sites, distant and near.

For the network administrator, the extended network offers additional challenges, such as security control and configuration management. Microsoft has added some new tools in Windows 2000 to help handle these issues. Configuration is managed through the Routing and Remote Access (RRAS) utility. Improved security mechanisms have been added; more authentication methods are accepted, and you can create remote access profiles to control remote users.

For the exam, you'll be expected to know how to configure connections; how to manage an RAS server (especially its security); and how to configure policies for remote access users. Procedures are included for installing an RAS server and how to create remote access policies.

Critical Information

Remote Access Service (RAS) servers connect remote users to the network through the *Routing and Remote Access Service (RRAS)*. A Windows 2000 Server computer that is running the Routing and Remote Access Service can authenticate and service requests from remote clients. This allows users to access resources remotely in the same manner as they access the resources locally.

This section covers dial-up remote access, when a remote access client uses the telecommunications infrastructure to create a temporary physical circuit (virtual circuit) to a port on a remote access server.

Configuring Inbound Connections

Inbound connections allow incoming calls from remote users access to the RAS server. *Outbound connections* allow users to dial out to external resources through the RAS server. Users can connect to the RAS server through a modem, ISDN connection, or direct connection (through a null-modem cable). *Demand-dial routing connections* support both inbound and outbound connections.

You configure inbound and outbound connections through the Ports Properties dialog box in the Routing and Remote Access utility. To access this dialog box, expand your computer in the Routing and Remote Access window, right-click Ports, and select Properties from the pop-up menu.

In the Ports Properties dialog box, highlight the RAS connection device you want to configure and click the Configure button. This brings up the Configure Device dialog box, where you specify whether the computer will be used for inbound connections only (the default setting) or for demand-dial routing connections. In addition, you can configure the telephone number that will be used for the device.

Managing RAS Server Properties

To configure the properties of an RAS server, right-click the server in the Routing and Remote Access utility and select Properties from the pop-up menu. The RAS server's Properties dialog box contains General, Security, and Event Logging tabs, as well as tabs for each protocol you've installed for remote access connections.

General Properties

The General tab allows you to enable the computer as a router or as an RAS server. For a router, you can specify whether the computer will route packets between two or more network segments.

Security Options

In the Security tab you select and configure an authentication provider and select an accounting provider.

AUTHENTICATION PROVIDER AND AUTHENTICATION METHODS

The authentication provider is the server that will provide authentication services for remote access or demand-dial users. You can choose from two types of authentication providers:

- Windows authentication uses a Windows 2000 local server, Windows 2000 domain controller, or Windows NT 4.0 domain controller to authenticate remote access requests.

- RADIUS authentication uses a RADIUS server to authenticate remote access requests. RADIUS stands for Remote Authentication Dial-In User Service.

To configure authentication methods, click the Authentication Methods button in the Security tab. This brings up the Authentication Methods dialog box, containing the options defined in Table 6.5.

TABLE 6.5: Remote Access Authentication Methods

Authentication Method	Description
Extensible Authentication Protocol (EAP)	A protocol that allows the RAS server and the remote access client to negotiate an authentication scheme, such as Generic Token Card, MD5-Challenge, Transport Level Security (used with Smart Cards), and S/Key. EAP is also designed to support emerging authentication technologies.
Microsoft Encrypted Authentication Version 2 (MS-CHAP v2)	An enhanced version of MS-CHAP that uses a higher level of security.
Microsoft Encrypted Authentication (MS-CHAP)	A nonreversible authentication protocol that uses an encrypted password authentication process.

TABLE 6.5: Remote Access Authentication Methods *(continued)*

Authentication Method	Description
Encrypted Authentication (CHAP)	A challenge-response authentication protocol used by non-Microsoft clients to provide challenge-response authentication using the Message Digest 5 (MD5) hashing scheme to encrypt the response sent from the RAS client to the RAS server.
Shiva Password Authentication Protocol (SPAP)	A form of authentication used by clients that connect to Shiva LAN Rovers.
Unencrypted Password (PAP)	A protocol that uses plain text passwords. This is the least secure authentication method.
Unauthenticated Access	Allows the remote computers to connect to your network without any authentication. *Use extreme caution if you choose to enable this option.*

NOTE Click the EAP Methods button in the Authentication Methods dialog box to configure options for MD5-Challenge, smart card, or other Certificate EAP protocols. You can add other EAP methods through remote access policies.

ACCOUNTING PROVIDER

The accounting provider is the server that will provide accounting services for remote access or demand-dial connections. You can specify that you will use Windows accounting, RADIUS accounting, or no accounting provider (None).

IP Options

The IP tab has options for enabling IP routing and allowing IP-based remote access and demand-dial connections. You can also configure IP address assignment in this tab. You can specify that remote clients will get their IP addresses from a DHCP server or from a static IP address pool. If you choose to use a static address pool, you'll configure the IP addresses in this dialog box.

IPX Options

If you have specified that the Internetwork Packet Exchange (IPX) protocol will be used for remote access connections, the RAS server's Properties dialog box will contain an IPX tab. Through this tab, you can allow IPX-based remote access and demand-dial connections, and enable network access for those connections.

IPX network number assignment is also configured through the IPX tab. You can choose automatic IPX address assignment or specify an address range. You can specify that the same network number should be used for all IPX clients, and you can allow remote clients to request an IPX node number. Normally, you specify that IPX addresses should be assigned automatically and leave these settings at default values. However, you may need to adjust the IPX settings if you'll be using File and Print Services for NetWare or if your computer is functioning as an IPX router.

PPP Options

The PPP tab has settings for configuring several *Point-to-Point Protocol (PPP)* options:

- *Multilink* connections allow several physical connections to be combined into a single logical connection. If you use multilink connections, you can specify whether the amount of bandwidth should be controlled using the *Bandwidth Allocation Protocol (BAP)* or the Bandwidth Allocation Control Protocol (BACP).

- Link Control Protocol (LCP) extensions are used to specify that LCP should send Time-Remaining and Identification packets as well as request callback during an LCP negotiation.

- You can specify that the Microsoft Point-to-Point Compression Protocol (MPPC) should be used to compress any data that is sent over the remote access or demand-dial connection.

Event Logging Options

The Event Logging tab allows you to configure how RAS server events are logged. You can choose to log errors only, log errors and warnings, log the maximum amount of information, or disable event logging. You can also enable PPP logging. If you enable PPP logging, all events related to the PPP connection process will be written to the *Windir*\Tracing\ppp.log file. This log file is useful for troubleshooting remote access problems.

Assigning Dial-in Permissions to Users

You assign permissions to users who can access an RAS server through any of the following locations: the user's Properties dialog box, in the Local Users and Groups utility on a member server, or in the Active Directory Users and Computers utility on a Windows 2000 domain controller. To open the Properties dialog box, access the appropriate utility, open the Users folder, and double-click the user account.

The options on the Dial-in tab allow you to configure the following dial-in properties. If a property is not available, that means your computer is not configured to support the option. You can

- Allow or deny remote access permission, and specify whether a remote access policy will be used (remote access policies are covered in the upcoming sections).

- Designate no callback, callback set by the caller, or to always use callback to a specified telephone number.

- Specify whether static IP address or static routes should be applied to the user's connection.

Remote Access Policies and Profiles

By defining a *remote access policy*, you configure who is authorized to access the RAS server. The remote access policy lets you create a dial-in profile that specifies access based on Windows 2000 group membership, time of day, day of week, and type of connection. You can also configure settings for options such as maximum session time, authentication requirements, and BAP policies. Remote access policies are set up through the Routing and Remote Access utility. Expand your computer, and then expand Remote Access Policies.

Managing Access Using Remote Access Policies

In Windows 2000, dial-in access is authorized based on the dial-in properties of a user account, and on remote access polices. Remote access policies include a set of conditions and connection settings that give you the flexibility to authorize connection attempts to RRAS. You can use these settings to either allow or reject connection attempts.

ACCESS BY USER ACCOUNT

If you wish to manage remote access on a per-user basis, you'll set the remote access permissions on the user accounts that are allowed to create remote access connections. This is done in the user account's Properties dialog box, by selecting the Allow Access setting. Additionally, you'll need to modify the profile properties of the default access policy, called Allow Access If dial-in Permission Is Enabled, for the needed connection parameters.

You can access this policy by double-clicking Remote Access Policies in the Routing and Remote Access window. To manage the properties of this policy, right-click it and select Properties from the pop-up menu. The Settings tab of the policy's Properties dialog box will appear.

You control who can access the remote access policy by clicking the Add button in the Settings tab. Set the Windows-Groups attribute from the Select Attribute dialog box that appears. After you add the Windows groups that the policy will apply to, you can specify whether the group is granted or denied remote access permission.

Click the Edit Profile button at the bottom of the Settings tab to display the Edit Dial-In Profile dialog box. The six tabs of this dialog box contain the dial-in options you can configure, as described in Table 6.6.

TABLE 6.6: Edit Dial-in Profile Options

Tab	Description
Dial-in Constraints	Specify when a connection is disconnected based on idle time, maximum session time, and day and time restrictions. You can also restrict dial-in access to a specific number and restrict dial-in media.
IP	Restrict IP address assignment and configures IP packet filters for the connection.
Multilink	Configure multilink settings and BAP settings.
Authentication	Configure the authentication methods allowed for the connection.
Encryption	Specify the encryption settings to be used by the RRAS connections.
Advanced	Specify the connection attributes to be used by the RAS server.

If the remote access server is providing dial-up remote connections only and no VPN connections, delete the default access policy and create a new remote access policy. This new policy can then be configured to deny or allow access permissions based on your requirements. You'll also set the conditions and connection parameters.

ACCESS BY POLICY

The Windows 2000 remote access server policy administrative model is intended for either stand-alone servers or members of a Windows 2000 native mode domain. To manage remote access by policy, set the parameter on user accounts to Control Access Through Remote Access Policy. Then you can modify the remote access policy to allow or deny access based on your needs. Any connection that does not match any configured remote access policy is denied, even if the user account parameter is set to Allow Access.

Necessary Procedures

Included here are the steps for installing RAS and creating a remote access policy. Your knowledge of these procedures will reinforce your ability to handle what is covered on the exam.

Installing an RAS Server

You install and configure your RAS server through the Routing and Remote Access utility.

1. Select Start ➤ Programs ➤ Administrative Tools ➤ Routing and Remote Access.

2. The Routing and Remote Access utility starts. In the left pane of the Routing and Remote Access window, right-click your server and select Configure and Enable Routing and Remote Access from the pop-up menu.

NOTE   You'll need to disable RRAS if it has been enabled.

---

3. When the Routing and Remote Access Server Wizard starts, click the Next button to continue.

4. The Common Configurations dialog box appears. Select the Remote Access Server option and click the Next button.

5. Next up is the Remote Client Protocols dialog box, which lists the protocols installed on your computer. If you wish to add other protocols to be used for servicing remote clients, select the No, I Need to Add Protocols option. Otherwise, accept the default selection, Yes, All of the Required Protocols Are on This List. Click Next to proceed.

6. If you specified that the RAS server should use the TCP/IP protocol, the IP Address Assignment dialog box appears. You can choose to assign IP addresses automatically or assign them from a specified range of IP addresses. If you choose the Automatically option, the IP addresses are assigned through a DHCP server or by the server that's automatically generating the addresses. Click the Next button to continue.

7. The Managing Multiple Remote Access Servers dialog box appears. This dialog box allows you to specify whether you will use a RADIUS server. If you have multiple RAS servers, you can set up a RADIUS server, which stores a central authentication database and allows you to manage the RAS servers from a single location. Click the Next button.

8. Finally, you'll see the Completing the Routing and Remote Access Server Setup Wizard dialog box. If you want to see Help information after you close the Wizard, select the check box in the dialog box. Make your selection and click the Finish button.

Creating a Remote Access Policy

Follow these steps to create a remote access policy for authorizing access the RAS server:

1. Start the Routing and Remote Access utility, make sure your computer is expanded, and right-click Remote Access Policies. From the pop-up menu, select New Remote Access Policy.

2. In the Add Remote Access Policy dialog box, enter a name for this policy. Click the Next button.

3. When the Conditions dialog box appears, click the Add button.

4. The Select Attribute dialog box appears next, where you can select the attributes desired for this user. Click the Add button.

5. When the Groups dialog box appears, click the Add button.

6. In the Select Groups dialog box, select the groups to whom you want to grant access permission and click the Add button. Then click OK.

7. You'll return to the Groups dialog box; click OK. In the Conditions dialog box, click the Next button.

8. Next you'll see the Permissions dialog box. You can specify whether the groups you have selected will be granted remote access permission or denied remote access permission. Click the Next button.

9. The User Profile dialog box appears, and you can specify additional user profile settings for the remote access policy. If you want to configure the profile for users who match the policy's conditions, click the Edit Profile button. This brings up the Edit Dial-in Profile dialog box.

10. After you have configured your remote access policy, click the Finish button.

Exam Essentials

Know the role of Remote Access Service (RAS).   The Remote Access Service (RAS) is used to connect mobile or off-site users to the network through the Routing and Remote Access Service (RRAS).

Know the role of Routing and Remote Access Service (RRAS). The Routing and Remote Access Service (RRAS) can authenticate and service requests from remote users.

Know what is configured in the Ports properties dialog box.   This dialog box allows you to specify whether the computer will be used for inbound connections or for demand-dial routing connections.

Know the authentication providers.   Authentication is provided by either Windows authentication or by RADIUS authentication.

Know the various authentication methods used for RAS.   The authentication methods are Extensible Authentication Protocol, Microsoft Encrypted Authentication Version 2, Microsoft Encrypted Authentication, Encrypted Authentication, Shiva Password Authentication protocol, unencrypted password, and unauthenticated access.

Know the RAS IP options. The IP options enable IP routing or allow IP-based remote access and demand-dial connections. Additionally, you can specify IP assignments from a DHCP server or a static IP address pool.

Know the RAS IPX options. The IPX options allow IPX-based remote access and demand-dial connections, and enable network access for those connections.

Know the PPP options. PPP options are used to set up multilink connections, with a specified amount of bandwidth available for the connections; Time-Remaining and Identification packets and request callback; and software compression.

Know where to set dial-in permissions. Dial-in permissions can be set through the user's Properties dialog box, in the Local Users and Groups utility on a member server, or in the Active Directory Users and Computers utility on a domain controller.

Know what can be set with remote access policies. A dial-in profile can specify access based on a Windows 2000 group membership, time of day, day of week, and type of connection. It can also set options such as maximum session time, authentication requirements, and BAP policies.

Key Terms and Concepts

Bandwidth Allocation Protocol (BAP)   A protocol that can control the amount bandwidth used in a multilink environment.

demand-dial routing connection   Support for both inbound and outbound connections on a RAS server.

multilink   Multilink connections allow several physical connections to be combined into a single logical connection.

Point-to-Point Protocol (PPP)   A line protocol used to connect remote users to an RAS server.

remote access policy   A policy that defines the parameters of users' access to resources through RAS.

Remote Access Service (RAS) server   A server configured to allow remote users to connect to the network.

Sample Questions

1. As network administrator, you have several users who need to connect to the network from remote locations using computers with a variety of operating systems. Which authentication method is most appropriate?

A. EAP

B. MS CHAP v2

C. SPAP

D. PAP

Answer: A. Extensible Authentication Protocol (EAP) allows the RAS server and the remote client to negotiate an authentication scheme.

2. You are the network administrator. Several users need to connect to the network from remote locations. They have several modems installed in their computers. You have enabled multilink to allow these users faster access, but you need to limit the amount of bandwidth each user can consume. Which setting allows you to do this?

A. BAP

B. LCP

C. SPAP

D. PAP

Answer: A. Bandwidth Allocation Protocol (BAP) specifies the amount of bandwidth available for a connection.

Install, configure, and troubleshoot Terminal Services.

- **Remotely administer servers by using Terminal Services.**
- **Configure Terminal Services for application sharing.**
- **Configure applications for use with Terminal Services.**

Windows 2000 requires significantly more computing power than any other Windows-based operating system to date. Administrators can devote countless hours upgrading machines and deploying all the features of Windows 2000. An alternative to this management burden is to deliver selected system features to users through a *Terminal Services* arrangement.

Rather than installing the full operating system on each machine in the network, you upgrade one machine to be a Windows 2000 Server and install the Terminal Services client on every other computer. The client can be run on just about any Windows-based computer or terminal, eliminating the need for costly hardware upgrades. The Terminal Services server handles the entire computing load for every Terminal Services client.

Another use of Terminal Services is for remote administration. Through Terminal Services, administrators can perform all types of administration tasks from virtually any client.

The exam focuses on your ability to configure Terminal Services, including the applications that will run in the server and how to share the applications for your users. You'll be expected to know how to administer Terminal Services and how to monitor user activity on the Terminal Server. This section covers the background information about how Terminal Services provides it functionality, and the steps of installing, configuring, and monitoring its activities. Learning the Necessary Procedures will help reinforce your knowledge of the various Terminal Services modes and what can be done in them. You'll also see how to license Terminal Services and how to configure clients to use Terminal Services.

Critical Information

Implementation of a Terminal Services arrangement requires a certain amount of planning. You'll need to make sure that the computer deployed as the *Terminal Services server* has adequate resources to handle all the users who will be connected to it. And the clients must be able to run the client software. You also need to purchase and configure all the proper licenses required to run the Terminal Services software.

After you've planned your Terminal Services configuration, you can begin deploying the server and client software. Terminal Services includes a configuration utility, a management utility, and a client creator tool for managing the server and clients.

The Terminal Services Application

You can run Terminal Services in either of two modes. In *remote administration mode,* administrators can perform management tasks from virtually any client on the network. In *application server mode,* users have remote access to applications running on the server. Using this mode, Terminal Services delivers the Windows 2000 Desktop environment to computers that might not otherwise be able to run Windows 2000 because of hardware or other limitations.

In application server mode, the server's GUI is transmitted to the remote client, and the client sends keyboard and mouse signals to the server. These client computers are called *thin clients.* Users log on through any client on the network and can see only their individual *session.* Terminal Services manages these unique client sessions transparently. Many types of hardware devices can run the thin-client software, including Windows-based terminals and computers.

Benefits and Features of Terminal Services

Terminal Services offers many benefits to the network using it.

- **Wider deployment of Windows 2000:** Rather than installing a full version of Windows 2000 on every desktop, you can deploy Terminal Services instead. Computers whose hardware might not be supported by the full version of Windows 2000 can still take advantage of many of Windows 2000's features.

- **Simultaneous operation of both the thin-client software and a stand-alone operating system:** With Terminal Services, network users can continue to use their existing computer systems, but they can also enjoy the benefits of the Windows 2000 Desktop environment.

- **Simplified application deployment:** Instead of installing and updating applications on every machine in the network, the administrator can install and update one copy on the Terminal Services server. Thus every user has access to the latest version of the application.

- **Remote administration of the server:** Terminal Services allows the administrator to manage the server remotely when necessary.

Terminal Services includes many features that make it easy to use and manage. These features are described in Table 6.7.

TABLE 6.7: Terminal Services Features

Feature	Description
Multiple logon support	Users can log on multiple times, simultaneously, either from many clients or from one client, and can log on to multiple servers as well. This allows users to perform several tasks at the same time.
Roaming disconnect support	A user can disconnect from a session without logging off. The session remains active while disconnected, allowing the user to reconnect at another time or from another client.
Performance enhancements	Enhanced use of caching improves performance significantly.
Clipboard redirection	Users can cut and paste among applications on the local computer, and applications on the Terminal Services server.
Automated local printer support	Printers attached to clients are automatically added and reconnected.

TABLE 6.7: Terminal Services Features *(continued)*

Feature	Description
Security	The logon process is encrypted, and administrators can specify the number of logon attempts and the connection time of individual users. Data transmitted between the server and client can be encrypted at three levels (low, medium, or high), depending on security needs.
Session remote control	Two users can view the same session concurrently. This helps support personnel diagnose problems and train users.
Network load balancing	Terminal Services can evenly distribute client connections across a group of servers, alleviating the load on any one server.
Windows-based terminals	Windows-based terminals that run on a modified version of Windows CE and Remote Desktop Protocol are available.
Client Connection Manager	Creates an icon on the Desktop that allows quick connectivity to servers for either single-program or full-Desktop access.
Terminal Services Licensing	Helps administrators track clients and their licenses.
Dfs support	Users can connect to a Dfs share and administrators can host a Dfs share from a Terminal Services server. (See the objectives for administering the Distributed File System, in Chapter 2.)
Terminal Services Manager	Used by administrators to query and manage sessions, users, and processes.
Terminal Services Configuration	Creates, modifies, and deletes sessions.
Integration with local users and groups and the Active Directory	Administrators can create Terminal Services accounts similarly to creating regular user accounts.

TABLE 6.7:   Terminal Services Features *(continued)*

Feature	Description
Integration with System Monitor	System performance of Terminal Services can be tracked by System Monitor.
Messaging support	Administrators can send messages to clients.
Remote administration	Users with appropriate permissions can remotely manage all aspects of a Terminal Services server.
Configurable session timeout	Administrators can configure how long a session can remain active or idle before it's disconnected.

Components of Terminal Services

Terminal Services consists of three components: the *Terminal Services server,* the *Remote Desktop Protocol,* and the *Terminal Services client.* The Terminal Services server communicates with the Terminal Services client by using the Remote Desktop Protocol.

The Terminal Services Server

Most Terminal Services operations take place on the Terminal Services server (or "Terminal server"). When Terminal Services is in application server mode, all applications are run on the server. The Terminal server sends only screen information to the client and receives only mouse and keyboard input. The server must keep track of the active sessions.

The Remote Desktop Protocol

When you install Terminal Services, the Remote Desktop Protocol (RDP) is automatically installed. RDP is the only connection that needs to be configured in order for clients to connect to the Terminal server. You can configure only one RDP connection per network adapter. Use the Terminal Services Configuration tool to configure the properties of the RDP connection, including encryption settings and permissions, and the amount of time that client sessions can remain active.

The Terminal Services Client

The *Terminal Services client* (or "Terminal client") uses thin-client technology to deliver the Windows 2000 Server Desktop to the user. The client only needs to establish a connection with the server and display the GUI information that the server sends. This process requires very little overhead on the client's part, and it can be run on older machines that would not otherwise be able to use Windows 2000.

Planning the Terminal Services Configuration

Before you can use Terminal Services, determine which applications will be shared and what kind of hardware you'll be using. The requirements for running a Terminal server are more substantial than for running a normal Windows 2000 server, especially if you're using application server mode. You must also consider the extent and cost of licensing a Terminal Services configuration. Each client that connects to the Terminal server must have a special Terminal Services client license.

Determining Client Applications

Applications used with Terminal Services are installed on a per-computer basis, rather than a per-user basis. They must be available to every user who accesses the Terminal server. Administrators can install applications on the Terminal server directly or from a remote session.

Terminal Services tends to require extra system resources to manage all of the client traffic. Be aware of certain program characteristics that might inordinately tax the server. Intel-based programs running on Alpha machines, video-intensive applications, MS-DOS applications, and constantly running bits of code (such as automatic spell checkers) can drain system resources.

NOTE Using 16-bit applications can reduce the number of users that a single processor can handle by 40 percent and can increase the amount of memory required for each user by 50 percent. Obviously, it's best to use 32-bit applications whenever possible.

Determining Hardware Requirements

You'll need a computer that can handle the Terminal Services loads for your Terminal server. (The requirements for Terminal Services clients are minimal.) Hardware requirements for a Terminal server depend on how many clients will be connecting at a time and the usage requirements of the clients. The following are some guidelines:

- A Terminal server requires at least a Pentium processor and 128MB RAM to perform adequately. You should also provide an additional 10–20MB RAM per client connection, depending on the applications in use. A Terminal server shares executable resources among users, so memory requirements for additional users running the same application are less than for the first user to load the program.

- Use a high-performance bus architecture such as EISA, MCA, or PCI. The ISA (AT) bus cannot move enough data to support the kind of traffic generated by a typical Terminal Services installation.

- Consider using a SCSI disk drive, preferably one that is compatible with Fast SCSI or SCSI-2. For the best performance, use a SCSI disk with RAID, which significantly accelerates disk-access time by placing data on multiple disks.

- Because many users will be accessing the Terminal server simultaneously, use a high-performance network adapter. The best solution is to install two adapters in your machine and dedicate one to RDP traffic only.

The Terminal Services client runs well on a variety of machines, including older computers and terminals that would not otherwise be able to run Windows 2000. The client software runs on the following machines:

- Windows-based terminal devices (embedded)

- Intel and Alpha-based computers running Windows for Workgroups 3.11, Windows 95, Windows 98, Windows NT 3.51, Windows NT 4.0, and Windows 2000

- Macintosh and Unix-based computers (with additional third-party software)

Determining Proper Licensing Requirements

Terminal Services uses its own licensing method. A Terminal client must receive a valid license from a Terminal Services *license server* before logging on to a Terminal server. This only applies to the application server mode. When remote administration mode is being used, two concurrent client sessions are allowed automatically; you don't need a license from a license server.

You can enable Terminal Services Licensing when you install Windows 2000 Server or later, through the Add/Remove Programs icon in Control Panel. When you enable Terminal Services Licensing, you can select between two types of license servers:

- An enterprise license server can serve Terminal servers on any Windows 2000 domain, but cannot serve workgroups or Windows NT 4.0 domains.

- A domain license server can only serve Terminal servers that are in the same domain. In Windows 2000 domains, domain license servers must be installed on domain controllers. In workgroups or Windows NT 4.0 domains, domain license servers can be installed on any member server.

To deploy Terminal Services, you'll be required to obtain the proper server and client licenses.

Installing and Configuring the Terminal Services Server

The Terminal server controls all Terminal clients connected to it. All Terminal Services operations take place on the Terminal server. The clients are nothing more than dummy windows that display information sent from the server and send mouse and keyboard information to the server.

After you install Terminal Services, many settings that control how users and sessions are handled by the Terminal server are configured through the Terminal Services Configuration utility. You use the Terminal Services Manager utility to view every server and session on the network and manually perform actions such as disconnecting from or sending messages to sessions.

You install Terminal Services through the Add/Remove Programs icon in Control Panel. Terminal Services can only be configured to support one mode at a time, either remote administration mode or application server mode. After you install Terminal Services, three new items are added to the Administrative Tools program group: *Terminal Services Client Configurator, Terminal Services Configuration,* and *Terminal Services Manager*. The Terminal Services Client Configurator is used to create 32-bit and 16-bit client software diskettes for use with client machines.

With the Terminal Services Configuration utility, you can change the properties of the RDP-TCP (Remote Desktop Protocol-Transmission Control Protocol) connection that is created when you install Terminal Services. You can also add new connections with this utility. To open Terminal Services Configuration, select Start ➤ Programs ➤ Administrative Tools ➤ Terminal Services Configuration. The main configuration window is shown in Figure 6.1.

FIGURE 6.1: The Terminal Services Configuration window

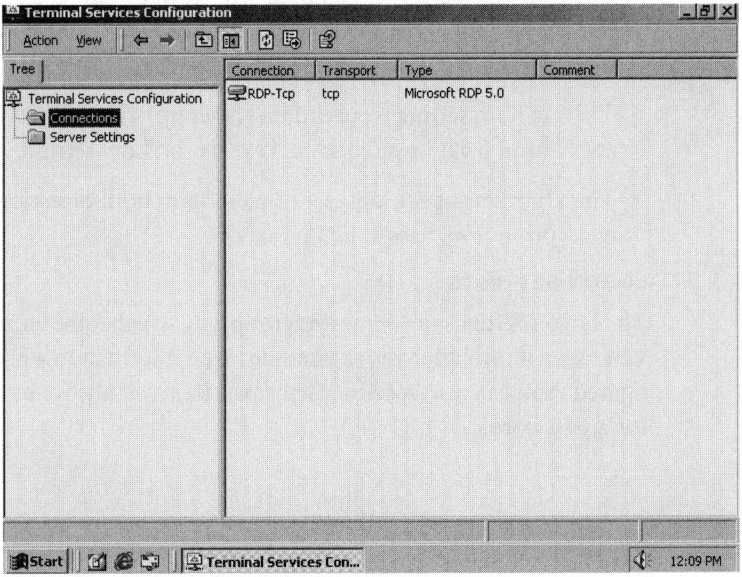

Managing Connections

To configure the properties for a specific connection, select the Connections folder, right-click the connection in the Terminal Services Configuration window, and select Properties from the pop-up menu. This brings up the RDP-TCP Properties dialog box.

GENERAL PROPERTIES

The General tab shows the connection type and transport protocol. In this tab, you can specify a comment for the connection, select the encryption level that will be used, and choose whether standard Windows authentication will be used. You'll see an option for another authentication method if another authentication package has been installed on the server.

Terminal Services uses the standard RSA RC4 encryption method when transferring data between the server and clients. The Encryption Level drop-down list offers three choices, from which you can pick depending on your needs:

- The Low setting secures all data sent from the client to the server, but not from the server to the client. Windows 2000-based clients use a 56-bit key. Earlier versions of the client use a 40-bit key.

- The Medium setting secures data traveling in both directions. This encryption level uses the same keys as the Low setting.

- The High setting secures data traveling in both directions. This encryption level uses a 128-bit key.

LOGON SETTINGS

The Logon Settings tab allows you to specify whether the client will provide logon information or whether the logon information will be preconfigured. You can also specify whether the user will always be prompted for a password.

SESSIONS SETTINGS

On the Sessions tab, you configure session timeout and reconnection settings. You can limit the amount of time that active, idle, and disconnected sessions remain running on the server. You also can set whether the session should end or be disconnected when the time limit is reached. A disconnected session is saved on the server, and the disconnected user can reconnect from any client without losing any data. Ending a session closes all of the user's applications immediately, usually resulting in lost data.

ENVIRONMENT SETTINGS

The Environment tab allows you to override the settings created in Client Connection Manager Wizard or the user profile, and start a specific program when the user logs on. You can also specify that no wallpaper will be displayed on the client, which speeds up screen redrawing.

REMOTE CONTROL OPTIONS

Remote Control allows you to view or control a user's session from another session. You cannot control a session from the Terminal server console. The Remote Control tab allows you to enable or disable remote control and indicate whether the user must give permission for remote control.

NOTE   You can access a session for remote control management through the Terminal Services Manager utility, as described in "Managing Terminal Services" later in this chapter.

CLIENT SETTINGS

The Client Settings tab allows you to configure connection settings and specify which options are disabled. By default, mappings set by a user in a session are lost when the user logs off. Terminal Services Configuration allows you to automatically restore the user's mappings every time he or she logs on. Users can map drives and Windows printers, and can set the main client printer as the default. The following options can be disabled/enabled in this tab:

- Drive mapping

- Windows printer mapping
- LPT Port mapping
- COM port mapping
- Clipboard mapping
- Audio mapping

NETWORK ADAPTER

The Network Adapter tab allows you to specify the network adapter that will support Terminal Service clients. You can also allow unlimited connections or set the maximum number of connections that can be made. You might choose to limit connections to conserve your server's resources and improve its ability to serve clients.

CONNECTION PERMISSIONS

In the Permissions tab you configure permissions (see Table 6.8) that allow or deny Terminal server access to users and groups.

TABLE 6.8: Terminal Services Connection Permissions

Permission	Actions Allowed
Query Information	Query sessions and servers for information
Set Information	Configure connection properties
Reset	End a session
Remote Control	View or control another session
Logon	Log on to a Terminal Services session
Logoff	Log off another user from a session
Message	Send a message to another session
Connect	Connect to another session
Disconnect	Disconnect another session
Virtual Channels	Use virtual channels, which provide access from a server program to client devices

Permission lists make permissions easier to administer. Three lists are available for connection permissions:

- Full Control, which includes all the permissions listed in Table 6.8

- User Access, which is limited to the Query Information, Logon, Message, and Connect permissions

- Guest Access, which includes the Logon permission

By default, the RDP-TCP connection that is installed with Terminal Services assigns Full Control to Administrators, and User Access to Users.

Managing Server Settings

Through the Terminal Services Configuration utility, you can also configure settings that apply to the server (see Table 6.9). To access the settings, select the Server Settings folder in the Terminal Services Configuration window.

TABLE 6.9:   Terminal Services Server Settings

Setting	Value	Description
Active Desktop	Enable/Disable	Turns Active Desktop on/off.
Delete Temporary Folders on Exit	Yes/No	Specifies whether temporary folders are deleted after a session ends.
Internet Connector Licensing	Enable/Disable	Allows anonymous users to open sessions across the Internet (this license must be purchased separately).
Permission Compatibility	Windows 2000/ Terminal Services 4.0	Specifies permission compatibility.
Terminal Server Mode	Application Server/ Remote Administration	Specifies the mode for the Terminal server.

TABLE 6.9: Terminal Services Server Settings *(continued)*

Setting	Value	Description
Use Temporary Folders per Session	Yes/No	Specifies whether temporary folders should be created for each session.

Managing Users of Terminal Services

In addition to Server settings, you can configure properties that apply to individual users. When you install Terminal Services, new tabs that are specific to Terminal Services are added to the user and group Properties dialog boxes. From these tabs, you can set properties such as connect-time limits. If you want these properties to apply to all of the users on a connection, use Terminal Services Configuration to override the individual user settings.

To set Terminal Services properties for an Active Directory user, open the Active Directory Users and Computers utility (by selecting Start ➢ Programs ➢ Administrative Tools ➢ Active Directory Users and Computers). Open the Users folder and double-click the user account. The following four tabs in the Active Directory user's Properties dialog box are Terminal Services properties:

- The Environment tab contains options for configuring the user's Terminal Services startup environment. This allows you to specify programs that should be started at logon, and any devices that the client should connect to at logon.

- In the Sessions tab, you can configure Terminal Services timeout and reconnection settings.

- The Remote Control tab allows you to configure Terminal Services remote control settings. You can enable/disable remote control and designate whether remote control access requires the user's permission.

- Use the Terminal Services Profile tab to set up a Terminal Services user profile. You can also specify the location of the Terminal Services home directory that will be used by the user.

Managing Terminal Services

The Terminal Services Manager utility helps you manage and monitor users, sessions, and processes that are connected to or running on any Terminal server on the network. With this utility, you can perform the following tasks:

- Display information about servers, sessions, users, and processes
- Connect to and disconnect from sessions
- Monitor sessions
- Reset sessions
- Send messages to users
- Log off users
- Terminate processes

To open Terminal Services Manager, select Start ➢ Programs ➢ Administrative Tools ➢ Terminal Services Manager. The main Terminal Services window is shown in Figure 6.2. The navigation pane on the left displays the domains, servers, and sessions. The details pane on the right has tabs that present information about the selected item in the navigation pane.

FIGURE 6.2: The Terminal Services Manager window

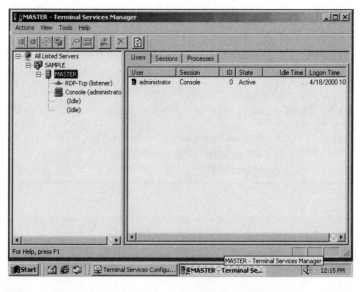

The options on the Actions menu allow you to perform several actions on sessions and processes. Most of these actions require special permissions. The Action menu options are described in Table 6.10.

TABLE 6.10: Terminal Services Manager Action Menu Options

Action	Description	Permission Required
Connect	Allows a user to connect to a session from another session. This option can only be used from a session; it cannot be used from the Terminal server console.	Full Control or User Access
Disconnect	Disconnects a user from a session. The session is saved, and all running applications continue to run.	Full Control
Send Message	Allows a user to send a message to any or all sessions.	Full Control or User Access
Remote Control	Allows a user to use the session to view or control another user's session. Sessions cannot be controlled from the Terminal server console	Full Control
Reset	Immediately ends a session. Any unsaved data is lost.	Full Control
Status	Displays information about a session, such as bytes sent and received.	Full Control or User Access
Log Off	Logs off a user from a session.	Full Control
End Process	Ends a process on a session. This is useful if a program has crashed and is no longer responding.	Full Control

Configuring Terminal Services Licensing

The first time a client attempts to log on to the Terminal server in application server mode, the server recognizes that the client has not been issued a license and locates a license server for this purpose. This license is a digitally signed certificate that will remain with the client forever and cannot be used by any other client.

Before you can begin using a license server, you must activate it through the Microsoft Clearinghouse using the Terminal Services Licensing tool.

TIP   While waiting for the registration process to be completed, you can issue temporary 90-day licenses to clients who need to use Terminal Services immediately.

After a license server is activated, you can begin installing *client license key packs*—sets of client licenses that the license server distributes to your clients. You install key packs either at the end of the license server activation process, or by right-clicking a license server in the Terminal Services Licensing tool and selecting Install Licenses from the pop-up menu. Terminal Services Licensing will contact Microsoft and request the number of keys that you specify. Microsoft sends the keys to the license server, and they'll be available for use immediately after they are received.

Setting Up Terminal Services Clients

The Terminal Services client software is a relatively small package that allows a wide range of machines to connect to a Windows 2000 Terminal server. The client installer should be distributed to every machine on the network that needs to use Terminal Services. There's a 16-bit version of the client for older machines and a 32-bit version for newer machines.

You can install the Terminal Services client software through a network share. The client installation files are located in \Windir\System32\Clients\Tsclient\Net.

Alternatively, you can create client installation disks through the Terminal Services Client Configurator utility if you cannot access a network share that contains the Terminal Services client software. Open this utility on the Terminal server by selecting Start ➤ Programs ➤ Administrative Tools ➤ Terminal Services Client Configurator. The Create Installation Disk(s) dialog box appears. Here you can specify that you will create installation disks for 16-bit or 32-bit Terminal Services clients. After you make your selection, click OK, and then insert the floppy disks when prompted.

After you've installed the Terminal Services client software on a Terminal client, you'll see a new program group called Terminal Services Client, which contains two items for connecting the client to the server:

- Use the Client Connection Manager utility to create predefined connections to a Terminal server.

- Use the Terminal Services Client utility for manual creation of Terminal Services connections.

TIP You can change the configuration of connections created through Client Connection Manager; right-click the connection and select Properties.

Running Terminal Server in Application Server Mode

When you have configured Terminal Services in application server mode, the Terminal clients you have installed will be able to access the applications running on the Terminal server. The following sections describe how to install applications on your Terminal server and configure applications for multisession use.

Installing Applications

The Registry and INI file mapping support that is built into Terminal Services causes programs to run correctly in Terminal Services, even if they were not designed to run in a multiuser environment. Terminal

Services automatically replicates the INI files and Registry settings from the system to each user. The INI files are placed in the user's home folder, or if no home folder is specified, in *Windir*\Documents and Settings*Username*.

To install applications on a Terminal server, use the Add/Remove Programs icon in Control Panel. Add/Remove Programs automatically runs the Terminal Services command change user, which ensures that the INI files and Registry entries are replicated and that the installed program will work properly for all Terminal Services clients. You should install the application on an NTFS partition, so that you can set permissions for the program.

Configuring Applications for Sharing

Terminal Services allows users to simultaneously run the same program. Because of this, applications that are run with Terminal Services must be configured for multisession use.

Most well-known applications have been tested for use with Terminal Services. Some require *compatibility scripts* that should be run after the program is installed to achieve the best performance on a Terminal server. The compatibility scripts may include notes on specific script capabilities and instructions on modifying them for custom installations. You can edit compatibility scripts in Notepad.

PER-USER DATA

In the multisession environment, each user is given an HKEY_CURRENT_USER Registry key, which stores per-user data. There is also a Registry key called HKEY_LOCAL_MACHINE, which stores information that is shared among users. Unfortunately, applications that assume one computer equals one user also assume that they can store user-specific data in HKEY_LOCAL_MACHINE. These applications also assume that they can store any file-based information, such as user preferences, in the System folder or the program directory. Always make sure that any per-user data is stored in HKEY_CURRENT_USER, in the user's home folder, or in a user-specified folder. Any global data should always be stored in either HKEY_LOCAL_MACHINE or in a specific location on the disk that is write-protected, such as the System folder.

Running terminal services in remote administration mode

If you install Terminal Services in remote administration mode, you'll be able to perform every administrative function from a client, just as if you were actually at the Terminal server console. Remote administration mode allows only two concurrent connections to the Terminal server, but you don't need additional Terminal Services client licenses to use this mode. It does not install any application-sharing features, which significantly decreases the overhead associated with running Terminal Services. This is important when your server is mission-critical and can't be burdened with extraneous processes.

If you already have Terminal Services installed in application server mode, you can switch to remote administration mode through the Add/Remove Programs icon in Control Panel.

Troubleshooting Terminal Services

When you are running Terminal Services in application server mode, you might find that installed applications do not work properly on Terminal clients. You may encounter this problem if the application was installed before Terminal Services was installed. To fix this problem, uninstall the application, and then reinstall it using the Add/Remove Programs icon in Control Panel.

Another problem that may occur is that the automatic logon connections won't work for Windows NT 4.0 Terminal clients. To fix this, run the Terminal Services Client Connection Manager utility. Choose automatic logon and specify the username, password, and domain.

Necessary Procedures

The procedures in this section cover the modes in Terminal Services, installing the necessary licenses, and configuring client connections.

NOTE Install Terminal Services in remote administration mode if you want to be able to perform administrative tasks from any client on the network; otherwise, you'll have to work from the Terminal server console.

Installing Terminal Services in Remote Administration Mode

1. Select Start ➢ Settings ➢ Control Panel. Double-click the Add/ Remove Programs icon.

2. In the Add/Remove Programs window, click Add/Remove Windows Components.

3. The Windows Components Wizard starts. Check the Terminal Services box and click the Next button.

4. Now you'll see the Terminal Services Setup dialog box. Make sure the Remote Administration Mode radio button is selected and click the Next button.

5. The Configuring Components dialog box appears. If the Windows 2000 Server CD is not already in your CD-ROM drive, you'll be prompted to insert the CD. Files will be copied, and the Terminal Services components will be configured. This may take a few minutes.

6. When the Completing the Windows Components Wizard dialog box appears, click the Finish button.

7. When prompted, click the Yes button to restart your computer and make the changes effective.

Installing Terminal Services in Application Server Mode

NOTE Install Terminal Services in application server mode when you want to give users remote access to applications running on the server.

Take the following steps to install Terminal Services in application server mode (this assumes remote administration mode is *not* installed):

1. Select Start ➢ Settings ➢ Control Panel. Double-click the Add/ Remove Programs icon.

2. In the Add/Remove Programs window, click the Add/Remove Windows Components option.

3. The Windows Components Wizard starts. Check the Terminal Services box and click the Next button.

4. In the first Terminal Services Setup dialog box, select the Application Server Mode radio button and click the Next button.

5. In the second Terminal Services Setup dialog box, you select the default permissions for application compatibility. The Permissions Compatible with Windows 2000 Users option provides the highest level of security. The Permissions Compatible with Terminal Services 4.0 Users option provides the highest compatibility for legacy applications. Make your selection and click the Next button.

6. You might be notified that certain applications may not work properly after installing Terminal Services in application server mode. After Terminal Services Setup is complete, you should reinstall these applications. If an application doesn't support network access, it won't work with Terminal Services. Click the Next button to continue.

7. Next up is the Configuring Components dialog box. If the Windows 2000 Server CD is not already in your CD-ROM drive, you'll be prompted to insert the CD. Files will be copied and the Terminal Services components will be configured. This may take a few minutes.

8. When the Completing the Windows Components Wizard dialog box appears, click the Finish button.

9. When prompted, click the Yes button to restart your computer and make the changes effective.

Configuring Terminal Services Licensing

Follow these steps to set up licensing arrangements for Terminal Services (the server):

1. Select Start ➢ Settings ➢ Control Panel and double-click the Add/Remove Programs icon.

2. In the Add/Remove Programs window, click the Add/Remove Windows Components option.

3. The Windows Components Wizard starts. Check the Terminal Services Licensing check box and click the Next button.

4. Next you see the Terminal Services Setup dialog box. Specify the mode that Terminal Services will use (this is used to verify that Terminal Services is running in application server mode) and click the Next button.

5. In the Terminal Services Licensing Setup dialog box, specify whether the license server will be available for your enterprise or for your domain or workgroup. Click the Next button.

6. If your Windows 2000 Server CD is not already in the CD-ROM drive, you'll be prompted to insert the CD so that the necessary files can be copied.

7. When the Completing the Windows Components Wizard dialog box appears, click the Finish button. Close the Add/Remove Windows Components window, and then close Control Panel.

8. Select Start ➢ Programs ➢ Administrative Tools ➢ Terminal Services Licensing.

9. Right-click your license server and select Activate Server from the pop-up menu.

10. The Licensing Wizard starts. Click the Next button.

11. The Connection Method dialog box appears. You can choose to connect to the Microsoft Clearinghouse via the Internet, the World Wide Web, telephone, or fax. In this example, we'll connect by telephone. Select the Telephone option and click the Next button.

12. In the Country/Region Selection dialog box, select your country or region and click the Next button.

13. In the License Server Activation dialog box, type in the license number provided by Microsoft (or leave this blank; you have 90 days to provide a valid number). Click the Next button.

Installing the Terminal Client through a Network Share

Take the following steps to install the Terminal Services client software on the computer that will connect to a share on the Terminal server:

1. Run the `Setup.exe` program in the `\Windir\System32\Clients\Tsclient\Net\Win32\disks\disk1` folder to install the client on the Terminal server.

2. The Terminal Services Client Setup window opens. Click the Continue button.

3. In the Name and Organization Information dialog box, type in your name and organization and click the OK button.

4. When the Confirm Name and Organization Information dialog box appears, check to see that the information is correct and click the OK button.

5. The License Agreement dialog box appears next. Click the I Agree button to agree to the license agreement.

6. In the Terminal Services Client Setup dialog box that appears next, specify the location where the Terminal Services client will be installed. To continue, click the large button to the left of the description, "Setup will install all of the Terminal Services client components in the specified destination folder."

7. The next dialog box asks if you want all users of this computer to have the same initial settings. Click Yes to install the client software for all users, or click No to install the software for only the current user.

8. When the installation is complete, you'll see a message to this effect. Click the OK button.

Creating a Client Connection

To create a connection using the Client Connection Manager utility, take the following steps:

1. Select Start ➤ Programs ➤ Terminal Services Client ➤ Client Connection Manager.

2. In the Client Connection Manager window, select File ➢ New Connection.

3. The Client Connection Manager Wizard starts. Click the Next button.

4. You start with the Create a Connection dialog box. Specify the connection name and the name or IP address of the Terminal server. Click the Next button to continue.

5. Next up is the Automatic Logon dialog box. Here you can specify that the user will log on automatically. If you enable automatic logon, you'll specify a username and password. After you make your selection, click the Next button to continue.

NOTE   Enabling automatic logon poses a security risk and should be used with caution.

---

6. The Screen Options dialog box appears next, where you configure the screen area for the client window. Only the options that are valid for your configuration will be available. You can also specify full-screen mode for display of the connection. Click the Next button to continue.

7. In the Connection Properties dialog box, you can enable data compression (which is used if you will connect by modem or through a slow network connection) and select whether you want to cache bitmaps. Then click the Next button.

8. In the Starting a Program dialog box, specify whether a program should be started automatically when a Terminal Services connection is opened. Click Next to continue.

9. In the Icon and Program Group dialog box, you can change the icon and program group that will be used for the Terminal client. Make your selections and click the Next button.

10. When the Completing the Client Connection Manager Wizard dialog box appears, click the Finish button.

11. The connection you created appears in the Client Connection Manager window. Double-click this connection to access the Terminal server.

12. If you didn't enable automatic logon, you'll see the Log On to Windows dialog box. Type in a valid username and password and click the OK button.

13. You are attached to the Terminal server as a Terminal client, and you'll see the Terminal Services Client Desktop. When you're done with your Terminal Services session, close the Terminal Services Client Desktop to access the Disconnect Windows Session dialog box, and disconnect.

Exam Essentials

Know the difference between the Terminal Services modes. Terminal Services can be run in two modes. Remote administration mode allows administrative tasks to be performed from any client on the network. Application server mode gives users remote access to applications running on the Terminal Services Server.

Know the benefits of running Terminal Services. Terminal Services has many benefits, including wider deployment of Windows 2000, simultaneous operation of both thin-client software and a stand-alone operating system, simplified application deployment, and remote administration of the server.

Know the Terminal Services features. Terminal Services features include multiple logon support, enhancements to system performance, Clipboard redirection, security, network load balancing, automated local printer support, session remote control, and remote administration.

Know the Terminal Services components. Terminal Services consists of a Terminal Services server, the Remote Desktop Protocol, and Terminal Services clients.

Know the requirements for a Terminal Services server. A Terminal Services server requires at least a Pentium processor and 128MB

RAM. Additional RAM is required for each client connection. You should also consider a high-performance network adapter card, high-performance bus architecture, and SCSI disk drives.

Know the requirements for a Terminal Services client.   Terminal Services clients can be run on a variety of machines, including Windows-based terminal devices; computers running Windows for Workgroups 3.11, Windows 95, Windows 98, Windows NT, and Windows 2000; and computers running Unix and Macintosh.

Know how to manage connections.   Connections are managed from the Connections folder in the Terminal Services window. On the General tab, you can specify for each connection the type and transport protocol used, and the encryption level used. The Logon Settings tab controls what logon information the user must provide. The Sessions tab controls session timeouts and reconnections settings. In the Environment tab, you determine the user profile settings.

Know what client settings are available.   The Client Settings tab in the Connections folder allows you to automatically restore the client's mappings at every logon. You can control each of the following mappings: drive, Windows printer, LPT port, COM port, Clipboard, and audio.

Know the options for configuring network adapters.   You can control the number of connections allowed on a network adapter card: an unlimited number or a specified maximum number.

Know what tasks are done through the Terminal Services Manager utility.   Terminal Services Manager helps you manage and monitor users, sessions, and processes that are connected to or running on any Terminal Services server.

Know the process to install client license key packs.   Before you can begin using Terminal Services, you must activate the license server. This is done through the Microsoft Clearinghouse. After the license server is activated, you can begin to install client license packs.

Know how to install Terminal Services client software.   You can install the Terminal Services client software through a share on the network, or by creating Terminal Services client installation disks.

Know how to install applications in the Terminal Services environment. Use the Add/Remove Programs icon in Control Panel to install applications on a Terminal Services server. This ensures that the application is properly installed.

Know how to optimize applications in the Terminal Services environment. Applications can be optimized for Terminal Services by using compatibility scripts after the application has been installed.

Key Terms and Concepts

application server mode   A Terminal Services mode that gives users access to applications running on the server.

compatibility script   A script that is run to optimize certain applications; required by some applications in order to run on a Terminal Services server.

client license key packs   The licenses that are distributed to Terminal Services clients by a license server.

license server   Terminal Services using its own licensing method, controlled by a license server. Clients must receive a valid license before they can connect to a server.

remote administration mode   A Terminal Services mode that gives administrators the ability to perform administrative tasks on the server.

remote control   Remote control allows a Terminal Services user to view or control another user's session.

Remote Desktop Protocol (RDP)   The protocol that supports clients' connections to a Terminal Services server.

session   Created for a user when he or she logs on to the Terminal Services server.

Terminal Services client   A client that is accessing a session on a Terminal Services server over thin-client technology.

Terminal Services server   A Windows 2000 server that is running Terminal Services.

Terminal Services Client Configurator   The utility that creates installation disks for Terminal Services clients.

Terminal Services Configuration   The utility that manages the RDP-TCP connections, as well as adds new connections.

Terminal Services Manager   The utility with which you manage and monitor Terminal Services users, sessions, and processes.

thin client   A Terminal Services client with a small-bandwidth signature. The server sends GUI information to the client using a video compression technology. The client sends keyboard and mouse signals to the server for processing.

Sample Questions

1. You are the network administrator. You are beginning to deploy applications that will be available through thin-client technologies. In what mode does the Terminal Services server operate to give users access to the applications?

   A. Session mode

   B. Thin-client mode

   C. Remote administration mode

   D. Application server mode

   Answer: D. Application server mode gives users access to applications running on the Terminal Services server.

2. You need to monitor the processes that are running on the Terminal Services server. Which utility will show you this information?

   A. Terminal Services Client Configurator

   B. Terminal Services Manager

   C. Terminal Services Configuration utility

   D. Performance Monitor

   Answer: B. The Terminal Services Manager allows you to monitor users, sessions, and processes.

Install, configure, and troubleshoot network adapters and drivers.

By adding a network adapter to your system, Windows 2000 adds a permanent local area connection. Configuring and trouble-shooting a network adapter is very similar to adding any other device. Microsoft will address this topic only lightly on the exams. You should know how to configure and troubleshoot these devices. In Necessary Procedures, you'll find the steps to view the parameters that are set on the network adapter.

Critical Information

Network adapters are hardware devices that connect computers to a network. Network adapters are responsible for providing the physical connection to the network, and the physical address of the computer. Like all other hardware devices, network adapters need a driver in order to communicate with the Windows 2000 operating system.

Installing a Network Adapter

Before you install a network adapter, read the instructions that accompany the hardware. If your network adapter is new, it should be self-configuring, with Plug-and-Play capabilities. A network adapter that supports Plug and Play should work the next time you start up the computer.

NOTE New devices will auto-detect needed settings and be self-configuring. Older devices rely on hardware setup programs to configure the hardware. And on *really* old devices you'll have to manually configure the adapter by setting switches or jumpers.

If the network adapter is not Plug-and-Play compatible, the operating system should detect the new piece of hardware after you install it, and will start a Wizard that leads you through the process of loading the adapter's driver. If this Add New Hardware Wizard does not start automatically, you can add the network adapter through the Add/ Remove Hardware icon in Control Panel.

Configuring a Network Adapter

After you install a network adapter, you configure it through its Properties dialog box. To access this dialog box, select Start ➤ Settings ➤ Control Panel ➤ Network and Dial-up Connections ➤ Local Area Connection ➤ Properties, and click the Configure button. Alternatively, you can right-click My Network Places and choose Properties, then right-click Local Area Connection and choose Properties, and then click the Configure button.

In the network adapter's Properties dialog box, the properties are grouped on four tabs: General, Advanced, Driver, and Resources.

General Network Adapter Properties

The General tab contains the name of the adapter, the device type, the manufacturer, and the location. The Device Status box reports whether or not the device is working properly. If it isn't, you can click the Troubleshooter button to have Windows 2000 display some general troubleshooting tips. You can also enable or disable the device through the Device Usage drop-down list options.

Advanced Network Adapter Properties

The contents of the Advanced tab will vary depending on the network adapter and driver you are using. To configure options in this dialog box, choose the property you want to modify in the Property list box on the left, and specify the value for the property in the Value box on the right.

NOTE The settings on the Advanced tab of the network adapter Properties dialog box typically won't need to be changed except as instructed by the manufacturer.

Driver Properties

The Driver tab of the network adapter Properties dialog box provides the following information about your driver:

- Driver provider, usually Microsoft or the network adapter manufacturer

- Date the driver was released

- Driver version, useful in determining if you have the latest driver installed

- Digital signer, which is the company that provides the digital signature for driver signing

By clicking the Driver Details button at the bottom of the Driver tab, you can access additional information about the driver. The Driver File Details dialog box lists the following:

- Location of the driver file, useful for troubleshooting

- Original provider of the driver, usually the manufacturer

- File version, useful for troubleshooting

- Copyright information about the driver

The Uninstall button at the bottom of the Driver tab removes the driver from your computer, and you'd do this if you were going to replace the driver with a completely new driver. Normally, however, you'll update the driver rather than uninstalling it.

To update a driver, click the Update Driver button at the bottom of the Driver tab. This starts the Upgrade Device Driver Wizard, which steps you through the process of upgrading the driver for an existing device.

TIP If you cannot find the driver for your network card or the configuration instructions, look for the latest drivers at the card vendor's Web site. Typically you'll also find a list of Frequently Asked Questions (FAQ) about the hardware.

Resource Properties

Each device installed on a computer uses computer resources. Resources include interrupt request (IRQ), memory, and I/O (input/ output) settings. The Resources tab of the network adapter Properties dialog box lists the resource settings for your network adapter. This information is important for troubleshooting, because if other devices are trying to use the same resource settings, your devices will not work properly. The Conflicting Device List box at the bottom of the Resources tab shows any conflicts.

Troubleshooting Network Adapters

If your network adapter is not working, the problem may be with the hardware, the driver software, or the network protocols. Following are some common causes for network adapter problems:

Network adapter not on the HCL	If the device is not on the official HCL, contact the vendor.
Outdated driver	Make sure that you have the most up-to-date driver for your adapter. Check for the latest driver on the vendor's Web site.
Network adapter not recognized by Windows 2000	Check Device Manager to see if Windows 2000 recognizes your adapter. If you don't see it listed, you'll need to install it manually (through the Add/Remove Hardware icon in Control Panel). Also verify that the adapter's resource settings don't conflict with the settings of other devices (check the Resources tab of the network adapter's Properties dialog box).
Hardware not working properly	Run any diagnostics that come with the adapter. If everything seems to work properly, make sure the cable is good and that all applicable network hardware is installed properly and is working. This is where it pays off to have spare working hardware (such as cables and extra network adapters) on hand.

| Improperly configured network protocols | Make sure your network protocols have been configured properly. |

TIP You can also check Event Viewer to see if you find any messages that give you a hint about what is causing a network adapter error.

Necessary Procedures

When you need access to the properties of a network adapter, follow these steps:

1. Select Start ➤ Settings ➤ Control Panel ➤ Network and Dial-up Connections ➤ Local Area Connection ➤ Properties, and then click the Configure button.

2. In the General tab of the connection's Properties dialog box, click the Configure button under Connect Using.

3. In the General tab of the network adapter's Properties dialog box, verify that the Device Status box shows "This device is working properly."

4. Click the Advanced tab. Note the properties that are available for your driver.

5. Click the Driver tab. Note the driver date and version information. Click the Driver Details button to see the location of your network adapter's driver file. Click OK to close the Driver File Details dialog box.

6. Click the Resources tab. Note the resources that are being used by your network adapter. Verify that the Conflicting Device List box shows "No conflicts."

Exam Essentials

Know the difference between Plug-and-Play and other devices.
Plug-and-Play devices should work immediately after you've installed them and restarted the machine. Non-Plug-and-Play devices will launch a wizard to walk you through the process of installation.

Know how to configure network adapters. Network adapters are configured through their Properties dialog box.

Know how to view resources used by a network adapter. The Resources tab of the network adapter's Properties dialog box shows resources such as IRQ, memory, and I/O settings.

Know how to troubleshoot network adapters. Some common causes of a malfunctioning network adapter are that the adapter isn't supported on the official HCL; the driver is outdated; or that the hardware isn't working properly, isn't recognized by Windows 2000, or is improperly configured.

Key Term and Concept

network adapter   Hardware used to connect a computer to the network.

Sample Questions

1. You have just added a network adapter to your system. When you reboot the system, the network adapter fails to initialize. Where do you check to see if the device is working properly?

A. General Network Adapter Properties

B. Advanced Network Adapter Properties

C. Driver Properties

D. Resource Properties

Answer: A. The General Network Adapter Properties tab of the network adapter's Properties dialog box will show you if the device is working properly, in the Device Status section.

2. You have just added a network adapter to your system. Upon rebooting the system, the network adapter fails to initialize. Where do you go to troubleshoot the device? Select all that apply.

A. General Network Adapter Properties

B. Advanced Network Adapter Properties

C. Driver Properties

D. Resource Properties

Answer: A, C, and D. The General Network Adapter Properties tab of the network adapter will show you if the device is working properly in the Device Status section. The Driver Properties will show the date and location of the driver. The Resource Properties will show you the resources that are being used for the device. The Conflicting Device List box will show any conflicting devices.

Chapter

7

Implementing, Monitoring, and Troubleshooting Security

For network administrators, security is always a primary concern. This chapter covers the many security-related features that are part of Windows 2000 Server. One objective covers the Encrypted File System, which can protect files on the hard drive yet is transparent to the end users. The chapter also includes important topics such as security policies, auditing, account policies, and the analysis tools that are part of the Security Configuration and Analysis MMC snap-in. All of these features are designed to prevent unauthorized access to your vital files and systems.

Because security is one of the principal selling features of Windows 2000, this Microsoft certification exam will, of course, cover this topic in depth. You'll be expected to know how to configure policies, both local and system, and how these policies will interact. You'll have to know how to implement auditing, and the mechanisms of the Encrypting File System. Finally, you'll need a solid familiarity with using the Security Configuration tool set to make sure you've taken advantage of Windows 2000 security features and implemented an effective security posture to protect your network.

Encrypt data on a hard disk by using Encrypting File System (EFS).

With Windows 2000's Encrypting File System (EFS), the data in NTFS files is encrypted on disk. The encryption technology used is public-key based and runs as an integrated system service, making it easy to manage, difficult to attack, and transparent to the user. Because EFS is a new technology, Microsoft will test your understanding of it. You'll be expected to know how EFS adds security to files and what happens to files if they are moved to unencrypted partitions.

Critical Information

Data encryption is a way to increase the safety of stored data. Encryption is the process of translating data into code that is not easily accessible. Once data has been encrypted, a password or key is required to decrypt the data. Unencrypted data is known as *plain text*; encrypted data is known as *cipher text*.

The Encrypting File System

The *Encrypting File System (EFS)* is the Windows 2000 technology that is used to store encrypted files on NTFS partitions. Encrypted files add an extra layer of security to your file system.

The default configuration of EFS allows users to begin encrypting files without any administrative efforts. EFS goes to work when a user specifies that a folder or file on an NTFS partition should be encrypted. EFS will automatically create a public-key pair when the encryption attribute is selected. Each file is encrypted with a randomly generated key, which is then used to decrypt the file when the user needs to access the file. The encryption follows the file, even when it is moved to an unencrypted volume.

The encryption is transparent to the user, who has access to the file. However, when other users try to open the file, they won't be able to decrypt it—even if they have Full Control NTFS permissions. Instead, they will receive an error message. Without the public-key pair, you cannot open and read an encrypted file.

You encrypt and decrypt files through a volume's Properties dialog box or by using the CIPHER command-line utility. The steps for both these procedures are included in the coverage of this objective.

Using the CIPHER Utility

CIPHER is a command-line utility that can be used to encrypt and decrypt files on NTFS volumes. The syntax for the CIPHER command is as follows:

```
CIPHER /[command parameter] [filename]
```

Table 7.1 lists the command parameters associated with the CIPHER command.

TABLE 7.1: CIPHER Command Parameters

Parameter	Description
/e	Specifies that files or folders should be encrypted.
/d	Specifies that files or folders should be decrypted.
/s:dir	Specifies that subfolders of the target folder should also be encrypted or decrypted based on the option specified.
/I	Causes any errors that occur to be ignored. Without this switch, the CIPHER utility stops whenever an error occurs.
/f	Forces all files and folders to be encrypted or decrypted, regardless of their current state. Normally, if a file is already in the specified state, it is skipped.
/q	Runs in a quiet mode and displays only the most important information.

Necessary Procedures

The two procedures explain how to encrypt and decrypt files or folders using either Windows Explorer or the CIPHER command.

Setting Properties to Encrypt a Folder or File

To encrypt a folder or a file, take the following steps:

1. Open Windows Explorer by selecting Start ➤ Programs ➤ Accessories ➤ Windows Explorer.

2. In Windows Explorer, find and select the folder or file you wish to encrypt.

3. Right-click the folder or file and select Properties from the pop-up menu.

4. In the General tab of the Properties dialog box, click the Advanced button.

5. When the Advanced Attributes dialog box appears (see Figure 7.1), check the Encrypt Contents to Secure Data check box. Then click the OK button.

6. The Confirm Attribute Changes dialog box appears next. Here, specify whether you want to apply encryption to this folder only (Apply Changes to This Folder Only), or to apply encryption to the subfolders and files within the folder as well (Apply Changes to This Folder, Subfolder, and Files). Then click the OK button.

FIGURE 7.1: The Advanced Attributes dialog box is accessed from the folder's Properties dialog box.

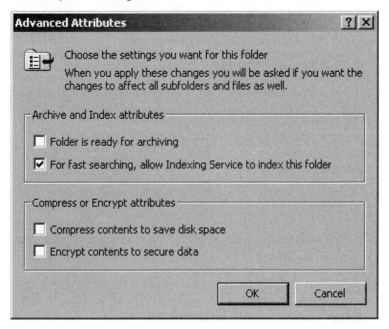

To decrypt folders and files, repeat the steps just above, but uncheck the Encrypt Contents to Secure Data option in the Advanced Attributes dialog box.

NOTE By default, the Administrator has rights to access the properties of another user's encrypted folder or file and decrypt it. This allows an Administrator to recover a file if the user who encrypted it is unavailable to decrypt it (for example, because that user left the organization).

Using the CIPHER Utility to Manage Date Encryption

1. Select Start ➤ Programs ➤ Accessories ➤ Command Prompt.

2. In the Command Prompt dialog box, type **C:** and press Enter to access the C: drive.

3. From the C:\> prompt, type **cipher**. You will see a list of folders and files and the state of encryption.

4. Type **MD TEST** and press Enter to create a new folder named Test.

5. Type **cipher /e test** and press Enter. You will see a message verifying that the folder was encrypted.

Exam Essentials

Know the role of the Encrypting File System. EFS encrypts data in NTFS partitions. This increases data security.

Know how to encrypt files. You can use a volume's Properties dialog box to encrypt a file, or you can use the CIPHER command.

Key Terms and Concepts

CIPHER   A command-line utility that can be used to encrypt files on NTFS volumes.

cipher text   Data that has been encrypted.

data encryption   The process of translating data into code that is not easily accessible.

Encrypting File System (EFS)   The Windows 2000 technology that is used to store encrypted files on NTFS partitions.

public key   Public key is a scheme that uses a pair of keys for encryption: a public key, which encrypts data, and a corresponding private (secret) key for decryption of data.

plain text   Data that has not been encrypted.

Sample Questions

1. What Windows 2000 Server service do you use to manage data encryption?

A. DFS

B. EFS

C. QMS

D. TRS

Answer: B. The Encrypting File System (EFS) is used to manage data encryption in Windows 2000.

2. You are the network administrator in a company that has decided to increase the security of the data stored on its servers. Which of the following will help you accomplish this? Select all that apply.

A. Using CIPHER to encrypt the files

B. Editing the file's Properties to allow encryption

C. Editing the folder's Properties to allow encryption

D. Editing the volume's Properties to allow encryption

Answer: A, D. You can use either the volume's Properties dialog box or the CIPHER command to encrypt files.

Implement, configure, manage, and troubleshoot policies in a Windows 2000 environment.

- Implement, configure, manage, and troubleshoot Local Policy in a Windows 2000 environment.
- Implement, configure, manage, and troubleshoot System Policy in a Windows 2000 environment.

*P*olicies give the network administrator the means to control users' actions on the network. Local policies control what the user can do after they log on to the system. You can set options for a local audit policy, user rights assignments, and control of access to the floppy disk or CD-ROM. System policies control the computer's system configuration and the user's work environment.

Microsoft places a strong focus on the capabilities of policies and will expect that you know how to implement them. That includes understanding the settings, setting up the policies, and managing them. You'll also need to know how to anticipate the effective results when multiple policies interact, based on established precedence.

Critical Information

In Windows 2000, you use Group Policy to define configurations for groups of users and computers. You can create specific desktop configuration for each group of users and computers. The settings for Group Policy include options for Registry-based policies, security settings, software installation, and folder redirection. Group Policy settings are contained in Group Policy Object (GPO), which in turn is part of the Active Directory. All of these settings are controlled using the Group Policy snap-in in the MMC. The Local Computer Policy snap-in lets you create local polices that govern user rights and audit policies.

Local Policies

When you want to control the actions a user can perform after logging on, you use *local policies*. With local policies, you can implement auditing of the user's operations, specify the user's rights, and set up security options. Auditing is covered in the objective "Implement, configure, manage, and troubleshoot auditing."

User rights fall into two general categories: logon rights and privileges. *Logon rights* control who can log on to a computer and how. The logon methods are from the keyboard, from the network, as a service, and as a batch file. Logon rights can also be specified to allow or deny logon to a computer. *Privileges* limit access to system resources and can override permissions set on a particular object. Some examples of privileges are to back up files and directories, to add workstations to a domain, and to change system time.

Security options offer a wide variety of controls for computers. You can design policies that log users off when their logon hours expire; that disable the Ctrl+Alt+Del for logon, forcing users to use smart card logon; and that halt a computer's operations if you're unable to audit.

To set up and maintain local policies, you'll first need to add the Local Computer Policy snap-in to the MMC. From the MMC, to access the Local Policies folders, follow this path: Local Computer Policy, Computer Configuration, Windows Settings, Security Settings, Local Policies. Figure 7.2 shows the MMC with the Local Policies folders displayed in the right-hand pane: Audit Policy, User Rights Assignment, and Security Options.

FIGURE 7.2: Accessing the Local Policies folders in MMC

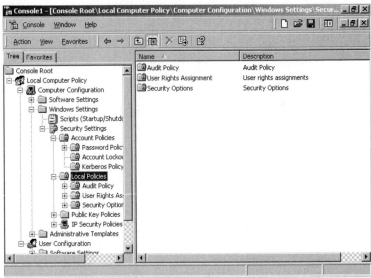

System Policies

Through *system policies,* you can control the network computers' system configuration and the users' work environment. System policies work by editing the Registry to reflect the policy settings. You can set system policies for specific users, groups, and computers, as well as for all users and all computers. By default, no system policies are used unless an Administrator creates them. These policies are configured through the System Policy Editor, a GUI invoked with the POLEDIT command.

System policies are commonly associated with Windows NT 4.0 In Windows 2000, it is recommended that you use Group Policy to manage users' Desktop settings. However, you can still use the System Policy Editor (POLEDIT.EXE) to manage system policies in Windows 2000. In the Windows family of operating systems, system policy files work together as follows:

- System policy files created in Windows 2000 or Windows NT 4.0 will work with Windows 2000 and Windows NT 4.0 clients.

- System policy files created in Windows 98 or Windows 95 will work with Windows 98 and Windows 95 clients.

You can configure system policies for the following:

Default User	Sets defaults for any user who logs on from an NT computer (writes to the HKEY_CURRENT_ USER portion of the Registry)
User	Allows you to create a customized system policy for a specific user (writes to the HKEY_ CURRENT_USER portion of the Registry)
Group	Similar to a User system policy, but you can apply this system policy to a group of users (writes to the HKEY_CURRENT_USER portion of the Registry)
Default Computer	Sets default settings for any Windows 2000 or Windows NT 4 .0 computer in the domain (writes to the HKEY_LOCAL_MACHINE portion of the Registry)
Computer	Allows you to create a customized system policy for a specific computer (writes to the HKEY_LOCAL_MACHINE portion of the Registry)

NOTE   In order to manage system policies for specific users and groups, your Windows 2000 Server computer must be configured as a domain controller.

Configuring User and Group System Policies

Desktop and system settings are controlled through the system policies that you apply to all users (through the Default User icon), to a specific user, or to a group. The options for user and group system policies are described in Table 7.2.

NOTE The system policy options refer to Windows NT because they were primarily designed for controlling NT clients. Using the term "Windows NT" supports backward compatibility.

TABLE 7.2: User and Group System Policy Options

Options	Descriptions
Control Panel	Specifies display settings, such as hiding the Screen Saver and Appearance tabs of the Display Properties dialog box
Desktop	Configures wallpaper and color schemes
Shell	Configures restrictions such as hiding Network Neighborhood, and not saving settings when the user exits
System	Sets restrictions such as disabling the Registry editing tools, and running only allowed Windows applications
Windows NT Shell	Configures Windows NT custom folders and specifies restrictions relating to the NT shell
Windows NT System	Specifies whether or not to parse AUTOEXEC.BAT, and whether or not to run logon scripts synchronously.

TIP By default, the system looks for system policies on the authenticating domain controller in the NETLOGON share in a file called NTCONFIG.POL. If you want your system policy to be enforced systemwide, make a note of this filename and share name, because they must be explicitly specified when you create the system policy.

Determining Effective System Policy

When a user has multiple system policies assigned through user and group memberships, the following conditions determine which system policy takes precedence:

- If the user has user system policy options configured, these policies are in the HKEY_CURRENT_USER portion of the Registry. This allows specific user policies to take precedence over any existing Default User or group system policies. Thus a group system policy will not be used if a user system policy exists.

- If the user is a member of any groups that have system policy options configured, and the user does not have any user system policy options defined, the group system policies will be merged into the HKEY_CURRENT_USER portion of the Registry by priority. If multiple group policies have been defined, you can specify group priority in the System Policy Editor options.

- If the user does not have any user or group system policies that apply, the HKEY_CURRENT_USER portion of the Registry will be updated with any changes made to the Default User system policy.

- If a user profile and a system policy are both present and have conflicting settings for the same options, the system policy options will overwrite the user profile configuration in the Registry.

Configuring Computer System Policies

You can also manage computer settings through system policies. Following are some of the options you can configure:

- Network settings, which control system policy updates

- System settings, for running items at startup

- Windows NT Network settings, which control creation of hidden drive shares

- Windows NT Printers settings, which control printer configuration options

- Windows NT Remote Access settings, which control remote access options

- Windows NT Shell settings, which control custom shared objects such as Desktop items and the Start menu

- Windows NT System settings, which are used to configure logon and file system settings

- Windows NT User Profiles settings, which are used to configure user profiles

Necessary Procedures

The following procedure gives you the steps to create and configure a system policy for a user or group.

WARNING It is much easier to edit user configurations through the System Policy Editor, which is a GUI interface, than it is to edit the text-based Registry. However, when you use the System Policy Editor, you are editing your Registry, so be careful. Back up your Registry before making any changes.

---

1. Select Start ➢ Run, type **POLEDIT** in the Run dialog box, and click the OK button.

2. In the System Policy Editor window, select File ➢ New Policy.

3. The System Policy Editor displays icons for Default Computer and Default User. Select Edit ➢ Add User (or Add Group).

4. The Add User (or Add Group) dialog box appears. You can type in the name of the user/group, or click the Browse button to select from a list of available users/groups. After you add the user/group, click the OK button.

5. The user/group you selected appears in the System Policy Editor window. To edit or view the policy settings for the user/group, double-click the user/group.

6. The policies are listed on the Policies tab of the user/group Properties dialog box. Click an option that you want to configure.

7. You see a list all of the policies that can be defined. Click the check boxes to configure the options as follows:

- A grayed-out check box indicates that no policy is applied.

- A check mark indicates that the policy should be applied. This is considered a True value.

- A blank (or white) check box indicates that the policy should not be applied. This is considered a False value.

8. Repeat steps 6 and 7 to configure each option you want to modify. After all of the options have been configured, click the OK button in the Policies tab.

9. When you have finished editing all of the user and group policies, save the policies by selecting File ➤ Save.

Exam Essentials

Know what local polices cover.   Local policies allow you to implement auditing, set user rights, and set security options.

Know how system policies interoperate with clients.   System policies for Windows 2000 or Windows NT will work with Windows 2000 *and* Windows NT clients.

Know for whom you can configure system policies.   System polices can be set for the Default User, users, groups, Default Computer, and computer.

Know when system policies apply.   By default, no system policies are used. After system policies are created, the domain controller looks for the `NTCONFIG.POL` file in the NETLOGON share.

Know how to determine effective system policy.   User policies take precedence over group policies. The order of multiple group policies can be set in the System Policy Editor. Group policies take precedence over the Default User. The Default User policy takes precedence over a user profile.

Key Terms and Concepts

local policy   A local policy controls what a user can do after logon. Local policies implement auditing settings, user rights, and security.

NETLOGON share   A share on the domain controller that can contain the `NTCONFIG.POL` file.

`NTCONFIG.POL`   The file that holds the system policy information.

system policy   System policies control the computer's system configuration and the user's work environment.

Sample Questions

1. A system policy can be applied to which types of users? Select all that apply.

A. All users

B. A specific user

C. A group of users

D. A computer

Answer: A, B, C, and D. A system policy can apply to Default User, User, Group, Default Computer, and Computer.

2. Local policies control what kind of user actions? Choose all that apply.

A. Logon

B. Auditing

C. Security

D. Computer system configuration

Answer: B and C. A local policy controls what a user can do after logon. Local policies implement auditing settings, user rights, and security.

Implement, configure, manage, and troubleshoot auditing.

Audit policies give network administrators the ability to track and manage what users are doing in the network. Audit policies are set as part of local policies, as discussed in the preceding objective. Although auditing is a good tool for monitoring system security, Microsoft's exams typically test this area very lightly. You'll be expected to know the basics of what audit policies do and how you set them up.

Critical Information

The *audit policies* allow you to watch what your users are doing. You audit the events that pertain to user management. By tracking certain events, you can create a history of specific tasks such as user creation, and successful or unsuccessful logon attempts. You can also identify security violations that arise when users attempt to access system management tasks for which they aren't authorized.

When you define an audit policy, you can choose to audit success or failure of specific events. The success of an event means that the task was successfully accomplished. The failure of an event means that the task was not successfully accomplished.

By default, auditing is not enabled, and it must be manually configured. Once auditing has been configured, you can see the results of the audit through the Event Viewer utility. Table 7.3 describes the Audit Policy options.

WARNING   Auditing too many events can degrade system performance due to the high processing requirements of auditing operations. A substantial amount of disk space is consumed, as well, to store the audit log. You should use this feature judiciously.

TABLE 7.3: Audit Policy Options

Policy	What It Tracks
Audit Account Logon Events	User logons, logoffs, and network connections
Audit Account Management	User and group account creation, deletion, and management actions
Audit Directory Service Access	Directory service accesses
Audit Logon Events	Events related to logon, such as running a logon script or accessing a roaming profile
Audit Object Access	Access to files, folders, and printers
Audit Policy Change	Any changes to the audit policy
Audit Privilege Use	Any changes to user authorizations to define or see the results of auditing
Audit Process Tracking	Events such as activating a program, accessing an object, and exiting a process
Audit System Events	System events such as shutting down or restarting the computer; events that relate to the Security log within Event Viewer

Necessary Procedures

Here are the steps to set up an audit policy that allows you to monitor logons and account management changes:

1. Select Start ➢ Programs ➢ Administrative Tools ➢ Security and expand the Local Computer Policy snap-in. (On a domain controller, it will be Local Security Policy.)

2. In the tree on the left side of the MMC, expand the folders as follows: Computer Configuration, Windows Settings, Security Settings, Local Policies, and Audit Policy.

3. Open the Audit Account Logon Events policy. In the Local Policy Setting field, specify Audit These Attempts. Check the boxes for Success and Failure. Click the OK button.

4. Open the Audit Account Management policy. In the Local Policy Setting field, specify Audit These Attempts. Check the boxes for Success and Failure as necessary. Click the OK button.

Exam Essentials

Know how to enable an audit policy.   Audit policies are manually configured in the MMC, in the Local Computer Policy snap-in.

Know where to view the results of auditing.   The results of an audit policy can be examined in the Event Viewer utility.

Key Term and Concept

audit policy   A policy that allows you to see what your users are doing. This policy determines what will be displayed (such as logon attempts, failed attempts, etc.) in the Security log of Event Viewer.

Sample Questions

1. As network administrator, you want to see if unauthorized users are trying to gain access to your computers. Which policy should you set up?

A. Audit Account Logon Events successes

B. Audit Account Logon Events failures

C. Audit Logon Events successes

D. Audit Account Logon Events failures

Answer: B. By auditing account logon events, you track user logons and logoffs. By selecting failures, you can see if someone is trying to hack onto the computer.

2. You are the network administrator. You want to see who is using your new color laser printer. Which policy should you set up?

A. Audit Account Logon Events

B. Audit Process Tracking

C. Audit Logon Events

D. Audit Object Access

Answer: D. By auditing object access, you can observe access to files, folders, and printers.

Implement, configure, manage, and troubleshoot local accounts.

One of the most fundamental tasks in network management is the creation of user and group accounts. Without a user account, a user can't log on to a computer, a server, or a network. Unless group accounts are established, the administrator will have a more difficult job of granting users' rights to network resources.

Windows 2000 Server supports local and Active Directory users and groups, so you can manage users from a local perspective as well as through the Active Directory. This exam focuses only on the local user and group accounts; the Active Directory accounts are covered on other exams. Active Directory accounts are mentioned here briefly in the context of their use with user and group accounts.

Critical Information

Windows 2000 supports two kinds of users: local users and Active Directory (domain) users. A computer running Windows 2000 Professional or Windows 2000 Server (configured as a member server) has the ability to store its own user accounts database. The users stored at the local computer are known as *local users*. The Active Directory is a directory service available with the Windows 2000 Server platform. It stores information in a central database so that users can have a single user account for the network. The users and groups stored in the Active Directory's central database are called *Active Directory users or domain users.*

NOTE For detailed discussion of the Active Directory, refer to *MCSE: Windows 2000 Directory Services Administration Study Guide,* by Anil Desai with James Chellis (Sybex, 2000).

If you maintain local user accounts, an account is required on each computer to which the user needs access within the network. For this reason, domain user accounts are more commonly used to manage larger networks.

On Windows 2000 Professional computers and Windows 2000 member servers, you create and manage local user accounts through the Local Users and Groups utility. On Windows 2000 Server domain controllers, you manage user accounts with the Microsoft Active Directory Users and Computers utility.

Built-in User Accounts

When you install Windows 2000 Server, several built-in user accounts are created by default. Table 7.4 describes the built-in user accounts and indicates which environment (local or domain) contains the built-in account.

TABLE 7.4: Built-in User Accounts

Built-in User	Description	Environment
Administrator	An account that has full control over the computer. You provide a password for this account during Windows 2000 installation. This account can perform all tasks, including creating users and groups, managing the file system, and setting up printing.	Local and domain

TABLE 7.4: Built-in User Accounts *(continued)*

Built-in User	Description	Environment
Guest	Allows users to access the computer even if they don't have a unique username and password. Because of the inherent security risks associated with this type of user, Guest account is disabled by default. When enabled, it is usually given very limited privileges.	Local and domain
ILS_Anonymous_ User	An account used by the ILS service. ILS supports telephony applications that use features such as caller ID, videoconferencing, conference calling, and faxing. To use ILS, Internet Information Services (IIS) must be installed.	Domain
IUSR_ *computername*	An account that provides anonymous access for IIS (on a computer that has IIS installed).	Local and domain
IWAM_ *computername*	An account used for IIS to start process applications (on a computer that has IIS installed).	Local and domain
Krbtgt	An account used by the Key Distribution Center service.	Domain
TSInternetUser	An account used by Terminal Services.	Domain

TIP By default, the name Administrator is given to the account with full control over the computer. You can increase the computer's security by renaming the Administrator account and then creating an account named Administrator without any permissions. This way, even if a hacker is able to log on as Administrator, the intruder won't be able to access any system resources.

Using the Local Users and Groups Utility

The Local Users and Groups utility helps you create, delete, and rename user accounts, as well as change passwords. There are two methods for accessing this utility:

- Load the Local Users and Groups utility as a Microsoft Management Console (MMC) snap-in.

- Access the Local Users and Groups utility through the Computer Management utility.

If your computer doesn't have the MMC configured, the quickest way to access Local Users and Groups is through the Computer Management utility. Right-click My Computer and select Manage from the pop-up menu to open the Computer Management window. In the System Tools folder, you'll see the Local Users and Groups folder. Expand that folder to access the Users and Groups folders within the utility (see Figure 7.3).

FIGURE 7.3: Local Users and Groups in Computer Management

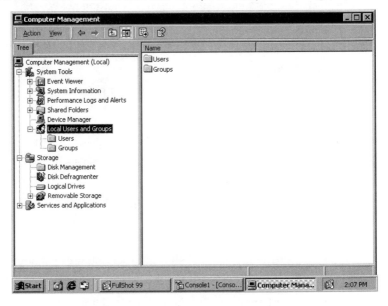

NOTE The procedures for many basic tasks of managing local users—such as creating, disabling, deleting, and renaming user accounts—are the same for both Windows 2000 Server and Professional.

Creating New Users

To create users on a Windows 2000 Server computer, you must be logged on as a user with permissions to create a new user, and you must be a member of the Administrators group or Power Users group.

To create a new user, open the Local Users and Groups utility, highlight the Users folder, and select Action ➢ New User. This opens the New User dialog box. In this dialog box, the User Name field is required. All of the other settings in the New User dialog box are optional.

TIP You can also create users through the command-line utility NET USER. For more information about this command, type **NET USER /?** from a command prompt.

USERNAMES

The only real requirement for creating a new user is that you must provide a valid username. "Valid" means that the name must be structured according to the Windows 2000 rules for usernames. However, it's also a good idea to have your own rules for usernames, which, along with the Windows 2000 rules, can form your naming convention.

Here are the Windows 2000 rules for usernames:

- Must be between 1 and 20 characters
- Must be unique among all other user and group names stored within the specified computer
- Cannot contain any of the following characters:

    * / \ [ ] : ; | = , + ? < > "

- Cannot consist exclusively of periods or spaces

Keeping these rules in mind, choose a naming convention to be your consistent naming format. You should also provide a mechanism that will accommodate duplicate usernames. This mechanism should be able to readily identify the user without using a duplicate user account name.

TIP   Naming conventions should also be applied to names for objects such as groups, printers, and computers.

SIDS

When you create a new user, a *security identifier (SID)* is automatically created on the computer for the user account. The username is a property of the SID. Clearly, using SIDs would make administration a nightmare. Fortunately for your administrative tasks, you see and use the username rather than the SID.

Usage of SIDs has several advantages. Because Windows 2000 uses the SID as the user object, you can easily rename a user while still retaining all the properties of that user. SIDs also ensure that if you delete and re-create a user with the same username, the new user account will not have any of the properties of the old account because it is based on a new, unique SID.

OPTIONS FOR NEW USER ACCOUNTS

Table 7.5 describes the text fields and check boxes in the New User dialog box.

TABLE 7.5:   New User Account Options

Option	Description
User Name (required)	Defines the username for the new account. Choose a name that is consistent with your naming convention. Usernames are not case sensitive. This is the only required field in the dialog box.

TABLE 7.5: New User Account Options *(continued)*

Option	Description
Full Name	Typically, the user's first and last name. Default entry in this field is the same as the entry in the User Name field.
Description	Typically used to specify a title and/or location, but can be used for any purpose.
Password	Assigns the initial password for the user. For security purposes, it's not advisable to use readily available information about the user. Passwords can be up to 14 characters and are case sensitive.
Confirm Password	Confirms that you entered the password the same way twice, to verify that you typed it correctly.
User Must Change Password at Next Logon	If enabled, forces the user to change the password at the first logon. This security option is selected by default.
User Cannot Change Password	If enabled, prevents a user from changing the password. Useful for Guest and other accounts that are shared by more than one user. By default, this option is off.
Password Never Expires	If enabled, specifies that the password will never expire, even if a password policy has been set up. For example, you might select this for a service account for which you don't want the administrative overhead of managing changing passwords. By default, this option is off.
Account Is Disabled	If enabled, specifies that this account cannot be used for logon purposes. For example, you might turn this on for template accounts or for an account not currently being used. It helps keep inactive accounts from becoming threats to security. By default, this option is off.

NOTE   Make sure that your users know that usernames are *not* case sensitive, but passwords *are*.

Disabling and Deleting User Accounts

When a user account is no longer needed, it should be disabled or deleted. If you choose to disable an account, you can later reenable it to restore it with all its associated user properties. An account that is deleted can never be restored.

WARNING   User accounts that are not in use are a security risk, because an intruder could access your network though an inactive account.

It's wise to disable an account if a user will not be working with it for a period of time because of a vacation or other leave of absence. Another reason to disable an account is if you're planning on putting another user in that same function, so that the new person will have access to the same resources as the previous user.

You disable a user account by checking the Account Is Disabled check box in the user's Properties dialog box. To access the Properties, double-click the user account in the Users folder of the Local Users and Groups utility. You can also access a user's Properties by highlighting the user account and right-clicking.

You should delete a user account if you are sure that the account will never be needed again. To delete a user account, open the Local Users and Groups utility, highlight the account you wish to delete, then select Delete.

Because user deletion is a permanent action, you'll be prompted to confirm your action. Once you've clicked the Yes button here, you won't be able to re-create or access the account again (unless you restore your local user account database from a backup).

NOTE The Administrator and Guest accounts cannot be deleted. The *initial user* account can be deleted.

Renaming Users

Once a user account has been created, you can rename it at any time. When you rename a user account, it retains all the associated user properties of the previous username. Remember, the name is a property of the SID.

You might want to rename a user account because the user's name has changed or to correct a misspelling. You can rename an existing user's account for a new user to whom you want to assign the same properties, as when someone is hired to take an ex-employee's position.

To rename a user account, open the Local Users and Groups utility, highlight the user account you wish to rename, and select Action ➤ Rename. Edit the username and press Enter to complete the action.

NOTE Renaming a user does not change any "hard-coded" names, such as the user's home directory. If you want to change these names as well, you must modify them manually.

Changing a User's Password

What do you do if a user forgets the password and can't log on? You can't just open a dialog box and see the old password. However, as the Administrator, you *can* change the user's password. To do this, open the Local Users and Groups utility, highlight the user account, and select Action ➤ Set Password. Type in the new password to set it, and then again to confirm it.

Managing Local User Properties

For more control over user accounts, you can configure user properties. Through the user Properties dialog box, you can change the original password options, add the users to existing groups, and specify user profile information.

To open the user's Properties dialog box, access the Local Users and Groups utility, open the Users folder, and double-click the user account. The Properties dialog box has tabs for the four main categories of properties:

- The General tab contains the information that you supplied when you set up the new user account, including any Full Name and Description information, the selected password options, and whether or not the account is disabled. If you want to modify any of these properties after you've created the user, simply open the Properties dialog box and make the changes on the General tab.

- The Member Of tab is used to manage the user's membership in groups. It displays all the groups that the user belongs to. From here, you can add the user to an existing group by clicking the Add button, or remove that user from a group by clicking the Remove button.

- The Profile tab lets you set properties to customize the user's environment, as explained in the next section.

- The Dial-in tab is used to define dial-in properties such as remote access permissions and callback options. These options are used in conjunction with remote access servers and virtual private network (VPN) servers.

Setting Up the Local User Environment

The Profile tab allows you to customize the user's environment by specifying the following items for the user: the user profile path, a logon script, and a home folder.

SETTING A PROFILE PATH

User profiles contain information about the Windows 2000 environment for a specific user. For example, profile settings include the Desktop arrangement, associated program groups, and screen colors that users see when they log on.

If the configuration option is a personal preference, it is most likely a part of the user profile. Configuration options that relate to the computer are not a part of the user profile, however. For example, the mouse driver is not a part of a user profile. But the properties of the mouse configuration—such as the speed, pointer, and mouse button settings—reflect the user's personal preferences and are a part of a user profile.

By default, when a user logs on, a profile is opened for a user. The first time users log on, they receive a default user profile. A folder that matches the user's logon name is created in the Documents and Settings folder; this folder holds a file called NTUSER.DAT, as well as subfolders that contain directory links to the user's Desktop items. Any changes that the user makes to the Desktop are stored on the local computer when the user logs off.

The Profile Path option in the Profile tab is used to point to another location (other than the default local location) for profile files. This allows users to access profiles that have been stored on a shared network folder. Profiles can thus be used for an individual or shared between a group of users. To specify a path, just type it into the Profile Path text box.

USING LOGON SCRIPTS

Logon scripts are files that run every time a user logs on to the network. They are usually batch files, but they can be any type of executable file.

You might use logon scripts to set up drive mappings or to run a specific executable file at logon. Logon scripts are also useful for compatibility with non–Windows 2000 clients who want to log on but still maintain consistent settings with their native operating system.

To run a logon script for a user, enter the script name in the Logon Script text box in the Profile tab of the user's Properties.

NOTE   Logon scripts are not commonly used in Windows 2000 networks because Windows 2000 automates much of the user's configuration. On the other hand, this isn't the case in older NetWare environments (for example), and administrators must use logon scripts to configure the user's environment.

SETTING UP HOME FOLDERS

Users normally store their personal files and information in a private folder called a *home folder*. In the Profile tab of the user's Properties, you can specify the location of a home folder as a local folder or a network folder.

To specify a local path folder, choose the Local Path option and type the path in the text box next to that option. To specify a network path for a folder, choose the Connect option and specify a network path using a UNC (Universal Naming Convention) path. In this case, a network folder should already have been created and shared.

Local Group Accounts

On a Windows 2000 member server, you can use only local groups. A *local group* resides on the Windows 2000 member server's local database.

On a Windows 2000 domain controller in the Active Directory, you can have security groups and distribution groups. A *security group* is a logical group of users who need to access specific resources. You use security groups to assign permissions to resources. A *distribution group* is a logical group of users who have common characteristics. Applications and e-mail programs can use distribution groups.

Windows 2000 domain controllers also allow you to select a *group scope,* which can be domain local, global, or universal.

- *Domain local groups* are used to assign permissions to resources. Local groups can contain user accounts, universal groups, and global groups from any domain in the tree or forest. A domain local group can also contain other domain local groups from its own local domain.

- *Global groups* are used to organize users who have similar network access requirements. Global groups can contain user and global groups from the local domain.

- *Universal groups,* used to organize users logically, appear in the global catalog (a special listing that contains limited information about every object in the Active Directory). Universal groups can contain users from anywhere in the domain tree or forest, other universal groups, and global groups.

On Windows 2000 Professional computers and Windows 2000 member servers, you create and manage local groups through the Local Users and Groups utility. On Windows 2000 Server domain controllers, you manage groups with the Microsoft Active Directory Users and Computers utility.

Built-in Group Accounts

When you install Windows 2000 Server, several built-in group accounts are created by default. Table 7.6 describes the built-in group accounts and indicates which environment (local, domain, or global) contains the built-in account.

TABLE 7.6: Built-in Group Accounts

Built-in Group	Description	Environment
Account Operators	Members can create domain user and group accounts, but can only manage the user and group accounts they create.	Domain
Administrators	Has full rights and privileges. Its members can grant themselves any permissions they don't have by default, to manage all objects on the computer (including the file system, printers, and account management).	Local and domain

TABLE 7.6:   Built-in Group Accounts *(continued)*

Built-in Group	Description	Environment
Backup Operators	Members have rights to back up and restore the file system, even if the file system is NTFS and members have not been assigned permissions to the file system. However, they can only access the file system through the Backup utility. To directly access the file system, Backup Operators must have explicit permissions assigned. This group has no members by default.	Local and domain
Guests	Has limited access to the computer. Allows you to let people who are not regular users access specific network resources. As a general rule, most administrators do not allow Guest access because it is a potential security risk. By default, the Guest user account is a member of the Guests local group.	Local and domain
Power Users	Has fewer rights than the Administrators group, but more rights than the Users group. Power Users can create users and groups, but can only manage the users and groups they create. They can also create network shares and printers.	Local
Print Operator	Members can administer domain printers.	Domain

TABLE 7.6: Built-in Group Accounts *(continued)*

Built-in Group	Description	Environment
Replicator	Intended to support directory replication, a feature used by domain servers. Only domain users who will start the replication service should be assigned to this group. This group has no members by default.	Local and domain
Server Operators	Members can administer domain servers.	Domain
Users	Used by end users who should have very limited system access. If you have installed a fresh copy of Windows 2000 Server, the default settings for this group prohibit users from compromising the operating system or program files. By default, all users who have been created on the computer, except Guest, are members of the Users local group.	Local and domain
Cert Publishers	Members can manage enterprise certification and renewal agents.	Global
DHCP Administrators	Has administrative rights to manage Dynamic Host Configuration Protocol (DHCP) servers.	Domain
DHCP Users	Has the necessary rights to use DHCP services.	Domain
DnsAdmins	Has administrative rights to manage Domain Name System (DNS) servers.	Domain
DnsUpdateProxy	Has permissions that allow DNS clients to perform dynamic updates on behalf of other clients, such as DHCP servers.	Global

TABLE 7.6: Built-in Group Accounts *(continued)*

Built-in Group	Description	Environment
Domain Admins	Has complete administrative rights over the domain.	Global
Domain Computers	Contains all the workstations and servers that are a part of the domain.	Global
Domain Controllers	Contains all the domain controllers in the domain.	Global
Domain Guests	Has limited access to the domain. This group is provided so that you can let people who are not regular users access specific network resources.	Global
Domain Users	Contains all the domain users. This group should have very limited system access.	Global
Enterprise Admins	Has complete administrative rights over the enterprise. This group has the highest level of permissions of all groups.	Global
Group Policy Creator Owners	Has permissions to modify group policy for the domain.	Global
RAS and IAS Server	Contains the Remote Access Service (RAS) and Internet Authentication Service (IAS) servers in the domain. Servers in this group can access remote access properties of users.	Domain
Schema Admins	Has special permissions to modify the schema of the Active Directory.	Global
WINS Users	Has special permissions to view information on the Windows Internet Name Service (WINS) server.	Domain

---

NOTE On a Windows 2000 Server domain controller, groups are located in the Users folder and the Builtin folder.

Creating New Local Groups

To create a group, you must be logged on as a member of the Administrators or Power Users groups. The Administrators group has full permissions to manage users and groups; members of the Power Users group can manage only the groups that they create.

When you create a local group, follow these guidelines for naming it:

- Use a descriptive name (for example, Accounting Data Users).

- The group name must be unique to the computer, different from all other group names and usernames that exist on that computer.

- Use up to 256 characters. Alphanumeric characters are easiest to manage. Do not use the backslash (\ ) character.

As when choosing usernames, you should consider your naming conventions when assigning names to groups.

Creating groups is similar to creating users and is a fairly straightforward process. After you've added the Local Users and Groups snap-in to the MMC, you expand it to see the Users and Groups folders. Right-click the Groups folder and select New Group from the pop-up menu. This brings up the New Group dialog box.

The only required entry in the New Group dialog box is the group name. Optionally, you can enter a description for the group and add (or remove) group members. When you're ready to create the new group, click the Create button.

Managing Local Group Membership

Once you've created a group, you can add members to it. A user can belong to multiple groups.

You can easily add and remove users through the group's Properties dialog box. From the Groups folder in the Local Users and Groups utility, double-click the group to bring up its Properties dialog box.

From there, you can change the group's description and add or remove group members. When you click the Add button to add members, the Select Users or Groups dialog box appears. In this dialog box, you select the user accounts you wish to add and click the Add button. Click the OK button to add the users to the group. To remove a member from the group, select the member in the group Properties dialog box Members list and click the Remove button.

RENAMING GROUPS

To change a group's name, use the familiar Windows method of right-clicking the group and choosing Rename from the pop-up menu. Type a new name and press Enter.

DELETING GROUPS

If you're sure that you will never want to use a group again, you can delete it. Once a group is deleted, you lose all permissions assignments that have been specified for the group. To delete a group, right-click it and choose Delete from the pop-up menu. You'll be warned that once a group is deleted, it cannot be restored. Click the Yes button to process the deletion.

NOTE   If you delete a group and give another group the same name, that new group won't be created with the same properties as the deleted group.

Necessary Procedures

The following procedures cover the steps to create, disable, delete, and rename user accounts. The process is similar for creating, deleting, and renaming group accounts.

Creating New Local Users

1. Open the MMC and expand the Local Users and Groups snap-in.

2. Highlight the Users folder and select Action ➢ New User. The New User dialog box appears.

3. In the User Name field, the user's name.

4. In the Full Name field, type the user's full name.

5. In the Description field, type a description of the user.

6. Click the Create button to add the user.

Disabling a User Account

1. Open the MMC and expand the Local Users and Groups snap-in.

2. Open the Users folder. Double-click a user to open the Properties dialog box.

3. In the General tab, check the Account Is Disabled box and click the OK button.

Deleting a User Account

1. Open the MMC and expand the Local Users and Groups snap-in.

2. Open the Users folder and highlight the user account.

3. Select Action ➤ Delete. You'll be prompted to confirm this user deletion.

4. If you're certain you want to permanently delete this user account, click the Yes button.

Renaming a User Account

1. Open the MMC and expand the Local Users and Groups snap-in.

2. Open the Users folder and highlight the user account.

3. Select Action ➤ Rename.

4. Type in the new username and press Enter. Notice that the original Full Name property is retained in the Local Users and Groups utility.

Exam Essentials

Know how to create a new user account.   Users are created in the MMC's Local Users and Groups snap-in.

Understand the difference between disabling a user account and deleting it. A disabled account can be restored with all of its permissions intact. A deleted account can never be re-created. You'd disable an account when a user is away for an extended period of time, or when you're planning to replace a user who leaves. Delete an account only if you're sure that it will never be needed again.

Know what user profiles contain. User profiles contain information about the Windows 2000 environment for a particular user. Every user can have an individual user profile that is configured to his or her preferences.

Understand how logon scripts are used. Logon scripts run every time a user logs on to the system. Typically, a logon script contains drive and printer mappings for non–Windows 2000 clients.

Know how to connect users with their home folders. A home folder is a user's private folder, generally located on a server so that the user data can be backed up regularly. A UNC path specifies the path to the home folder, in the Connect option of the Profile tab of the user's Properties.

Know how to manage local groups. Local groups are created and used to simplify user administration. You can create, control membership of, rename, and delete groups.

Key Terms and Concepts

Active Directory users The name of the database that stores the users and groups for an Active Directory.

distribution group A logical group of users in the Active Directory who have common characteristics.

domain local group A group scope used to assign permissions to resources. Local groups can contain user accounts, universal groups, and global groups from any domain.

global group A group scope used to organize users who need similar network access.

home folder   A user's private folder on a server, used to store critical files.

local group   A group account residing in the local member server's database.

local user   A user account residing in the local member server's database.

logon script   A file that is run every time a user logs on. It generally contains information to set up drive and printer mappings.

security group   A logical group that needs access to specific resources and will require the same permissions for the resource.

security identifier (SID)   The unique identifier on user and group accounts. The username is a property of the SID.

universal group   A group scope used to logically organize users; it appears in the global catalog.

user profile   The Windows 2000 environment information for a specific user.

Sample Questions

1. Lucy, the VP of Finance, is leaving the company. Joe will be her replacement, but he won't start until two weeks after Lucy leaves. What is the best way to handle the account situation for these two users?

   A. Create a new account for Joe when he arrives.

   B. Delete Lucy's account. Create a new account for Joe when he arrives.

   C. Rename Lucy's account for Joe.

   D. Disable Lucy's account until Joe arrives. Then rename the account.

   Answer: D. In this situation, the best solution is to disable the account until the new person arrives and then rename the account. This preserves all the permissions that have been assigned to the account.

2. You are the network administrator. Your users need to access resources on a NetWare server every time they log on. What, if anything, can be done to make automatic access possible for these users?

A. Use user profiles.

B. Create home folders for the users on the NetWare server.

C. Use logon scripts to set up drive mappings.

D. There is nothing you can do. They'll need to access the resources manually.

Answer: C. Logon scripts can set up drive and printer mappings. They can be run every time the user logs on.

Implement, configure, manage, and troubleshoot Account Policy.

Account policies govern what happens during the logon process. You have control over this process to implement security as necessary for your organization. Account policies control password restrictions and account lockout parameters. In domain controllers, the Kerberos 5 security protocol adds an additional level of security.

In the past, Microsoft has tested this topic only lightly; however, with the growing use of Kerberos policies, you can expect an increased level of coverage on the exams.

Critical Information

Account policies are used to specify the user account properties that relate to the logon process. They allow you to configure computer security settings for passwords, account lockout specifications, and Kerberos authentication within a domain.

In the MMC snap-in for Group Policy, you reach the Account Policies folders through the Local Computer Policy item. Expand Local Computer Policy, then Computer Configuration, Windows Settings,

Security Settings, and Account Policies. On a Windows 2000 member server, you'll see two folders: Password Policy and Account Lockout Policy. On a Windows 2000 Server computer configured as a domain controller, you'll see three folders: Password Policy, Account Lockout Policy, and Kerbcros Policy.

Password Policies

Password policies ensure that security requirements are enforced on the computer.

NOTE The password policy is set on a per-computer basis; it cannot be configured for specific users.

Table 7.7 describes the password policies that are defined on Windows 2000 member servers. On Windows 2000 domain controllers, all of these policies are configured as "not defined."

TABLE 7.7: Password Policy Options

Policy	Description	Default	Minimum	Maximum
Enforce Password History	Tracks user's password history	Remember 0 passwords	Same as default	Remember 24 passwords
Maximum Password Age	Maximum number of days user can keep valid password	42 days	1 day	Up to 999 days
Minimum Password Age	Number of days password must be kept before it can be changed	0 days (password can be changed immediately)	Same as default	999 days

T A B L E   7 . 7 :   Password Policy Options *(continued)*

Policy	Description	Default	Minimum	Maximum
Minimum Password Length	Minimum number of characters required for password	0 characters (no password required)	Same as default	14 characters
Passwords Must Meet Complexity Requirements	Allows you to install password filter	Disabled	Same as default	Enabled
Store Password Using Reversible Encryption for All Users in the Domain	Specifies higher level of encryption for stored user passwords	Disabled	Same as default	Enabled

The password policies are used as follows:

- The Enforce Password History option prevents users from repeatedly using the same password. When their password expires or is changed, users must create a new password.

- The Maximum Password Age option requires users to change their password after the maximum password age is exceeded.

- The Minimum Password Age option prevents users from changing their password several times in rapid succession in order to defeat the purpose of the Enforce Password History policy.

- The Minimum Password Length option ensures that users create a password and specifies a length requirement for that password. Note: If this option isn't set, users are not required to create a password.

- The Passwords Must Meet Complexity option prevents users from picking passwords from items found in a dictionary of common names.

- The Store Password Using Reversible Encryption for All Users in the Domain option imposes a higher level of security for user passwords.

Account Lockout Policies

Account lockout policies are used to specify the maximum number of invalid logon attempts that will be tolerated. You configure the account lockout policies so that after *x* number of unsuccessful logon attempts within *y* number of minutes, the account will be locked for a specified amount of time or until the Administrator unlocks the account. Table 7.8 describes the account lockout policies.

NOTE Usage of account lockout policies is similar to banks' implementation of ATM access code security. You have a certain number of chances to enter the correct access code. If someone steals an ATM card, they won't be able to keep guessing the access code until they get it right. Typically, after three unsuccessful attempts at your access code, the ATM machine takes the card. Then you must request a new card from the bank.

TABLE 7.8: Account Lockout Policy Options

Policy	Description	Default	Minimum	Maximum
Account Lockout Threshold	Number of invalid attempts allowed before account is locked out	0 (disabled; account will not be locked out)	Same as default	999 attempts
Account Lockout Duration	Period of lockout if Account Lockout Threshold is exceeded	0 minutes; but if Account Lockout Threshold is enabled, 30 minutes	Same as default	99,999 minutes

TABLE 7.8: Account Lockout Policy Options *(continued)*

Policy	Description	Default	Minimum	Maximum
Reset Account Lockout Counter After	Period for which unsuccessful logon attempts are remembered	0 minutes, but if Account Lockout Threshold is enabled, 5 minutes	Same as default	99,999 minutes

Kerberos Policies

Kerberos (version 5) is a security protocol used in Windows 2000 Server to authenticate users and network services. This is called dual verification, or *mutual authentication*. When a Windows 2000 Server is installed as a domain controller, it automatically becomes a *key distribution center (KDC)*. The KDC is responsible for holding all of the client passwords and account information. Kerberos services are also installed on each Windows 2000 client and server.

The Kerberos authentication involves the following steps:

1. The client requests authentication from the KDC using a password or smart card.

2. The KDC issues the client a ticket-granting ticket (TGT). The client can use the TGT to access the ticket-granting service (TGS), which allows the user to authenticate to services within the domain. The TGS issues service tickets to the clients.

3. The client presents the service ticket to the requested network service. This service ticket authenticates the user to the service and the service to the user, for mutual authentication.

The *Kerberos policies* are described in Table 7.9.

TABLE 7.9: Kerberos Policy Options

Policy	Description	Default Local Setting	Effective Setting
Enforce User Logon Restrictions	Any logon restrictions will be enforced	Not defined	Enabled
Maximum Lifetime for Service Ticket	Maximum age of a service ticket before it must be renewed	Not defined	600 minutes
Maximum Lifetime for User Ticket	Maximum age for a user ticket before it must be renewed	Not defined	10 hours
Maximum Lifetime for User Ticket Renewal	Period during which a ticket may be renewed before it must be regenerated	Not defined	7 days
Maximum Tolerance for Computer Clock Synchronization	Maximum discrepancy for clock synchronization between the client and the KDC	Not defined	5 minutes

Necessary Procedures

Following are the steps for setting password and account lockout policies.

Setting Password Policies

1. Select Start ➢ Programs ➢ Administrative Tools ➢ Security and expand the Local Computer Policy snap-in.

2. Expand the folders as follows: Computer Configuration, Windows Settings, Security Settings, Account Policies, Password Policy.

3. Open the Enforce Password History policy. In the Effective Policy Setting field, specify the number of passwords to be remembered. Click the OK button.

4. Open the Maximum Password Age policy. In the Local Policy Setting field, specify the number of days allowed before password expiration. Click the OK button.

Setting Account Lockout Policies

1. Select Start ≻ Programs ≻ Administrative Tools ≻ Security and expand the Local Computer Policy snap-in.

2. Expand the folders as follows: Computer Configuration, Windows Settings, Security Settings, Account Policies, Account Lockout Policy.

3. Open the Account Lockout Threshold policy. In the Local Policy Setting field, specify the number of invalid logon attempts allowed before the account will lock. Click the OK button.

4. Open the Account Lockout Duration policy. In the Local Policy Setting field, specify the number of minutes for which the account will remain locked. Click the OK button.

5. Log off as Administrator. Try to log on as another user with an incorrect password until you see the error message stating that the account has been locked.

6. When the lockout message appears, log on as Administrator.

7. To unlock the account, open the Local Users and Groups snap-in in the MMC. Expand the Users folder, and double-click the user. In the General tab of the Properties dialog box, deselect the Account Is Locked Out check box. Then click OK.

Exam Essentials

Know how to set account policies.   Password policies are set in the Group Policy snap-in for the MMC.

Know the options for password policies.   Password policies are set to enforce security on the computer. Options are enforce password history, maximum password age, minimum password age, minimum password length, passwords must meet complexity requirements, and store password using reversible encryption.

Know the options for setting account lockout policies.   Account lockout policies are set to prevent unauthorized users from gaining access to the computer. Options are policy account lockout threshold, account lockout duration, and reset account lockout counter.

Know how Kerberos authentication works.   Kerberos is a security protocol that is automatically installed on all Windows 2000 Server domain controllers. The protocol holds all the client passwords and account information.

Know the options for setting Kerberos policies.   The Kerberos options that you can control are enforce user logon restrictions, maximum lifetime for service ticket, maximum lifetime for user ticket, maximum lifetime for user ticket renewal, and maximum tolerance for computer clock synchronization.

Key Terms and Concepts

account lockout policy   A policy that governs when an account will be locked out and for how long. This policy is designed to prevent unauthorized users from hacking into the computer.

account policies   Policies that govern the properties associated with the logon process.

Kerberos policy   A security protocol used in Windows 2000 Server to authenticate users and network services.

Key Distribution Center (KDC)   The Key Distribution Center (KDC) is responsible for holding the account information and client passwords for a domain. When a Windows 2000 Server is installed as a domain controller, that server is automatically a KDC.

password policy   A policy that governs password requirements, such as password age and length.

Sample Questions

1. Which policies can you control on a Windows 2000 member server?

A. Password policy

B. Account lockout policy

C. Kerberos policy

D. Logon policy

Answer: A, B. A Windows 2000 member server can set password policies and account lockout policies. A Windows 2000 domain controller can set Kerberos policies as well.

2. You are the network administrator. You are trying to implement tighter security. What options can you set in the Password Policy?

A. Maximum password length

B. Maximum password age

C. Password must meet complexity requirements

D. Account lockout duration

Answer: B, C. Password policy options are enforce password history, maximum password age, minimum password age, minimum password length, passwords must meet complexity requirements, and store password using reversible encryption.

Implement, configure, manage, and troubleshoot security by using the Security Configuration Tool Set.

The Security Configuration tool set is a collection of features (under the Security Configuration and Analysis MMC snap-in) that help you verify whether you have properly implemented security. These features are not designed to replace system tools such as User Manager, Server Manager, and so on, which address various aspects of system security. Rather, the goal of Security Configuration is to complement these other management tools. To this end, Security Configuration defines an engine that can interpret a standard configuration file (a security template) and perform the required operations automatically in the background. The analysis tool in the tool set is designed to provide information about all system aspects related to security.

Microsoft's Windows NT and Windows 2000 product families have excelled in their ability to implement security. An entire exam (70-217, Implementing and Administering a Microsoft Windows 2000 Directory Services Infrastructure) has been constructed to test your knowledge of Windows 2000 security features overall. Here in this exam for the Windows 2000 Server, you'll be expected to know how to use security templates and how to determine if you have implemented security by doing a security analysis.

Critical Information

Windows 2000 Server includes a utility called Security Configuration and Analysis, which you can use to configure and analyze the computer's local security settings. This utility works by comparing your actual security configuration to a security template configured with your desired settings. To provide comprehensive security administration and information, the Security Configuration tool set helps you configure and analyze all of the following: account policies, local policies, restricted groups, system services, file and folder sharing, system Registry, and directory security. The Security Configuration and Analysis utility is an MMC snap-in. After you've added it to the MMC, you can use the tool set to run the security analysis process.

The following steps are involved in the security analysis process:

1. Using the Security Configuration and Analysis utility, specify a working security database that will be used during the security analysis.

2. Import a security template that can be used as a basis for configuring your local security.

3. Perform the security analysis. This compares your configuration against the template that you specified in step 2.

4. Review the results of the security analysis.

5. Resolve any discrepancies indicated by the analysis.

Importing a Security Template

The Security Configuration and Analysis database *(security database)* is a computer-specific data store that is generated when one or more configurations are imported to a particular computer. There is an initial database created when a computer has a clean installation of Windows 2000. This database is referred to as the local computer policy database. Initially, it contains the default out-of-the-box security configuration of your system. After specifying the working security database, your next step in security analysis is to import a security template. The template is used as a comparative tool and contains information about the desired security level. The Security and Configuration Analysis utility compares the settings in the template to your current security settings in the security database.

You do not set up security through the security template. Rather, the template is where you organize security attributes in a single location.

TIP   As an administrator, you can define a base security template on a single computer and then export it to all the servers in your network.

Creating a Security Template

You create security templates through the Security Templates snap-in in the MMC. These templates contain the items listed in Table 7.10.

T A B L E   7 . 1 0 :   Security Template Configuration Options

Security Template Item	Description
Account Policies	Configurations to be used for password policies, account lockout policies, and Kerberos policies
Local Policies	Configurations to be used for audit policies, user rights assignments, and security options
Event Log	Configuration settings that apply to Event Viewer log files

TABLE 7.10: Security Template Configuration Options *(continued)*

Security Template Item	Description
Restricted Groups	Allows you to administer local group memberships
Registry	Security for local Registry keys
File System	Security for the local file system
System Services	Security for system services and the startup mode used by local system services

After you add the Security Templates snap-in to the MMC, you can open a sample security template and modify it, as follows:

1. In the MMC, expand the Security Templates snap-in and then expand the folder for *Windir*\Security\Templates.

2. Double-click the sample template that you want to edit. Several sample templates are available, including basicsv (for basic server) and basicdc (for basic domain controller).

3. Make any desired changes to the sample security template. Changes to the template are not applied as settings to the local system by default. The settings in the template are simply a specification for how you would like the system to be configured.

4. When you've made all needed changes to the sample template, save the template by highlighting the sample template file, right-clicking, and selecting the Save As option from the pop-up menu. Specify a location and a filename for the new template. By default, the security template will be saved with an INI extension in the *Windir*\Security\Templates folder.

Opening a Security Template

A configured security template can be imported for use with the Security Configuration and Analysis utility. In the MMC, right-click the Security Configuration and Analysis utility and select the Import Template option from the pop-up menu. Then highlight the template file you wish to import and click the Open button.

Performing a Security Analysis

The next step is to perform a security analysis. To run the analysis, simply right-click the Security Configuration and Analysis utility and select the Analyze Computer Now option from the pop-up menu. You'll see a Perform Analysis dialog box in which you specify the location and filename for the error-log file path that will be created during the analysis. When the analysis is complete, you'll be returned to the main MMC window. From there, you can review the results of the security analysis.

Reviewing Security Analysis

The results of the security analysis are stored in the Security Configuration and Analysis snap-in, under the configured security item. Figure 7.4 shows an example of security analysis results for password policies.

FIGURE 7.4: Viewing the results of a security analysis

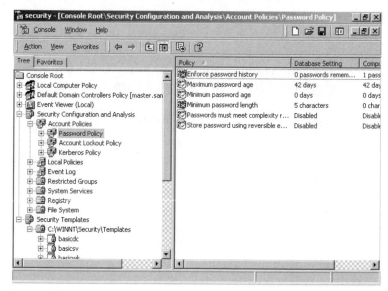

The policies that have been analyzed will have an × or a check mark at the left, as shown in Figure 7.4. An × indicates that the template specification and the actual policy do not match. A check mark tells you that they do match. If any security discrepancies are indicated, you should use the Group Policy snap-in to resolve the security violation.

Necessary Procedures

These procedures guide you through the use of the Security and Configuration Analysis snap-in. They cover specifying a security database, creating or importing a template, and how to look at the data collected during the security analysis.

Adding the Security and Configuration Analysis Snap-in

1. Select Start ➢ Programs ➢ Administrative Tools ➢ Security.

2. Select Console ➢ Add/Remove Snap-in.

3. In the Add/Remove Snap-In dialog box, click the Add button. Highlight the Security Configuration and Analysis snap-in and click the Add button. Then click the Close button.

4. In the Add/Remove Snap-In dialog box, click the OK button.

Specifying a Security Database

1. In the MMC, right-click the Security Configuration and Analysis snap-in and select the Open Database option from the pop-up menu.

2. The Open Database dialog box appears. In the File Name text box, type the name of the database you will create and click the Open button. By default, this file will have an SDB (for security database) extension. The Import Template dialog box appears. Select the template that you want to import. You can choose a predefined template through this dialog box, or a customized template file you've created (as described in the next procedure). Make your selection and click the Open button.

Creating the Security Template

1. In the MMC, select Console ➢ Add/Remove Snap-in.

2. In the Add/Remove Snap-In dialog box, click the Add button. Highlight the Security Templates snap-in and click the Add button. Then click the Close button.

3. In the Add/Remove Snap-In dialog box, click the OK button.

4. Expand the Security Templates snap-in, then expand the WINNT\Security\Templates folder.

5. Double-click the basicsv file.

6. Select Account Policies, then Password Policy.

7. Edit the password policies as follows:

   a. Set the Enforce Password History option to the number of passwords to be remembered.

   b. Enable the Passwords Must Meet Complexity Requirements option.

   c. Set the Maximum Password Age option to the number of days.

8. Highlight the basicsv file, right-click, and select Save As.

9. In the Save As dialog box, place the file in the default folder and name the file. Click the Save button.

Importing the Security Template

1. Highlight the Security Configuration and Analysis snap-in, right-click, and select the Import Template option.

2. In the Import Template dialog box, highlight the desired security template and click the Open button.

Performing and Reviewing the Security Analysis

1. Highlight the Security Configuration and Analysis snap-in, right-click, and select the Analyze Computer Now option.

2. In the Configure System dialog box, accept the default error log file path and click the OK button.

3. When you return to the main MMC window, double-click the Security Configuration and Analysis snap-in.

4. Double-click Account Policies, and then double-click Password Policy. You will see the results of the analysis for each policy, indicated by an × or a check mark next to the policy.

Exam Essentials

Know how to perform a security analysis.   Start by specifying a working security database. A security template is then imported, to be used for comparison. The analysis is then performed and the results are analyzed. Any discrepancies are noted in the results.

Know the use of a security template.   The security template is a comparative tool used by the Security and Configuration Analysis utility to compare existing security settings to the template settings.

Know how to review the security analysis results.   The results of security analyses are stored in the Security and Configuration Analysis snap-in of the MMC. An × indicates any discrepancies.

Know how to resolve discrepancies.   Discrepancies are resolved with the Group Policy snap-in.

Key Terms and Concepts

security analysis   The process of analyzing the local computer's security settings.

Security and Configuration Analysis   A utility for analyzing and helping to configure the computer's local security settings.

security template   A comparative set of security settings used with Security and Configuration Analysis.

Sample Questions

1. Where do you find the Security Configuration and Analysis utility?

   A. MMC

   B. Administrative Tools

   C. Control Panel

   D. Computer Management

   Answer: A. The Security Configuration and Analysis utility is an MMC snap-in.

2. You are reviewing the results of the security analysis. How do you know which items did not match the template settings?

   A. The items are grayed out.

   B. There are check marks beside the items.

   C. There is an × beside these items.

   D. They are listed separately.

   Answer: C. The comparison results will have either a check mark or an × besides the security items. Items with the × did not match the template.

Index

Note to the Reader: Throughout this index, **boldfaced** page numbers indicate primary discussions of a topic. *Italicized* page numbers indicate illustrations.

K

W

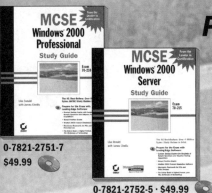